For Leigh
with best wishes

Bill

October 1997

DEVELOPING CORPORATE COMPETENCE

THIS BOOK IS DEDICATED TO KATHLEEN
FOR A LIFETIME OF FAITH AND SUPPORT,
WHO DIDN'T LIVE QUITE LONG ENOUGH
TO SEE THIS PROJECT BEAR FRUIT

DEVELOPING CORPORATE COMPETENCE

A High-Performance Agenda for Managing Organizations

❖

William Tate

Gower

Published by
Gower Publishing Limited
Gower House
Croft Road
Aldershot
Hampshire GU11 3HR
England

Gower
Old Post Road
Brookfield
Vermont 05036
USA

British Library Cataloguing in Publication Data
Tate, William
  Developing Corporate Competence: A High-Performance Agenda for Managing
  Organizations
  Agenda for Management Performance
  I. Title
  658.4

ISBN 0–566–07670–5

Library of Congress Cataloging-in-Publication Data
Tate, William, 1942–
    Developing corporate competence: a high-performance agenda for managing
    organizations
    William Tate.
        p.   cm.
      Includes index.
      ISBN 0–566–07870–5
      1. Industrial management.   2. Organizational effectiveness.
      3. Performance.   4. Executive ability.   I. Title.
      HD31.T275   1995   95–1057
      658—dc20

Typeset in ITC Garamond Light by Poole Typesetting (Wessex) Ltd, Bournemouth, and printed in Great Britain by Hartnoll's Ltd, Bodmin.

CONTENTS

bureaucracy — Redesigning bureaucracy — Administration
versus managing — Keeping the checkers in check —
References

FIGURES

PREFACE

❖

C an do – chooses not to! Can do – not allowed to! Why are we so obsessed with what individuals are capable of doing, yet largely uninterested in what they choose and choose not to do, and what they are allowed and not allowed to do? Why do we fail to consider what good it actually does their organizations? Why do we shy away from examining what really goes on inside their organizations to ensure that capability is used freely, wisely and fully?

As surely as centralization follows decentralization (I was going to say darkness follows light), recovery from Britain's perennial economic woes is always claimed to hinge on individual training 'to raise skills' or nowadays 'competence', especially that of managers. Only this time round we have Lead Bodies to help us – not a dead weight, however you pronounce it. I served on one, and they are doing a fine job. But too much is expected of competence and its counterpart qualification, an NVQ. We deceive everyone, including ourselves, if we believe the sum of individual competence is automatically corporate competence. It is no such thing. If only it were that simple. Personal competence development is ineffective unless linked to the organization's real problem context and – more importantly – unless we also take parallel care of the organization's own development. If we do that, we will convert 'can do' into 'choose to do' and 'allowed to do'. If we do not, can-do competence will be corrupted by unchannelled personal motives and unmanaged organizational forces.

Think about it. All our experience tells us that the fact that people have and can demonstrate a skill doesn't mean they will do so in the cut and thrust of daily political reality. We all know managers who are able to communicate, but for whom it suits their mean purpose to hoard information for reasons of personal power, or cases where organizations' protocol often requires managers to pass matters up to the boss rather than liaise spontaneously with their counterparts across departmental boundaries. The raw talent of traders in the financial derivatives market may go unrestrained. 'Can do' is but a fraction of the messy story.

The financial services industry scandals in 1994 presented organization psychologists and other students of management with a classic case-study of the personal versus corporate competence dichotomy – the sale of personal pension plans which offered people a worse deal than the occupational schemes from which they were induced to transfer their funds. Their bosses' myopic logic said the salespeople obviously weren't competent. Therefore either sack them or retrain them. Both actions were carried out on a huge scale after the insurance companies were found out.

The response was unfair to the alleged culprits. It also placed an unfair burden on the trainers. It conveniently overlooked the obvious: that insurance salespeople might be competent to identify which policies they would not want to buy if they were in their clients' shoes, but may choose to press them on their clients nevertheless. They might do so out of personal choice, or it might be what everybody expects, part of a below-the-surface conspiracy, an organization- or industry-wide culture 'undiscussible'. Now, rather late in the day, insurance companies are beginning to admit that their practice of hiring desperate salespeople on a commission-only basis for short periods of service while they exploit their social contacts might be a significant factor.

My book, *Developing Managerial Competence: A Critical Guide to Methods and Materials,* focuses on the individual manager. It offers a constructive critique of the range of means and products available for developing individual managerial competence, and how best to choose and exploit them, especially new techniques and technologies in the field of open and work-based learning. This book, *Developing Corporate Competence: A High-Performance Agenda for Managing Organizations*, was written contemporaneously and picks up the logical argument where the first book leaves off. In other words, it is concerned with an organization's all-round management competence and how to develop it. If achieved, I call this *corporate competence*.

Ideally, developers' work should lead to performance improvement at several levels – individual managers, inter- and intra-management teamwork, and management of the organization as a whole. This clearly means going beyond attending to managers merely as individuals (however senior) – the limited and limiting focus we find in so much management development activity. It is all very well for developers to concentrate on the individual, but that should not blind us to the individual-in-context. It is that context which calls the tune, and the piper is the organization. So the search is on for the most direct ways of bringing together development action, organization problems and business results.

Providing that link requires much more than a well-considered strategy for developing individuals in a way which meets the organization's needs. The full potential of management development needs to reach beyond describing that context alone and seeing that the manager's development accommodates it. It must also include performance-permitting and performance-enhancing action developed through the relevant management *systems* – the appraisal system, the climate system, the career system and the reward system, and several more as we shall see. These management development approaches, processes and interventions are aimed at the level of the *management of the organization's business*, where the emphasis is on management *activity* rather than simply the management *population*, the game more than the players. It is here that the disciplines of management development and organization development join forces.

Development's remit must also extend beyond mere development, contra-dictory though that sounds. Developers also need to know what talent they have, when and how to obtain more of it, how to hang on to it, and where to place it for maximum impact.

OVERVIEW OF THE CONTENTS

PART ONE	Chapter 1	Models, concepts and definitions
	Chapter 2	

PART TWO	Chapter 3	Analysing needs and diagnosing problems
	Chapter 4	

PART THREE	Chapter 5	Interventions, methods and action
	Chapter 6	
	Chapter 7	

PART FOUR	Chapter 8	Working to develop the organization
	Chapter 9	
	Chapter 10	
	Chapter 11	

PART FIVE	Chapter 12	Strategies for the future
	Chapter 13	

The first two chapters supply the spine onto which all the ideas in the later chapters can be firmly grafted. In Chapter 1, 'Developing a Model Foundation', we discuss various models used in connection with root concepts about managers and management, and about their development. The problem is that too many devel-opers and most of their clients are content with poor imitations of the real develop-ment product; at the heart of this chapter is a quest for the holy grail of true management development – what would it actually look like if we could see it? We also apply the principle and practice of mission and goals statements to delineate the field of development activity.

In Chapter 2, 'To Train or to Educate? That is the Question', we consider the fundamental choice of how to balance the development activities between training and education. This issue is often fudged, even ignored entirely, yet we are talking about whether we want managers who comply or who question, who do as they are told or who think for themselves. This chapter exposes the underlying assumptions behind these implicit or explicit choices and then relates them to the systematic training model and the integrated learning model.

The next two chapters, in Part Two, examine analytical processes at different levels and in novel ways. Chapter 3, 'Establishing Managers' Development Needs', takes a sceptical view of conventional ways of identifying managers' and management's problems and needs. My thesis is that much current analytical practice contributes little to the organization's diagnosis and ultimately its performance. So the chapter suggests how readers may become the wise master of these techniques rather than their obedient servant.

Chapter 4 takes this a step further by 'Diagnosing Organizational Needs'. Although this and the previous chapter are here split into two, they are two sides of the same coin. The process of analysing management's needs should be a seamless process whereby performance problems which have their roots in organizational obstacles and shortcomings, rather than in managers' personal capabilities, should be open to scrutiny at the same time.

The next section of the book aims to help developers make the best possible use of various intervention techniques and methods. In Chapter 5, 'Choosing Development Interventions', we examine two respected tools of the developer's trade, action learning and process consulting. These have been chosen because they intervene in a way which directly integrates individuals' development needs with those of the business. Faddish approaches to team building then receive a broadside, redressed by a searching, problem-targeted methodology.

In Chapter 6, 'Managing Performance', we concentrate on the performance management approach to monitoring and developing management effectiveness, how to extract the best from appraisal systems, how to balance concern for managers' results against management practices, and how to differentiate between and exploit monetary rewards and incentives in order to achieve a desired outcome. As collaborative managerial teamwork assumes more importance, the chapter suggests how this can be fostered using appraisal devices.

Chapter 7, as its title 'Refocusing Career Management' implies, stakes out controversial new ground, suggesting that being absorbed with healthy managers is far from healthy. It calls for companies to recognize the potential they already have and not flush away valuable experience with every cost-cutting exercise or de-layering fashion that comes along. The chapter examines the shift from jobs to people, and questions the growing use of computerized career planning techniques. It finally redefines a relevant role for Career Management for the future.

The next four chapters which form Part Four of the book, change the emphasis from developing individuals and teams to developing the organization's culture and climate in a way that allows management to perform at the optimum level. Here I am using the term 'management' as the activity as well as the participant members. I suggest some ways of giving managers the kind of organizations they need and deserve to achieve mutual prosperity and fulfilment.

Chapter 8 begins the process by drawing the connections between the different levels of management performance, individual and system, in 'Linking Development to Organization Performance'. It questions why developers arrive at different perceptions of their role. It then draws various models of organizations, and examines where management development activity is concerned with particular boxes in these models. Finally, it suggests ways of using these concepts to provide context and material for developers' activity.

Chapter 9, called somewhat dramatically 'The Fall and Rise of the Organization', helps developers understand the natural forces of decay which eat away inside organizations – at standards, relationships, morality, leadership, etc. – unless they are forever vigilant and continually seek opportunities for renewal. An aspect we are all familiar with, but rarely act positively about beyond moaning and the occasional skirmish, is that of seeping bureaucracy. This disease clogs our organizations' arteries, or at the risk of mixing metaphors, it is the flesh-eating bug gnawing remorselessly at the soft underbelly of its vulnerable host. This chapter shows how to engage battle with bureaucracy, indeed how to wage a strategic war aimed at its root causes.

Chapter 10, 'Developing a Positive Environment', differentiates between climate and culture and examines the distinctive nature of the developer's interest in each. It places climate and culture in the context of organization models, and relates these concepts to various degrees of change in organizations, from fairly limited through to transformational. It then suggests some practical ways for developers to promote a healthy climate and culture.

Chapter 11 takes the popular theme of 'Building a Learning Organization', puts it under the spotlight and comments on how companies' concepts of training and attitudes towards resources link with the theme. It examines companies which claim to be learning organizations, and then suggests what developers can do to help further the cause of this valuable concept.

The purpose of the final two chapters, Part Five, is to help developers pull together ends and means. Chapter 12, 'Forming a Development Strategy', shows readers how they can exploit the many ideas in this book by making strategic changes to their own development practice. It examines different strategies, and offers advice on formulating a vision and on how to identify and choose from options. It also presents a format for conducting a wholesale review of training, and discusses how best to make suitable organizational arrangements for its delivery.

Chapter 13, 'Developing the Organization to *Be*', rounds off the book by overlaying its ideas with a value framework. In advocating a more open climate, its purpose is to bring meaning to development action in terms that will serve the interests of a wide definition of stakeholders.

THE BOOK'S AUDIENCE

This book is aimed at organization and management developers, trainers, educators, facilitators, consultants, agencies and institutions as well as learning material producers and designers, both working internally or externally. It will be of prime interest to those who take an integrated and strategic view of development, as opposed to the all-too-familiar focus on the individual manager, often independent of context.

This book is for those who accept the idea that management development is not the same as manager development, nor merely managerial teamwork. Corporate competence requires acceptance of the notion that management development includes directly developing the *corporate management of the business* at a level beyond individual managers, one which encompasses the managers' environment, including management systems and climate.

If some of the ideas in this book can reach beyond developers to their clients, in other words directly to the power holders and those who run our businesses, it will be a much-needed bonus.

THE BOOK'S APPROACH

This book is practical in the way it discusses difficult and complex issues, and practical in suggesting what to do about them. Without implementation and some change or decisions by readers, the book's ideas serve little purpose. I also recognize that today most people in worthwhile jobs feel under considerable pressure. Even finding time to read a book like this can present a problem – though I agree with Charles Handy that too many managers have their priorities wrong and sacrifice reading first; their organization culture often contributes to this and induces a sense of guilt that reading is not work. Nonetheless, I have done my best to accommodate this with an easy style, without compromising on the tough content. Kurt Lewin's timeless dictum 'There is nothing so practical as a good theory' sits comfortably here.

I have tried to make some use of features found in good open learning, within the inevitable constraints of conventional book publishing. For example, you will find important points summarized as Key Tips in the practical sections of the book. More importantly, you are prompted at appropriate points by activities and questions. These allow you to consolidate learning by engaging in health checks, or reflecting and making decisions or analyses of your own. This way I hope you may be better able to capture and record your thoughts and personal learnings. Of course, not all of these activities will apply to everyone – that depends on your individual role and responsibilities – so make use of them only when they appear helpful.

I make no grand claim to originality. In keeping with the honoured tradition of the sixteenth-century French writer Michel de Montaigne ('I have only made up a bunch of other men's flowers, providing of my own only the string that ties them together'), I have drawn on the best models, concepts and approaches which are most apposite to management development as I have defined it here. My contribution is to untie the mysteries, give them a thought-provoking twist, and repackage them with suitable case-study material and the fruits of many years' experience. I have then sought to present the result in an accessible, provocative and practical manner which I hope will provide many useful ideas and insights.

THE PURPOSE OF THE BOOK

Wherever possible, this book aims to question the prevailing orthodoxy, to redefine the developers' ambit, to make readers sit up and react – probably disagree – then start to ponder, reflect and think afresh. There is so much that is untapped, unseen and unquestioned in our organizations which is crying out for the developers' touch. Hence the title, *Developing Corporate Competence: A High-Performance Agenda for Managing Organizations*.

Like its companion book, *Developing Managerial Competence: A Critical Guide to Methods and Materials*, if one word more than others indicates the single strand of values, it is 'open' – openness to new ideas and possibilities; open to extending our discipline of development in new directions; opening up for discussing the undiscussed and the undeveloped recesses in the management of our organizations; openness to learning from whatever quarters the opportunities arise.

This book aims to stir, stimulate, challenge and unsettle. At times it unashamedly engages with some of the darker forces in the management of organizations, and exposes some of the dubious values and shallowness of many accepted practices which ultimately contribute little and achieve no lasting change and improvement.

As you should by now sense, whilst the book's coverage is fairly diverse and touches a number of aspects of management development, it is anything but a repackaging of what has been written elsewhere. In each area, the book quickly seeks to move beyond what many people already know, to expose the real issues, how to tackle them, and how to exploit development's full potential. This book seeks to delve below the surface of much of the management development industry, its offerings and its protagonists, and asks awkward questions about their purpose, their values and their direction. Much of what we practise and much of what we buy is squandered because we don't think it through. We fail to anchor it in business reality, integrate it with other reinforcing action, and engage it with real everyday organization dilemmas.

There are currently several vitally important issues which are receiving little useful discussion and remain low profile. There are easy pickings to be made by those merely seeking to illuminate the problems, the waste of human assets, the corruptions of power, and the widespread abuses in management. You read about these in the newspapers. Yet where is management development? Usually relegated to the wings for a bit part, threatening no one, forsaking its calling at centre stage. Who is prepared to go there? Who is prepared to let them? Who knows what 'there' is? If *Developing Managerial Competence* holds the spotlight, it is *Developing Corporate Competence* which carries the torch.

This is not supposed to be an easy read. If it does its job, the book will give conventional trainers and developers some sleepless nights. It invites readers to play a part in challenging much of the current restricted thinking and lobby for a wider discussion and a more relevant agenda – both inside and outside their companies and institutions – on the kind of development which those who give 'their all' for business and for their employers richly need and deserve, but all too often do not receive. My hope is to turn some people away from their current vision of management development and free them to embark on a more fulfilling and more relevant journey. If that sounds arrogant, only you can judge when you have finished reading whether it was justified.

The author is always interested to hear from readers concerning their own experiences and views in relation to the ideas expressed in this book. He can be contacted at the address given below.

Fernleigh House
The Terrace
Wokingham
Berkshire RG40 1BP
United Kingdom
Tel: 01734 773443

William Tate

June 1995

ACKNOWLEDGEMENTS

I would like to acknowledge the help of many friends, colleagues and fellow learners, some whose personal contribution to life's lessons in the hard-knocks school of business is individually long-forgotten but which undoubtedly left its hidden mark only to surface again between the lines of these pages.

I am also indebted to the career chances offered by Nick Georgiades, to the support of Gerard Egan at Loyola University of Chicago, and other academics, consultants and writers on both sides of the Atlantic. In particular I should like to thank Shafi Parwani for his help with the text, and Mel Williams and Nicola Connor for supplying case material.

I would also like to thank the numerous fellow authors and publishers for allowing me to quote from their books and publications. Finally, I could not have completed this project without the proof-reading help of my sharp-eyed wife, Pauline, and the full support of my developing family.

I would also like to thank the following for permission to use copyrighted material:

Addison-Wesley Publishing Company for material from: C. Argyris and D. A. Schön (1978), *Organizational Learning: A Theory in Action Perspective*. © 1978 Addison-Wesley Publishing Company Inc. Reprinted by permission of the publisher.

American Management Association for extracts, J. Harvey (1974), 'The Abilene Paradox: The Management of Agreement', *Organizational Dynamics*, Summer. © 1974 American Management Association. All rights reserved.

John Wiley and Sons Inc., New York for extracts from: H. Hornstein (1986), *Managerial Courage: Revitalizing your Company Without Sacrificing your Job*. © H. Hornstein 1986.

Oxford University Press for extracts from John Kay (1994) *Foundations of Corporate Success*.

Sage Publications Ltd for extracts from: D. Boje (1994), 'Organizational Story-telling', *Management Learning* **25** (3); J. Gosling and D. Ashton (1994), 'Action

Learning and Academic Qualifications', *Management Learning* **25** (2). © 1994 by permission of Sage Publications Ltd.

Extracts from *Senior Management Standards*, published by the Management Charter Initiative, are Crown copyright material and are reproduced with the permission of the Controller of HMSO.

William Tate

PART ONE
MODELS, CONCEPTS AND DEFINITIONS

❖

1

DEVELOPING A MODEL FOUNDATION

OVERVIEW

This opening chapter takes the various themes concerning manager, management and organization development treated in this book, and discusses them in terms of conceptual models, to provide a firm foundation upon which to build the ideas in the later chapters.

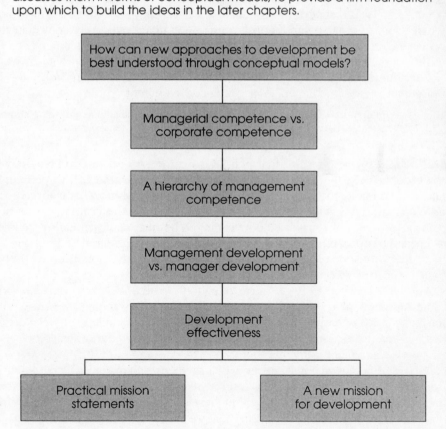

INTRODUCTION

C onfusingly, the word 'management' has two rather different meanings – the body of people who manage, and what they are paid to do. Actually it is more complicated than that. The individual management action or managing that managers are paid to *do* personally is not the same as the wider management of the business.

These subtly different shades of meaning and most people's loose usage of the word 'management' may partly explain the common assumption that if we attend to 'what managers do' we will inevitably arrive at 'management'. Hence, for many people, *manager* development has erroneously come to mean *management* development. This apparently simple point contains one of the biggest practical hurdles for many developers and their clients to jump.

For example, what do we find dominating the market? Products for developing individual managers, case-studies about the development of individual managers and good-practice codes biased towards individual managers' development. In this book I am challenging that predominant development orientation and practice – if not the heart-felt belief of many developers – that the prime route to management competence is through individual managers and their personal learning. My fundamental premise is that developers, and national agencies, need to see a greater role for developing other organizational components that collectively contribute to management – in parallel and integrated with managers' own development, and in some cases even separately.

I profoundly agree with the view expressed by Professor John Storey in his thorough review of the field of management development:

> Both in terms of practice and theorising, the field of management development in Britain has been stunted by conventional views on what constitutes its proper realm of concern.[1]

This book is my response to that rightful concern. I am seeking to break down some of those self-imposed boundary walls and jump some of the perimeter ditches wherein lie too many unchallenged assumptions about what management development can be allowed to mess with. If after reading this chapter you are not persuaded (that is, if you started out needing to be) that management's potential, its needs and opportunities can and should at times be considered as distinct from that of individual managers, then I suggest you read no further. The rest of the book is constructed on that basic conceptual foundation.

We therefore need to begin our exploration of the book's key concepts with some important matters of definition. Such clarity of understanding is best achieved through the use of models. These can take several forms, including the well-known mission statements. Later we shall examine the concept and the general scope and limits of development using this approach.

We shall differentiate managers from management, and managerial competence from corporate competence, then contrast manager development with management development. The nuances behind these terms provide a rich seam to tap for propounding a new way forward. But, first, we shall explore a very basic model of corporate competence.

MANAGERIAL COMPETENCE VERSUS CORPORATE COMPETENCE

The name of the game here is **corporate competence**. To play it means unlocking the secret which will enable us to translate *can-do* competence into *choose-to-do* and *allowed-to-do*, which together can enable us to achieve our goal.

Management developers tend to be mainly interested in 'can do' – many of them exclusively so. They seek to enhance managers' capability which the latter can then apply to job problems and organization needs as and when they arise. (Note that my use of 'can do' here is not the same as in a 'can-do' culture, where it means an optimistic or positive environment where people generally believe anything is possible.) 'Choose-to-do' and 'allowed-to-do' both place demands on the organization to do its part. 'Choose-to-do' can be thought of as *bottom up*; it refers to individual managers' inclination to make full and wise use of their capability in a way which suits their employer's goals. While this has to come from within, organizations can do much to encourage this motivational force and reinforce its continued application. By contrast, 'allowed-to-do' can be thought of as *top down*, which the organization can facilitate in a variety of ways as shown below.

> Organization facilitation. Through a purposeful context and problems to solve, a supportive framework, an absence of needless restrictions and boundaries, a lack of obstacles to performance (e.g. bureaucracy), appropriate checks and balances etc.
> ↓
> **allowed-to-do**

INDIVIDUAL (**can-do**) COMPETENCE → CORPORATE COMPETENCE

> **choose-to-do**
> ↑
> Personal motivation and values. Through clear vision, goals and challenges, a positive fear-free climate, constructive performance management feedback, relevant selection and appointment decisions, fair recognition and reward system, etc.

My premise is that developers need to be concerned with providing the missing organizational ingredient to add to raw capability. This might mean removing obstacles to performance, for example, or enabling the manager to hone his or her skills on real-life problems for which the organization is known to want solutions. Without such a direct concern and involvement on the part of developers, performance may remain cocooned at the potential stage, unable to reach maturity and fly.

Viewed in this way, many approaches to development are problematical. They are often generic and concerned with developing a broad range of managerial skills and achieving a more qualified workforce. This has its place in the wider scheme of things, and may help individuals, but from the organization's perspective it is a scattergun which hits its target at random. But even tailored programmes can miss the mark. Much development is unconcerned with the realized norms of behaviour in the organization, whether they are dysfunctional or irrational, and whether they are actively managed for improvement. In other words, development activity in such instances is driven by its own externally modelled agenda.

Corporate competence, on the other hand, requires an internally driven agenda, as we shall see in later chapters. It calls for a sound diagnosis which places managers' scope and needs in the context of what the organization itself needs and is able to provide and achieve. That requires us to master the art of examining competence – in the widest meaning of that word – from the organization's end of the telescope. Developing corporate competence which is applied in practice therefore means integrating managerial capability with its organizational purpose and context, especially with real problems that managers are paid to solve; and then actively ensuring the delivery of performance through the organization's systems and a positive climate.

A HIERARCHY OF MANAGEMENT COMPETENCE

Those who have read my book *Developing Managerial Competence: A Critical Guide to Methods and Materials*[2] will, I hope, have accepted that the process of functional analysis (breaking down what managers do into small elements) cannot provide an adequate total definition of management competence. That process can only provide *some* of what we can *see* of what *individual* managers do. As shown in Figure 1.1, *what a manager does* occupies Level 1 on a continuum, progressing through to the *management of the organization and business* in Level 5. The development labels used in conjunction with each of the steps is shown beneath each one.

This continuum in Figure 1.1 is not a proposed training/development activity progression. It merely differentiates between the various terms, concepts and interests, and places them in a hierarchy of the totality of competent management from a developer's perspective. The five levels form a hierarchy in the sense of representing the developer's ability to imagine a progression of management competence (from managerial through to corporate) and its implications for development through a sequence of increasing complexity, sophistication, challenge and opportunity.

Levels 1 and 2, covering the basics and the higher art of managerial competence respectively, are expanded fully in *Developing Managerial Competence*.[2] The Management Charter Initiative's management standards provide a definition of Level 1. Work by John Burgoyne, among others, to define Level 2 is also discussed in my book referred to above. The *higher art of managing* includes, for example, handling and creating change, balancing chaos and control, and knowing when to shelve one's competence in favour of an openness to the new. This book answers the question: what can developers do to give managers at Levels 1–3 the best

FIGURE 1.1 HIERARCHY OF MANAGEMENT COMPETENCE

MANAGERIAL COMPETENCE	→		→	*CORPORATE COMPETENCE*
1 **WHAT A MANAGER DOES**	**2** **THE HIGHER ART OF MANAGING**	**3** **INTACT UNIT TEAMWORK**	**4** **COLLECTIVE MANAGEMENT TEAMWORK**	**5** **MANAGEMENT OF THE ORGANIZATION AND BUSINESS**
A foundation of generic management skills. Centred on the individual. Initial focus of national initiatives on individual managers' competence and discussion on national training targets for managers. Assumed a major problem area in the national debate on the country's poor economic competitiveness. Certificate and Diploma level primarily. Many companies' development interest limited to this level and assumed sufficient, particularly where a heavy orientation towards skill training and competences.	The less tangible meta-qualities, attributes and sensibilities which differentiate excellence from competence, particularly at higher levels, and which complement fundamental skills. Should hope to find uniqueness and capitalize on it. Involves acquiring experience and wisdom. Requires an understanding and management of the non-rational aspects of the organization as well as the rational. Concerned with managing careers and sound leadership appointments. Relevant to development activity at higher educational levels/qualifications.	The handling, composition and intra-group performance of intact teams within functions. Not simply concerned with individuals having good team skill and understanding, important though that is. The most common focus for team-building and team-development activity.	How the wider company management team works together for a common corporate goal. Concerned with interdepartmental purposes and relationships, and cross-functional working and collaboration, and how the vertical and horizontal team together deliver business results and continual renewal. Relatively neglected.	The full range of options available to senior managers for improving the management of their part of the organization and business. Has implications for developing organizational capability (via the management climate, systems, rewards, etc.) and not just personal capability, and for directly assessing management competence at the corporate level.
Manager development	*Manager development*	*Management development*	*Management development and organization development*	*Management development and organization development*

7

chance of success? A basic premise is that *potential* is only worth having and developing if it is manifested as *performance* of the kind that benefits the client organization. But the book's main concern is the later stages of full management and organization development, Levels 4 and 5.

My hierarchical representation of management competence has a number of strands in common with John Burgoyne's 'Levels of Maturity of Organisational Management Development' put forward in 1988 in *Personnel Management*, as shown in Figure 1.2.[3] The two models (in Figures 1.1 and 1.2) are complementary. Burgoyne, like me, is concerned with the excessive emphasis on the individual's development and 'too little on management development for the organisation as a whole'. But his definition of management development as 'the management of managerial careers in an organisation context' stops short of the broader definition I have adopted which gives management development a role in tackling wider problems in managing a business successfully.

Whereas Burgoyne equates management and its development with *managers*, in Level 5 of my hierarchy I additionally equate management with the *activity* and *systems* of management. Burgoyne's interest in the organization is, quite rightly, in ensuring that the development of managers takes place in the context of an accepted organization strategy for development. He talks about developing managers for the purpose of 'implementing' corporate policy. This sounds to me rather too passive, reactive and compliant. It also might imply business stability and consequently little need to develop managers to be proactive in managing change. It also suggests that 'corporate policy' comes down from top management in a classical hierarchical manner – not the way of the future.

My own definition of the further reaches of development activity as an aspiration is more radical. It is less hierarchically structured, less deferential and more involving. My definition and interest extends to including strategies for developing the way the business is healthily managed. So, drawing on the example of the beleaguered insurance companies quoted in the book's Preface, those problems are management *system* problems (e.g. the value system and the reward system) which must be of direct concern to developers. It is not sufficient for a model to note and relate managers' development to their working context: it has to develop that context.

ACTIVITY 1.1

Using the models, reflect on how broadly management development is defined and practised in your own business area. How widely shared are perceptions about development's valid scope?

LIMITS ON DEVELOPERS' ASPIRATIONS

Attaining this ideal position is another matter altogether. For a start, few developers possess either the skills or the courage. Nor are developers usually permitted such an important and political role. Burgoyne likewise didn't find developers operating

FIGURE 1.2 LEVELS OF MATURITY OF ORGANIZATIONAL MANAGEMENT DEVELOPMENT

1	2	3	4	5	6
No systematic management development	**Isolated tactical management development**	**Integrated and coordinated structural and development tactics**	**A management development strategy to implement corporate policy**	**Management development strategy input to corporate policy formation**	**Strategic development of the management of corporate policy**
No systematic or deliberate management development in structural or developmental sense, total reliance on natural, *laissez faire* uncontrived processes of management development.	There are isolated and *ad hoc* tactical management development activities, of either structural or developmental kinds, or both, in response to local problems, crises, or sporadically identified general problems.	The specific management development tactics which impinge directly on the individual manager, or career structure management, and of assisted learning, are integrated and coordinated.	A management development strategy plays its part in implementing corporate policies through managerial human resource planning, and providing a strategic framework and direction for the tactics of career structure management and of learning, education and training.	Management development processes feed information into corporate policy decision-making processes on the organization's managerial assets, strengths, weaknesses and potential and contribute to the forecasting and analysis of the manageability of proposed projects, ventures, changes.	Management development processes enhance the nature and quality of corporate policy-forming processes, which they also inform and help implement.

Reproduced by courtesy of *Personnel Management*

at his Level 6. But that is not sufficient reason to stop them from having the vision, setting a goal to move in this direction, and planning some first steps along the way. Later on, this book offers ideas on how developers might begin to make such progress.

DEVELOPMENT LANGUAGE

My levels 4 and 5 are where the fields of management development and organization development (OD) start to become indistinguishable for managers. Some readers may call these higher levels 100 per cent OD. Some might say they are not OD at all – OD as a process has always been difficult to define. I don't mind too much what label you give such development action. What I am keen to avoid is drawing too firm a demarcation between, on the one hand, the activity concerned with developing managers, and on the other hand, that concerned with developing managers' environment and management systems. (I am using the term 'systems' loosely here to include, for example, the managerial recognition and reward system.)

There are good reasons for melding the range of development activity as far as management is concerned. If you place the organization dimensions which affect the way the business is managed outside the management developer's purview, then two problems occur. First, the development of managers takes place at a remove from the most crucial management issues currently facing the organization and without regard to the many key factors which bear on managers' scope to perform; and therefore such development activity ultimately has little impact on results. Second, there is a good chance that nobody else will deal with such organization management issues, since few companies recognize it as a legitimate separate activity, or provide distinct resources for its conduct.

KEY TIP

❖   Avoid a sharp demarcation between the different aspects of development.

MANAGEMENT DEVELOPMENT VERSUS MANAGER DEVELOPMENT

Most so-called 'management development' is, as we have said, a misnomer: it is actually *manager* development. In other words, the emphasis is on individuals and their needs. Indeed much manager *development* can turn out to be something of a misnomer too: it is often straightforward manager *training*.

DISTINGUISHING DEVELOPMENT FROM TRAINING

By manager 'training', I mean an activity concerned with acquiring something specifically needed by the company for the person to perform acceptably in the current role. Development, by contrast, has the following characteristics:

O   It is centred on the person's general growth and state of being.
O   It may have wider applications beyond the predictable short term.
O   It may entail learning through such processes as work assignments.

For the sake of simplicity, I shall be generous here and use the term 'development' regardless of scope, motive, application and timescale.

CLOSED VERSUS OPEN SYSTEMS DEVELOPMENT

Apart from its usually narrow emphasis on individuals, the conventional approach to much development activity modestly assumes a highly restricted definition of its power and scope. Developers limit their aspirations by adopting a closed-system or self-contained view of what development can legitimately be associated with in the company. Many developers work in a unitary manner with just one box in the organization model – that marked *individual competence*. This box is mistakenly treated by the developers and the learners as though it can be isolated from the other boxes (such as the recognition system).

Developers frequently work with teams, but even here the emphasis is often on the manager's leadership of a team – again a case of individual competence. At best, development action generally stops short of my Level 4.

Far less often do we find the more ambitious extended model of management development, one which takes an open-systems perspective of the organization. At this more elevated level (i.e. 4 and 5) management development functions in a way which directly addresses problems which involve the collective successful management of the business. It therefore has to interact in an integrated and strategic manner with other variables in the organization system, such as the climate. Such development action is multi-pronged.

DEVELOPERS' LOW ASPIRATIONS

Why do most developers settle for so little?

1.   Management development at the Levels 4 and 5 is more difficult and challenging.
2.   It takes different skills and calls upon organization psychology as well as individual psychology.
3.   The developers lack the necessary access to the wider system and the company's problems.
4.   It is a political activity: it raises uncomfortable questions about the stewardship of those at the top, and the management culture they preside over, have enjoyed success under and with which they are presumably content.

Notwithstanding these obstacles, adopting the broader definition of management development can have a far more powerful impact on the business than mere manager development. There are several well-known problems experienced by those who choose to, or have to, work with the restricted definition:

○   It relies on a tacit and vain hope that the sum of any development of individual managers will somehow collectively solve the organization's management problems.

○   The process usually leaves out the top management or gives them only a token part.

○   The development action is often not adequately understood by others and learning is not reinforced by the boss and colleagues in the workplace.

○   The manager's organization (its structure, climate, processes, systems, rewards, IT and cultural norms) has not been prepared and is unsympathetic to any individual wanting to behave differently personally or wanting to change things.

Manager development often does benefit individuals personally, in either skill or career terms, and hopefully benefits the company a little. But it is not an organization change strategy and should not be mistaken as such. From the company's perspective, manager development lacks the power to grasp opportunities to make a real difference to the company's management and the business's performance. In hoping to achieve this much, it has to put its faith in individual managers' personal power and drive, usually against daunting odds which conspire to uphold the status quo.

ACTIVITY 1.2

What scope do you have for development to be used to integrate the range of vertical, horizontal and cross-functional relationships?

TRANSFERABLE SKILLS

For developers there can be a conflict of interest here. Managers are changing jobs less often as a matter of choice, and more often because their employer forces them to. Transferable skills which are not vested in one employer, or even one career, are a real asset. Manager development makes a useful contribution in this area, and the enhanced mobility of managers can benefit both parties (though it is more often seen as a one-sided deal in favour of the manager).

From this perspective too, manager development *is* a worthwhile activity, but it is clearly not all there is to management development. Moving the emphasis away from the individual and involving other people and other boxes in the organization model are some of the actions developers can take to make a greater impact.

DEVELOPMENT EFFECTIVENESS

Even if our only aim is manager development, there is more we can do to increase its chance of contributing to business success. What we are seeking is learning which is successfully carried through to organization action and ultimately to business value. There are many measures we can take – such as narrowing the gap between theory and practice, between off-the-job and on-the-job, and between learning-material and real-life. We can try to ensure that learning is not isolated from other performance factors in the organization, always remembering that employers are looking for an organization that serves the needs of the business.

BUSINESS VERSUS ORGANIZATION

In *Adding Value – A Systematic Guide to Business-Driven Management and Leadership*, Gerard Egan makes a nice but important distinction between **business** and **organization**.[4] He talks about the *business* as 'its mandate, what it is about, its strategic thrust'; it has an external orientation. Whereas the *organization* is 'the way the company or institution structures itself and deploys its human resources to serve the business'; this has an internal orientation. (I shall use the term 'company' to include all institutions across the public, private and voluntary sectors.)

Writing in *Management Today*, Egan offers an illustration showing where it is vital to think clearly about the important distinction between business and organization:

> One company after another blindly pursues restructuring – an *organizational* intervention – when the problems lie with the *business*, the poorly formed and executed strategies, the wrong set of products, poor service, ineffective marketing, and the like. A new structure will never rescue a lousy strategy or an inept marketing programme.[5] [my italics]

Since all human resource matters are by definition part of Egan's organization dimension, it follows that manager/management development action can be thought of as an organizational intervention rather than a business intervention. In other words, developers generally intend that the interests of the business should be addressed indirectly by acting upon factors within the organization dimension. For example, development effort often assumes that managers will acquire generic organization skills and knowledge (an internal focus) and then use this to tackle particular real business problems (an external focus).

We have to hope that the managers once working in their business environment will somehow find ways of making that full transition through to business value. And we assume that if the organization as a whole and all its members are thereby enabled to function fully effectively in the manner intended, then the interests of the business will be served.

In some cases the connection with the business is obvious; for example, development activity concerned with business meetings, negotiating with suppliers, dealing with investors, *putting the customer first* initiatives, etc.

In other cases the connection may be more tenuous. Here learnt skills may be wholly concerned with the internal smooth running of the organization machine; for example, improved staff briefings, better team relationships, good staff appraisals. As long as that internally focused application is not self-serving and truly – even if indirectly – serves the business, there is no problem with that. We simply take on trust that the business will ultimately be better off for having incurred the development effort and expenditure at the organization level.

TRANSFER OF LEARNING

There is, of course, usually a further (actually earlier) element of chance involved before the manager's new-found ability can be applied successfully to the organization and thence to serve the business. Most manager development activity works with abstract material, producing another level of indirectness of application, first to the real organization (e.g. from practising pseudo-meeting skills on a course to applying real-meeting skills at work), and then on to serve the ultimate business needs (e.g. meetings which develop sound business strategies).

Trainers talk about this optimistic bridging process as 'transfer'. By this they usually mean transfer from off-the-job to on-the-job, from course to workplace. But I have gone one step further in highlighting the second level of transfer – from internal organization action to business value (or business outcome, meaning or result); we shall see why in a moment.

First level of learning transfer

The first level of learning transfer (to the real workplace) is the more problematical, especially for the growing band of distance learners. But the problems of off-the-job learning are well-understood, as are the means for facilitating the transfer process. I discuss these and offer advice in *Developing Managerial Competence.*[2]

One of the best shortcuts is for the managers' learning to take place directly with the involvement of others, ideally work-group colleagues, but in practice the group of learners usually comprises a collection of like-minded strangers. This kind of linking-up may include developing the group members' interpersonal relationships, but that is only one particular application of collective learning.

Second level of learning transfer

The second level of learning transfer (on to business value) is less under the control of individual managers. But there are ways to shorten the odds, both in terms of the learning approach used and in terms of a wise choice of relevant learning material (in its widest sense), which we shall consider next.

INDIRECT OR DIRECT LEARNING

It is sometimes possible for development action to work closely from the outset at the direct level of business subjects. Here are a couple of examples.

CASE EXAMPLES: BUSINESS-LEVEL DEVELOPMENT ACTION

1. One well-known company that designed a management development programme aimed directly at the business level asked its managers to examine the changing nature of the competition. While learning the techniques and skills of competitor analysis, they were gaining a better understanding of their actual business, which they could then put to immediate use in their jobs.

2. Another company designed a course aimed at developing its managers' strategy-forming skills and produced business strategies which they could then take away with them.

ABSTRACT VERSUS REAL LEARNING MATERIAL

Abstract learning material

By abstract learning material I mean anything other than that which the learner is currently involved with on a regular work basis. It includes all generic material, texts, pre-written case-studies, games, simulations, outdoor pursuits, etc. The material is openly artificially developed and used for the purpose of providing learners with 'vehicles' from which to comprehend principles, acquire generic skills, etc. for onward transference and application to real-life work situations.

Real learning material

This category includes learners' own problems, contexts, colleagues, teams, relationships. Where case-studies are used these are current living case-studies, i.e. the real drama in learners' companies.

Inevitably, most formal learning for individual managers, especially where it leads to qualifications, will be of the abstract variety. But my thesis is that some of this learning is unnecessarily remote from learners' work lives, with the result that the transfer problems are greater than they sometimes need to be. If a client says 'my people need to be developed to be more commercial', then the developer should respond 'OK, let's examine some present business opportunities.'

Material takes the abstract form for a variety of well-recognized reasons – some good, some less good:

○   To make it safe for learners.
○   To optimize learning incidents.
○   To provide more time for practice and feedback.
○   Practical convenience for the provider.
○   Insufficient trainer skill and flexibility.
○   Lack of close access of the designer of the learning to the company's organization.
○   To have a familiar mass product to sell pre-packaged.

The degree to which the learning material is abstract varies, as shown in Figure 1.3. The use of abstract learning material can sometimes be confusing for learners, especially when it is the company's real material which the parties decide shall be used only for learning purposes and not to be acted upon subsequently.

FIGURE 1.3 FALSE–REAL LEARNING MATERIAL CONTINUUM

1 VISIBLY FALSE →	2 OSTENSIBLY → REALISTIC	3 POTENTIALLY → REAL	4 LIVE REALITY →
Patently removed from real work life (e.g. outdoor pursuits, and games such as how to survive on the moon).	Resembles typical work-type material, but not actually the learner's own or his/her company's.	Genuine learner's company material, but agreed for use only as learning opportunity.	The learners' own work problems and needs in context from which to learn *and* move forward.

CASE EXAMPLE: LEARNING MATERIAL

One company I know trains its heads of department in the skills of developing strategies for their own functional areas. To do this it uses the shared 'vehicle' of getting them to produce a radical business strategy for the company. They are then required to present their new business strategy to their board of directors. Having worked on this over several months, they become very attached to their strategy and consider it superior to the board's. They are then shocked when the board politely listens but does nothing with their strategy, correctly regarding it as no more than a learning exercise (i.e. Position 3, Potentially Real) because that is the deal they struck with the developers.

It is not sufficient for developers to claim to be able to avoid this kind of problem with good briefings. The problem arises because the chosen material could be real (i.e. Position 4, Live Reality), and the learners desperately want it to be.

ACTIVITY 1.3

Consider ways in which development might be used directly to impact business issues. What real current business problems could feature in development activities in place of abstract material?

CHOOSING LEARNING MATERIAL

In choosing and designing learning for maximum guaranteed pay-off to the business, we have seen that there are several dimensions for developers to consider, both in terms of subject areas and learning approaches:

O   Individual learning vs. group learning.

O   Stranger group vs. actual work-group.

O   Team capability vs. corporate capability.

O   Internal (organization) focus vs. external (business) focus.

O   Closed-system vs. open-system (i.e. integrated, multi-pronged action).

O   Abstract learning material vs. real learning material.

These can be plotted as a matrix, with the aim of indicating where there is the greatest chance of development action making an impact on the business, as shown in Figure 1.4.

FIGURE 1.4 DEVELOPMENT EFFECTIVENESS MATRIX

less direct impact	PROXIMITY TO BUSINESS MEANING INTERNAL/REMOTE FOCUS → EXTERNAL/CLOSE FOCUS	
INDIVIDUAL MANAGERS ↓	1 abstract closed	5 real closed
STRANGER GROUPS ↓	2 abstract closed	6 abstract/real closed
OWN WORK-TEAM ↓	3 abstract/real closed	7 real closed/open
WIDER ORGANIZATION	4 real open	8 real open

more direct impact

KEY TIPS

❖   Try to choose learning material which is as close as practicable to learners' real work context, and which involves their work colleagues if possible.

❖   Use multiple learning interventions to support and reinforce each other.

DIRECT LEARNING APPROACHES AND METHODS

There are several learning approaches or methods which also try to shortcut the transfer process. These include action learning and process consulting, which we shall look at in greater depth later in the book (Chapter 5).

Competence-based distance learning is a most interesting and popular example of an off- and on-the-job mix. It attempts to overcome the problem of using abstract learning material by extending its interest in the learning chain to the practical application in the workplace and basing its ultimate assessment on what happens there. This method is discussed in my book *Developing Managerial Competence*.[2]

There is also another class of development activity altogether, that which promotes learning through job experience (e.g. carefully planned career moves, taking part in taskforces with development in mind, etc.)

PLOTTING DEVELOPMENT ACTIVITIES

This basic matrix can be used to indicate where a range of typical development activities (methods and subjects) might fall. For several reasons, my own allocation (see Figure 1.5) of a sample of items to the sectors can be only a rough approxi-

---

FIGURE 1.5 DEVELOPMENT ACTIVITIES MATRIX

less direct impact

PROXIMITY TO BUSINESS MEANING
INTERNAL/REMOTE FOCUS → EXTERNAL/CLOSE FOCUS

INDIVIDUAL MANAGERS

1
Basic skill/knowledge courses
- presentation skills
- running meetings
- team leading
- time management
- coaching skills for managers
- business finance
- the role of supervision

Private counselling
- career advice
- work relationships
- stress

5
Learning by experience
- secondments
- shadowing
- special one-off projects
- taskforce participation
- changing work arrangements
- enlarging job responsibilities
- complete change of role

On-the-job coaching
Professional know-how
- law updates

Work-based learning

Competence-assessed distance learning

STRANGER GROUPS

2
Management games
- group dynamics
- team roles
- conflict resolution

Outdoor pursuits
- team-development

Business simulations

6
Strategic learning
- competitor studies
- strategy development
- partnership development

OWN WORK-TEAM

3
Live team enhancement

7
Action learning
Process consulting

WIDER ORGANIZATION

4
Management structural development
- decentralization
- hierarchical flattening
- business process re-engineering
- de-bureaucratization

Management systems development

8
Culture change programmes
- customer service initiatives
- internal customer concept
- TQM, JIT, etc.

Climate development

more direct impact

mation. The precise allocation depends on several factors. For example, the content material used may to a greater or lesser extent be false or real. And some individual skill modules can be developed in a group setting (indeed, they may have to be, as with learning chairmanship skills and appraisal skills, for example); but this learning group may or may not consist of working colleagues.

I posit that too great a proportion of development activities are to be found in the left-hand/upper sectors (1 and 2). This strikes me as unbalanced. Development's ability to improve the effectiveness of the company's performance would be enhanced by having more development action in the other sectors (3 to 8).

ACTIVITY 1.4

Plot for yourself where your current spread of development activities falls within the matrix. Where might an imbalance need to be redressed?

HOW BROAD CAN DEVELOPMENT BE?

All of the above discussion implies a fairly broad view about what potentially constitutes development. But just how broad? What are the limits?

CASE EXAMPLE: DEVOLVING POWER AS A DEVELOPMENT INTERVENTION

A company's management performance was limited by the negative exercise of power by a number of large and powerful head office 'support departments'. Line managers had no discretion and lacked the means to bring about action; they could only request it – especially of the personnel, finance and purchasing departments. No amount of effort at developing individual managers would have touched that problem. So manager development was not a solution.

As the consultant, I could see that a structural solution was needed in order to develop the company management performance capacity. What was needed was the decentralization of head office power and resources. This diagnosis was accepted and implemented.

It doesn't really matter whether or not readers are prepared to consider such drastic restructuring interventions as falling loosely under the 'development' banner (whether *management development* or *organization development*). What matters is that those looking for ways of developing the management of the business can, in one way or another, call on a wide variety of interventions, including structural ones. In other words, they need to take an holistic or systems-wide approach to performance-enhancing interventions.

If you accept this definition of development's remit, it can regrettably sometimes mean harming the careers of undeserving managers for the greater good of the company. This can be painful for those developers who like to regard the individual manager as their main responsibility, even as their personal client.

A NEW MISSION FOR DEVELOPMENT

Training has traditionally been put into its own neat box and told to stay there. Overt and fostered links with development activities, such as career planning, succession planning, appraisal, productivity issues, reorganizations, and the like, are still fairly uncommon. The organization structure, as well as past attitudes and the boundaries of professional disciplines have tended to encourage this.

But the scene is changing. Interest in outsourcing training, and the present high profile of training at the national level, are causing companies to take a closer look at it. The result is that trainers who remain in-house are able to come closer to real business issues and take a more proactive role. Yet this new view of training may not help with some of the structural barriers and limitations mentioned. In particular, there is a danger that the amount of publicity given to training, and exaggerated faith in its powers, may actually be at the expense of the work of developers.

Some companies are now beginning to loosen the ties round departmental boundaries, but most still use labels and compartments in a way which circumscribes full and open diagnosis, engagement and collaboration. Training departments are a prime example, or victim, of this segmentation practice.

The word 'training' itself is comfortingly suggestive of solutions and implies an emphasis on delivery. But this is to take a view from the wrong end of the telescope, and fails to look for what the customer needs. It can divert us from talking about problems that go much deeper than individuals' ability. The upshot is that many training departments' core activity is still running or sponsoring off-the-shelf programmes which individual managers are nominated for by their bosses or nominate themselves. These are generally interesting and popular, but they are rarely directly related to real problems or fundamental to the company's future. Nor are they even efficient or cost-effective. They are, at best, a partial answer.

Dedicated training departments can experience considerable resistance and difficulty gaining access to real-life management problems to solve, even where they do see their role in this way. When they *do* see problems, they are automatically disposed to seeing them in training terms. Yet the best solution to some organizational problems is often something quite different from training, such as moving people and even removing them altogether.

There is a need to broaden the range of actions available from the development function, and at the same time to give it wider access to the gamut of organizational, productivity, efficiency, structural, staffing and capability issues.

A STRUCTURAL ANSWER

One strategy for broadening the perspectives and relaxing the boundaries is to place training alongside wider development interests, making it formally part of a company's development strategy. Organization development, management development, training and education would then fall under a single roof with carefully planned terms of reference.

There is benefit here in bringing management development (MD) and organization development (OD) activities closer together. Rather like training, these too suffer from compartmentalization in some large companies (that is, those which show any understanding of, and give any kind of recognition to the legitimacy and practice of organization development).

But this suggested merger is not the only way to organize the various development activities. Management development is sometimes closely allied with recruitment and selection activity because of the shared interest in psychological assessment. This is a valid alternative organization structure strategy.

Also, the disciplines of MD and OD are distinct. MD draws on occupational psychology and is more interested in the individual and groups of individuals. OD draws on organization psychology and is more interested in the health and dynamics of the organization and how it affects its business. But there are many shared areas of interest, as we have seen. The following benefits may derive from placing these disciplines under one roof:

O   It removes management development's excuse for providing only *manager* development.
O   It facilitates synergy between the activities.
O   It develops an expanded toolkit for the practitioners, beginning with diagnosis.
O   It directly tackles real management issues affecting the business.
O   It gives OD a chance, without which it might lose out altogether.

PRACTICAL MISSION STATEMENTS

The suggested mission for a combined Management and Organization Development function is shown below. This was developed for a client in need of a significant turnaround of management culture, starting from a passive administrative base.

> *To provide a strategic focal point for the ongoing development of a modern and forward-looking organization and talented management team, promoting individual and collective management capability and company capacity, able to initiate and manage renewal and change.*

It may be helpful to contrast this with the parallel mission evolved for Personnel:

> *To provide appropriate professional personnel and employment services and policies to help departments achieve their business objectives.*

The Appendix at the end of this chapter contains fully expanded versions. The statement may be expressed in two parts, as is the case with those set out in the Appendix. Strictly speaking, only the first short sentence (as above) deals with **mission**, and the more lengthy elaboration which follows it appears as **goals**. Both components are necessary.

(Note that in the Appendix the aspect of career management appears summarized as just one element in the full M & OD Mission and Goals statement; this subject is covered in much greater detail in Chapter 7 'Refocusing Career Management'.)

Whether readers will find that the sample mission statements in the Appendix conform to their understanding of model mission statements is a personal matter. There are many and varied opinions about mission statements. There are expressive types of people who like mission statements to be very short and simple. They look for something which is memorable and catchy. Otis Lifts' 'To move people horizontally and vertically' is a prime example of this genre. Or they may seek something inspiring, as with mission statements which begin 'To be the best XYZ'.

To me these sound more like advertising slogans. I have come across allegedly serious examples such as 'To be the best finance department in the world', but how would this finance department differ from any other which also wants to be the best? To my mind, this simplistic approach produces statements which raise more questions than they answer.

From a somewhat analytical and rational approach, my own preference is for something which is the product of considerable debate. It is what has gone into generating the mission statement, and the process of involving the key stake-holders that matters more than its subsequent motivational impact. The statement should be able to answer interested parties' questions about the function's purpose and limits of its business.

ACTIVITY 1.5

Review your mission statement for the development function against the model set out in the Appendix. How might it be enhanced?

VISION VERSUS MISSION

We can still have slogans, but we should recognize them for what they are. Slogans probably come closer to qualifying as a forward *vision*, another point of confusion with mission. Statements of mission and goals should be about the short term. They should be unquestionably realistic and attainable if not already being practised. In contrast, visions are more concerned with longer-term aspirations and may not ultimately come about as envisaged. But they galvanize energy by indicating a bright future towards which people can take steps along the way.

REFERENCES

1. John Storey (1990) 'Management Development: A Literature Review and Implications for Future Research – Part II', *Personnel Review* **19** (1), p. 3.
2. William Tate (1995) *Developing Managerial Competence: A Critical Guide to*

Methods and Materials, Aldershot: Gower.

3. John Burgoyne (1988) 'Management Development for the Individual and the Organisation', *Personnel Management* (June).
4. Gerard Egan (1993) *Adding Value – A Systematic Guide to Business-Driven Management and Leadership*, San Francisco: Jossey-Bass, p. xx.
5. Gerard Egan (1993) 'The Shadow Side', *Management Today*, September.

APPENDIX: SAMPLE MISSION STATEMENTS

MANAGEMENT AND ORGANIZATION DEVELOPMENT

Mission

To provide a strategic focal point for the ongoing development of a modern and forward-looking organization and talented management team, promoting individual and collective management capability and company capacity, able to initiate and manage renewal and change.

Goals

○   To diagnose organization problems, within, between and across departments. To design, develop and help implement appropriate solutions that enhance the company's efficiency, effectiveness and capability.

○   To promote and develop a managerial culture which:
  ● emphasizes achieving results rather than carrying out processes;
  ● requires managers to manage rather than be administrators;
  ● shows impatience with poor performance, conformity and the status quo;
  ● gives power to line managers to win the business;
  ● emphasizes satisfying external and internal customer needs;
  ● experiments and trusts, and lets go of excessive control;
  ● displays flexibility and allows those best placed to take decisions and action;
  ● responds to the company's real financial and business environment;
  ● recognizes and optimizes its asset value in all its employees;
  ● tries to reach new standards of excellence and constantly improve.

○   To specify the ideal manager profile appropriate for future success, as an input to:
  ● appointment and promotion decisions;
  ● the identification and auditing of managerial talent;
  ● the design of training and development strategies, initiatives and programmes.

○   To design, implement and monitor the use of appropriate means of performance management, including appraisal, with respect to:
  ● objective-setting;
  ● appraisal interview skills;
  ● personal development plans;
  ● documentation;
  ● processes;
  ● feedback;
  ● ratings;
  ● rewards.

○   To encourage the use of a wide variety of imaginative and positive developmental and learning opportunities within departments, including:
  ● enlarging job responsibilities;

- undertaking special projects;
- taking part in taskforces;
- reorganizing the work arrangements;
- on-the-job guidance and coaching;
- mentoring;
- access to appropriate learning material;
- work shadowing;
- temporary job swaps with colleagues;
- short off-the-job training courses;
- educational studies;
- internal and external secondments;
- private counselling on personal matters;
- complete change of job role.

○ To design, plan, organize, conduct and evaluate in-house, off-the-job manager and management development, education and training programmes which enhance personal, inter- and intra-group competence, solve managers' real business problems and extend their personal vision. Sponsor and organize the use of external training and education provision where appropriate.

○ To encourage and provide the means of managers' access to relevant professional management literature, conferences, programmes and networks, which will keep them abreast of developments in their field. Scan the external world of management and thereby be the means by which the company can continually update its management aspirations.

○ To help plan managers' careers. Be a resource for career advice to individual managers. Advise top management on job rotation plans for managed experience. Plan and ensure key succession capability at senior levels. Ensure that decisions about who to retain and who to release take account of managerial talent as well as other considerations.

PERSONNEL

NB: This statement of Mission and Goals was produced for a large company structure in which development activity (Management and Organization Development) was separate from other Personnel services, and which was in the process of devolving all routine day-to-day employment administration to line departments.

Mission

To provide appropriate professional personnel and employment services and policies to help departments achieve their business objectives.

Goals

○ To provide functional coordination of the various line departments' own Employment Managers' work, by means of assisting with appropriate staffing, professional support and personal career development, and corporate employment policies, standards, documentation and advice, and the joint departmental monitoring of acceptable performance.

○   To manage a range of personnel specialisms at the centre whose expertise is applied corporately in the development of appropriate and up-to-date professional policies, practices, standards and documentation, and whose advice and services may be called upon by individual line departments, in respect of the following matters:

● Compensation and Benefits including job evaluation, job descriptions, salary structures, incentives and rewards, allowances and market data;

● Employee Relations including employment legislation, relations with organized labour, staff communications, employment contract and other business related to engagement, appointment, employment and termination;

● Recruitment and Selection including selection policies, standards and practices, job advertisements, interview skills training, assessment and testing, plus the direct handling of vacancies at higher levels;

● Manpower Planning including manpower forecasting, compiling and analysing data (e.g. wastage rates, age profiles), labour market supply and demand, quotas and targets, with a view to predicting and anticipating problems and proposing appropriate responses.

○   To provide a central Employment Administration Office service to handle the day-to-day employment affairs for (i) the top level of corporate management, and (ii) the small head office departments without their own Employment Manager.

○   To provide a corporate-wide range of personnel services, including such matters as the issue of ID cards, organization charts, etc.

In order to facilitate the achievement of these goals, the personnel department has the following aims:

1.   To achieve an appropriate balance between:

● the need to help individual line departments and their managers with local problems, while safeguarding the need for consistent corporate standards and practice where appropriate;

● the need to provide practical, speedy and expedient business solutions, along with the need for legally sound, well-considered and ethical professional personnel practice.

2.   To work in close cooperation with line departments, to provide support rather than control over matters concerned with their employees.

3.   To concentrate on developing and improving a specialist and advisory role rather than a routine day-to-day administrative role.

2

TO TRAIN OR TO EDUCATE?
THAT IS THE QUESTION

OVERVIEW

This chapter looks at a key choice for developers – that of training or education – when deciding what emphasis to give their activities when developing managers.

How can we best balance training and
education when developing managers?

Separating training
from education

Training or
indoctrination

Training vs. education
– how much?

Freedom
to learn

| Developers'
accountabilities | National training
trends | Systematic training vs.
integrated learning |

INTRODUCTION

W hat we are currently witnessing in the UK, especially with the advent of competences for management development (now even in some business schools), is a trend towards training at the expense of education. Sharpening bosses' accountability for the bottom-line, and raising the stakes for success or failure, are likely to push us further in this direction. This is a highly questionable trend.

But why is it happening? Is there a strategy to explain it? To some developers and commentators, the current national training scene appears somewhat conspiratorial, sinister and manipulative. There appears to be a hidden agenda. But the dynamics may be nothing of the sort. The string-pullers may simply be oblivious to the possible alternatives and their implications. After all, 'Britain's managers need more skills to compete in Europe' has an easy attraction. By comparison, the implications of non-training options for managers' development takes more comprehending. The alternatives are also less appealing to most employers. One option in particular – genuine education – requires stouter hearts and stronger stomachs.

Reaching beyond individual capability, management's performance may be enhanced by a host of both non-training and non-education options; in other words, interventions which aim to remove blockages, and interventions which aim to enhance *systems* of management. But more about this level of intervention later. In the meantime, we shall discuss development action aimed primarily at individual managers.

Underlying the choices about when and whether to use training or education are many moral assumptions as well as beliefs about how people learn. It is therefore not surprising that there are parallels to be drawn here with developers adopting either the traditional **systematic training model** or the more recently enunciated **integrated learning model** approach. We shall look critically at these models and propound an up-to-date set of beliefs for the development of managers.

But we begin by examining the stark options and sometimes painful choices to be exercised around training versus education. We show how these decisions are both dependent upon and crucially influential of management culture and style.

SEPARATING TRAINING FROM EDUCATION

To understand and illustrate these crucial choices, let's take an example with which readers will readily be able to identify: the work of airline pilots. Their world is clearly delineated: external stimuli are predictable 99 per cent of the time and the appropriate response is incontestable. To make these responses, pilots are therefore *trained*; they are not *developed*. Nor, as a generalization, are pilots educated (as a process, that is!), though they are, of course, required to have received a good education before being trained to fly. But they are not *educated* to fly.

One reason why training is the dominant learning process for pilots is that instances where they need to draw on personal reserves of creativity and imagination are rare. It does happen occasionally. One pilot whose aircraft had lost all control over the wing surfaces had to experiment with a wholly unconventional way of turning the aircraft by varying the amount of thrust from the two engines. Training had not prepared him directly for that eventuality. However, such novelty is, thankfully, rare.

But many managers feel they are faced with novel problems almost every day. Indeed, if the problems were always routine, would they even *be* managers? Would we need managers or just administrators? For these versatile managers, training can provide only *some* of their answers – the more predictable ones. They need something else to help them with the others.

One way of comparing demonstrated (output) competences and personal (input) competencies is to consider the former of greater interest to trainers, and the latter of greater interest to developers and educators. That begs the question of which of these alternatives companies should be more interested in for their managers. (These different types of competence are discussed in *Developing Managerial Competence*.[1])

FREEDOM TO LEARN

The humorist Stephen Fry captures the simple but profound spirit of the argument – as well as the spirit of the times:

> This new England we have invented for ourselves is not at all interested in education. It is only interested in training, both material and spiritual. Education means freedom, it means truth. Training is what you do to a pear tree when you pleach it and prune it to grow against a wall. Training is what you give to an airline pilot or a computer operator or a barrister or a radio producer. Education is what you give to children to enable them to be free from the prejudices and moral bankruptcies of their elders. And freedom is no part of the programme of today's legislators. Freedom to buy shares, medical treatment or council houses certainly, freedom to *buy* anything you please. But freedom to think, to challenge, to change. Heavens no.
>
> The day a child of mine comes home from school and reveals that he or she has been taught something I agree with is the day I take that child away from school.[2]

Leaving aside the party political dimension to this diatribe, and taking it out of its school context, Fry makes a telling point which we can translate to the world of business. All organizations are political by definition. There is always a hierarchy which gives power to some over others. Those with power over the company's ideology and resources sponsor or provide training for those below them. They decide what is good for others, invariably excluding themselves. It is an unusually confident leader who is comfortable having his authority, position, ideas or decisions challenged. It is even more rare to find a leader who believes that this kind of behaviour should be encouraged as healthy for the future of the organization. Yet this is precisely Fry's conclusion.

CONCOMITANT RISKS

Alan Mumford, in his book *Management Development – Strategies for Action*, claims that the purpose of development or learning is 'to encourage challenge and debate, either about the nature of the organisation or the individual.'[3] In case we missed the point, Mumford then sharpens our sense of how his 'development and learning' differs from training by posing a rhetorical question: 'Do those who offer such opportunities accept the dangers and risks involved, and do they make those to whom they are offering the opportunity aware of those dangers and risks?'

ACTIVITY 2.1

Identify where your current development opportunities present learners with high organizational expectations, and associated stresses and personal risks. How can you best ameliorate these and protect learners?

TRAINING OR INDOCTRINATION

Straightforward training is largely free of Mumford's political risks. But training does risk becoming a voice for propaganda. To take an example from the school context again, the devout speak of the need for more religious 'education' in children's upbringing. But its most ardent advocates (who usually criticize the study of *comparative religion*) don't mean education in Fry's liberalizing sense: they mean indoctrination. The latter is often found disguised inside education's cloak, but the two are polar opposites. What zealots really seek from learners is conviction and acceptance, not questioning. They want to close the mind to unacceptable possibilities, rather than open it up to doubt.

CERTITUDE VERSUS DOUBT

Certitude has a lot to answer for. Certitude is dangerous, especially in the particular context quoted. But it is also highly convenient for leaders, wherever they are. The strait-jacket of certainty ties people down, whereas the unleashing of doubt cuts their mental bonds and sets them free. What many 'teachers' are interested in is not education at all: it is training in disguise. Training inhabits the world of certitude; education thrives on, and fosters, doubt. Those who are sure they know the right answers for their communities know that freedom to question spells trouble.

Certitude may look like a friend but it is a charlatan; doubt seems like an unattractive companion but turns out to be a wise friend if only we will be trusting and understanding. Education helps us to see past the veneer of the press conference and through the public relations smoke screen. Education helps us to evaluate leadership without rose-tinted spectacles, and to respond appropriately to it. If training helps us manage, education helps us manage management.

TRAINING AS PROPAGANDA

Indoctrination and internal propaganda play a large part in managing most organizations. Company news-sheets are a branch of PR. Those in charge of them do not enjoy editorial freedom. I knew one company chairman who stipulated that his editor had to find some way of showing his photograph in each week's issue. Maybe this is inevitable. It makes some sense. People want to feel well led. No matter that their publications are sometimes sanitized and satirized as 'good news-sheets'.

Of rather more concern, many of what we call 'training' courses are really carefully managed propaganda events. Singing from the same songsheet sounds more harmonious and certainly makes life easier for the conductor, but we can only develop with managed discord. Keep a watch out for the misuse of propaganda under the guise of training.

TRAINING FOR CONSENSUS

Ask chief executives what they want from management development, and many will say they need to feel supported. Therein lies part of the problem. It may be what they want, but it is not what they need.

Certitude, training and compliance are natural bedfellows which bring warm feelings for leaders, wherever they are. To misquote the well-known advertising slogan, the appliance of compliance is easy and non-threatening. Compliance is a highly successful strategy for retaining and wielding power. It may also prove to be a successful business strategy, at least in a stable environment. But that does not make it healthy, especially over the long run.

Harmony leads to consensus, and on to yes-men. Just as training and education need balance, so do collaboration and conflict. Of course, in many companies, we find destructive conflict, both over ideas and their proponents. But over-friendly collaboration can easily lead to pacts and cover-ups (e.g. the production director privately agrees with the marketing director to keep quiet about the latter's gaffe so long as he does not raise his concerns with the managing director over the scheduling problem). In this way problems can get swept under the carpet.

The founder of RCA, David Sarnoff, said, 'Competition brings out the best in products, and the worst in people.' Probably true, but not the full story. As well as competition being good for products, I would add that organizations need healthy competition to develop ideas. Education is a way of promoting such a managerial culture. Education can open up the mind in the way that training can close it down.

TRAINING VERSUS EDUCATION – HOW MUCH?

Some trainers will quite reasonably argue (1) that managers need basic skills, e.g. in report-writing; (2) that they therefore need to be trained; (3) that this kind of training does not risk producing unthinking zombies; (4) that managers can't be left free to work out what they need; and (5) that someone else has to do that for them. I agree up to a point. Whilst there is much wrong with training, pear trees still need pleaching. The problem is more likely to be too little of what I am calling education, rather than too much training.

HIDDEN MOTIVES AND MESSAGES

But watch out. Even the most innocuous skills training can carry hidden messages. I remember when, about twenty-five years ago, I led a very basic course in how to run a committee, including how to table agenda items, how to raise points of order, how to write minutes, etc. I considered this to be nothing more than a skills course. What I failed to realize at the time was that I was imposing my own set of beliefs about the best way to transact business in the company. Behind the basic skills lies a set of unspoken and unconscious assumptions about when committees should be used, the pace of change, the use of bureaucracy, the provision of resources, the value of consensus decision making, etc.

Nowadays, we would say I was pursuing my own private agenda, but I hadn't progressed as far as considering my motives. I thought I was simply teaching useful skills. I certainly did not stop to ask whether the client (whoever that was) knew what I was doing, understood it, agreed with it, or even cared. (Nor did I ask myself whether what I was teaching stood any chance of being implemented, but that is a different issue, though a highly relevant one nonetheless.) If I had thought more about it, I would have believed it was helpful to produce people who would conform to my own norms of behaviour, but a set of norm-busters might have been more useful for the company.

INTERPRETATION BRIEFINGS

There is another aspect to explore. Some subjects may be capable of being treated in either an educational or a training manner. When the government enacts social legislation there is a need to make sure managers know about it, understand it, and are clear about how to interpret it. Is this education or training? If the purpose is to teach the party line, then it's not education; it's either training, a briefing or propaganda. We might well wonder what approach the Ministry of Defence used to 'train' its senior armed forces officers in how to interpret equal opportunities legislation! The more a company's culture is a **power culture** which relies on a command hierarchy, the more difficult it is for its leaders to let go, be open and allow its members to think for themselves.

KEY TIPS

❖   Ensure that propaganda can be justified, used positively and directed outwardly.

❖   Distinguish clearly between education, training, briefings, indoctrination/ propaganda.

❖   Be clear where you want to develop managers' ability to be free to think for themselves.

ACTIVITY 2.2

Consider your company's management style in terms of needing and favouring education versus training. What are the implications for development? What concerns do you have?

DEVELOPERS' ACCOUNTABILITIES

The attempt to manage the training agenda at national level on behalf of employers contrasts starkly with the traditional hands-off practice found inside many companies hitherto. Trainers were for too long given a largely free hand in their companies to decide for themselves what kind of learning experience was appropriate for their managers. Chief executives have a long record of showing little interest in whether or not they subscribe to a particular programme's underlying philosophy or values. In the words of Derek Hornby (now Sir Derek, erstwhile Chairman of both Rank Xerox (UK) Ltd and of The Institute of Management):

> The attention given to management development by top management was pretty cursory. It was considered 'a good thing', something that reputable companies did and, therefore, got management tolerance, but it was really administered and driven by the training specialist without the deep involvement of, or understanding by, line management.[4]

I remember the days when I ran a training department. My director supplied the executive board with monthly statistics on the number of trainees. I was even asked to shorten courses so that the number of people being trained would be larger.

Top management's interest in this area is changing now, partly as a result of the cunning way in which the government has talked prominent chief executives into taking up public roles in chairing Lead Bodies, Training and Enterprise Councils, etc.

The government's resultant successes have meant some loss of independence and freedom for trainers and developers. Their bosses are increasingly likely to ask 'why?' and 'what for?', not just 'how much?' Inconvenient though it is, trainers should welcome this higher political profile, sharper accountability and closer proximity to their companies' business centres of gravity.

ACTIVITY 2.3

Do your sponsors understand what the development function is doing and why? What could be done to improve their level of understanding? How free a hand do you have, and to what extent is this unhealthy?

BOUGHT-IN PACKAGES AND SERVICES

Developers and trainers have a clear responsibility to use thoughtfully the fast-growing market in bought-in packages and courses. The designers and producers likewise need to understand the deeper issues identified in this book. Sadly, we still find many trainers who buy in programmes, or send managers on external courses, without giving the philosophical aspects much thought.

KEY TIP

❖   Check out assumed values, beliefs and models underlying bought-in products and services.

NATIONAL TRAINING TRENDS

Some of these finer points were given attention in the late 1980s in the wake of some leading national reports on the making of managers, primarily those by Charles Handy,[5] and by Constable and McCormick.[6] But since then we seem to have mainly concentrated on short-term, individual, vocational skills training. We are behaving as though the manager's job is as highly circumscribed as that of the airline pilot. We seem not to recognize its unpredictability and ambiguity, and the growing need for managers to be able to take initiative in ways that training can never anticipate, and could not provide for even if we could foresee the need.

The pressure to ground learning in applied outputs tested at the workplace is also leading to a growing loss of distinction between institutional educators and company trainers. Vested interests aside, some regret this convergence for sound intellectual reasons. Others welcome it in the name of hard business reality and competition.

Oddly, examining the 1980s national debate to find the purpose of management education and training, it is hard to find any mention of Fry's 'freedom' or search for truth as a distinguishing or necessary feature. If you believe that freedom *is* a legitimate purpose of management education, then you won't find its pursuit encouraged in an approach which is oriented towards the workplace, training, action-skills and measurable outputs.

In Chapter 12, 'Forming a Development Strategy', there is a proposed action programme aimed towards the variously interested bodies and agencies concerned *inter alia* with these issues and some lessons that need to be learned.

NATIONAL CULTURE AND EDUCATION

Anthropologists argue that national culture is a determinant of education's purpose. In the more individualistic cultures (especially the UK and the USA) the purpose of education is equated with learning to cope with the unknown. In such societies, Geert Hofstede claims,

> The purpose of learning is less to know how to do, as how to learn … [whereas] in collectivist society there is a stress on adaptation to the skills and virtues necessary to become an acceptable group member … learning is more often seen as a one-time process.[7]

Hofstede does not talk separately about the purpose of *training*; he simply equates learning with education. Nevertheless, it still strikes me as ironical that in his definition of learning in a collectivist society he might instead have well been talking about current training trends! This is at a time when our culture is becoming ever more individualistic.

SYSTEMATIC TRAINING VERSUS INTEGRATED LEARNING

One of the issues to confront is the question of when (and if) it is appropriate to work to the systematic training model or a model more up to date and possibly more relevant to today's problems.

The systematic training model is an old model which was given immense impetus by the government's Industry Training Boards in the 1960s and 1970s. Most people recognize the model even if they cannot define it. According to the 1981 *Manpower Services Glossary of Training Terms*, systematic training is 'training undertaken on a planned basis as a result of applying a logical series of planned steps'.[8] Expressed in the most simple and general terms, these steps include the following:

○　　Agreeing a training policy.
○　　Identification of training needs.
○　　Development of training objectives and plans.
○　　Implementation of planned training.
○　　Validation, evaluation and review.

VALUES AND ASSUMPTIONS

There is a set of values and assumptions behind any such model – about the people who work in companies, about their organizations, and about work itself. For the systematic training model, these are described by Mike Pedler *et al.* in Figure 2.1.[9] Even before we squirm at the hypocrisy implied by the last item, the list in Figure 2.1 serves notice on the relevance of the systematic training model in today's climate. It may still have some applications, but by and large it both fails the comfort test as a way of regarding people and their behaviour, and it sounds far too stable and planned for the 1990s. As Martyn Sloman, writing in *Personnel Management*, says:

> it demands a precision of approach which fits uneasily into training objectives which arise from looser organization structures … does not consider issues that arise because of changing organizational relationships … defines training objectives narrowly, ignoring the link with development and other human resource benefits.[10]

To Sloman's misgivings I would add the following comments on the systematic training model:

○   It is paternalistic and too top-down driven.
○   It disregards various parties' interests in wide mobility through transferable skills.
○   It is too slow for a fast-moving business environment.
○   It regards individuals' capability as an isolated variable.
○   It places undue faith in training efficacy, especially where organization change is required.
○   It disregards learning by a variety of means (planned experience, reading, networking, etc.).
○   It is overly rational, denying the shadow side of organizational behaviour.
○   It assumes individuals and their training hold the key to raising productivity.
○   It neglects the part played by the wider system, either as (i) the true source of performance problems, (ii) targets for development action, (iii) opportunities to reinforce training.

FIGURE 2.1 SYSTEMATIC TRAINING: SOME UNDERLYING VALUES AND ASSUMPTIONS

- People are basically passive, dependent, needing extrinsic motivation.
- We can find ways of extrinsically motivating most people, but not everybody.
- People vary with respect to basic abilities and we can measure and remove this variation accurately, predicting job performance accordingly.
- People need to be shown what to do and how to do it (training).
- The output from well-planned training is predictable, constant, with little variation.
- We can measure this performance reliably and consistently.
- Any variation in performance is due almost entirely to the individual.
- Jobs can be broken down into minute parts and then put together again for skilled performance.
- Learning is about changing behaviour in a predictable and constant manner.
- The purpose of one's job is to play one's part in a well-organised, smoothly running structure of interlinked parts.
- The purpose of one's life is not a meaningful concept.
- The whole equals the sum of the parts.
- Cause and effect are closely linked in space and time.
- There are two sets of people and situations: those to whom the above assumptions apply and me.

Reproduced by courtesy of McGraw-Hill

There are various other so-called models, but these tend to consist of descriptions of various features to be found in companies' approaches to training, rather than discrete processes.[11]

As an alternative to the systematic training model, Pedler *et al.* propose the integrated learning model, whose values and assumptions are set out in Figure 2.2.[9] It is a fair bet that many people who read books like this will embrace the integrated learning model's values, perhaps regardless of the circumstances. However laudable this viewpoint may be, and however well it may apply to themselves, it may be unrealistic in coming to terms with senior line clients in their companies, even with government initiatives.

FIGURE 2.2 INTEGRATED LEARNING: SOME UNDERLYING VALUES AND ASSUMPTIONS

- People are basically creative, active, intrinsically motivated, and want to do well. Extrinsic motivators at best make no difference, usually make things much worse.

- While people do vary in basic abilities, we should note what they are good at and provide them with jobs that harness this.

- Diversity should therefore be recognised, respected, valued and appreciated in order to bring about creativity and richness in the company.

- People need a wide range of resources and opportunities to enable them to learn established ways and create new ones.

- The output from learning will vary: different people will learn different things in different ways.

- The only way to manage this variety is by providing a great variety of opportunities.

- It is difficult to measure performance. In any case, we need to provide opportunities for a wide variety of dialogue and feedback, not measurement.

- Variation in performance is almost entirely due to the system, not the individual.

- Jobs cannot be broken down into small parts. We need to work on continuous improvement and forever striving to delight my customer.

- The purpose of my job is to delight my customer.

- The purpose of my life is to gain fulfilment by developing to my full potential.

- All too often the whole is less than the sum of the parts. However, it has the potential to be more.

- Cause and effect are widely separated in space and time.

- These assumptions apply to me and everyone else.

Reproduced by courtesy of McGraw-Hill

PRACTICAL CHOICES

A practical way forward is to view the models as saying something selectively about the kind of learning and learners with which we are concerned. They may also say something about trainers versus developers. On this basis we might consider variants of the systematic training model as tolerable when talking about training for routinized, low-level job skills. Whereas, it seems to me, the integrated learning model is fundamental when it comes to self-development, adult education and the management population.

Given this last point, it is ironic that the currently high-profile competence approach for managers is being interpreted in ways that are immediately recognizable in the dated systematic training approach and the values and assumptions in Figure 2.1. A rather similar claim can be made for the National Training Awards.[11]

However many people may agree with the assumptions in Figure 2.2, it is likely that a larger number would behave unthinkingly as though they believed those in Figure 2.1 – and not simply for pragmatic reasons. The machinery of organizations has a habit of devouring our natural humanity. It is rather like the transformation that is said to take place in the most reasonable of people when they get behind the wheel of a car. The analogy might not be so far fetched. How often we hear 'but he's not really like that; if you meet him outside work he's good company and a devoted family man'?

The benefit of reflecting on these sets of assumptions is that they force us to confront the belief system which underpins our everyday actions. That sense of unease may be sufficient to make us feel compelled to change our practices.

Except where there is a tough new broom, change may not mean a radical abandonment of one model and its clear replacement with another. In any case, in many companies it will not have been apparent that one particular theoretical model was consciously driving everyday practice. Much of what goes on may have been a fudge somewhere on the continuum expounded by Ashridge Management College which places the **fragmented approach** to training at one end, and the **focused approach** at the other.[12] The level and degree of sophistication of the learners may cause variations too. The best way to proceed for the management population may therefore be a planned and gradual shift in favour of the integrated learning model.

BACK TO THE FUTURE

The ideas juxtaposed in Figures 2.1 and 2.2 are not new. Some of the values in these contrasting models come straight out of McGregor's 1960 *Theory X* (and Theory Y). Twenty years later in 1980 Marilyn Ferguson was putting forward a new learning paradigm in *The Aquarian Conspiracy* as a programme of transformation for the 1980s![13] (See Figure 2.3.) Progress in the world of work and training is sometimes frustratingly slow.

The term *paradigm shift* entered developers' vocabulary around that time and is a useful though difficult concept, defined as 'a fundamental change in the way we view the world and in how individuals, groups, and organizations relate to each other.'

FIGURE 2.3 EXAMPLES OF LEARNING PARADIGMS

Old learning paradigm

- Relatively rigid structure
- Priority on performance
- Emphasis on external world
- Concern with norms

New learning paradigm

- Belief that there are many ways to teach a given subject
- Priority on self-image as the generator of performance
- Inner experience seen as context for learning
- Concern with the individual's performance in terms of potential

---

ACTIVITY 2.4

Consider which model best describes your approach to learning. Would your company's values support the greater adoption of the integrated learning model in place of the systematic training model?

THE LEARNING ORGANIZATION

The values contained in the integrated learning model and those in Ferguson's 'new' paradigm are consistent with the forces behind the now-familiar learning organization. Whilst this concept is not an alternative training model as such, the learning organization does represent an alternative approach and a challenge to the systematic training model. Chapter 11, 'Building a Learning Organization', is devoted to this important subject.

REFERENCES

1. William Tate (1995) *Developing Managerial Competence: A Critical Guide to Methods and Materials*, Aldershot: Gower.
2. Stephen Fry (1992) *Paperweight*, London: Quality Paperbacks Direct, pp. 20–1.
3. Alan Mumford (1989) *Management Development – Strategies for Action*, London: Institute of Personnel Management.
4. Derek Hornby (1991) 'Management Development – The Way Ahead', in Mick Silver (ed.) *Competent to Manage – Approaches to Management Training and Development*, London: Routledge, p. 175.
5. Charles Handy (1987) *The Making of Managers*, London: National Economic Development Organisation.

6. John Constable and Roger McCormick (1987) *The Making of British Managers*, Corby: British Institute of Management.
7. Geert Hofstede (1991) *Cultures and Organizations: Software of the Mind*, Maidenhead: McGraw-Hill, p. 63.
8. Manpower Services Commission (1981) *Glossary of Training Terms*, 3rd edn, London: HMSO.
9. Mike Pedler, John Burgoyne and Tom Boydell (1991) *The Learning Company – A Strategy for Sustainable Development*, Maidenhead: McGraw-Hill, pp. 198–9.
10. Martyn Sloman (1994) 'Coming in from the Cold: A New Role for Trainers', *Personnel Management*, January.
11. Martyn Sloman (1994) *A Handbook for Training Strategy*, Aldershot: Gower, pp. 21–43, 168.
12. K. Barham, J. Fraser and L. Heath (1988) *Management for the Future*, Berkhamstead: Ashridge Management Research Group, p. 46.
13. Marilyn Ferguson (1980) *The Aquarian Conspiracy: Personal and Social Transformation in the 1980s*, Los Angeles: J.P. Tarcher Inc., pp. 289–91.

PART TWO
ANALYSING NEEDS AND DIAGNOSING PROBLEMS

❖

3

ESTABLISHING MANAGERS' DEVELOPMENT NEEDS

OVERVIEW

This chapter examines critically some of the present means of identifying managers' training and development needs and offers advice on how they can be used to optimum effect.

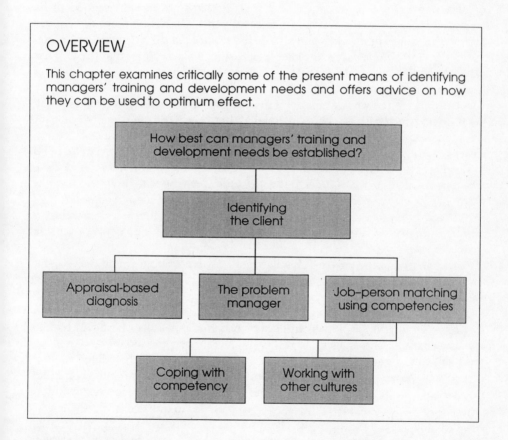

INTRODUCTION

D evelopers, trainers and consultants have to be able to respond to a wide range of client requests, including those concerning managers and supervisors. The requirement may be expressed as a straightforward need for development or enhancement, or managers might be said to have 'needs', or the client may regard a particular manager as an intolerable personal 'problem'.

Typically, the issue is already predefined in the client's mind, frequently in the form of the proposed solution, often training. This risks bringing the kind of discomfort faced by trained mechanics who are upset when car owners tell them what the problem is. Diagnosticians appreciate a few clues and want to know all the symptoms, but can feel uncomfortable if put in a strait-jacket by customers whose main virtue is their wallet. But in practice the encounter with the client is rarely problematic from this point of view, because many of those called in to help equally see their role in fairly narrow terms as providers of solutions of the kind for which their clients typically ask.

Clients' issues may concern an individual, a small group or, less often, be organization-wide. A blind spot is that the problems are usually claimed to be wholly and directly about people, whereas they may actually be only partially and indirectly about people *per se* and also include factors in the organization system. A second blind spot is that many clients persist in the false hope that training has magical powers and is the solution to such basic human problems as 'our customer service staff don't smile'.

To respond to the variety of potential client approaches, the good diagnostician needs to be armed with questions like 'Could they do it if their life depended on it?' We need to know when to train people and when to move people, since it is often easier to choose those who have it, rather than train those who haven't. We need to be able to distinguish between *those who can do but choose not to*, and *those who can do but aren't permitted to* (by the system). We need to be able to sort out *those who could and will (if given the wherewithal)*, and *those who could and won't*, and *those who will never be able to*. And where there are obstacles to performance, we need to be able to find whether they lie within people or outside them.

This chapter and the next are closely related. Both are about needs analysis, but this one is primarily about managers themselves and their inherent learning needs, and the next takes in wider organization dimensions.

These two target areas tend to be separated in practice, even though that is theoretically undesirable and an artificial dichotomy, especially where we are talking about groups of managers. In reality the factors become intertwined, making them difficult to disentangle and treat independently. Clients may well tell you the problem is to train individuals, when it may actually be an organization problem (e.g. structure, climate etc.), moreover one still waiting to be diagnosed and understood. Nonetheless, what you are allowed to consider in practice is usually heavily circumscribed at the outset by the client's limited *wants*, by expectations of what you are capable of providing, or by what you formally represent (e.g. a training department).

What neither of these chapters is about is explaining or advocating conventional Training Needs Analysis (TNA). Martyn Sloman's *A Handbook for Training Strategy* gives an account of the various techniques.[1] Methods available include structured interviews, critical incident method, repertory grid, job analysis and self-directed approaches. Despite their wide popularity, all these forms of TNA carry too narrow a definition and are so conceptually circumscribed at the outset (even before taking account of the practicalities) that they close the mind to the wider organizational dimensions and possibilities. Here we want to open up the mind. So these two chapters' titles imply an aim of meeting needs, whatever they are, rather than carrying out fixed processes. As part of that aim, we shall examine some currently popular ways of analysing needs and comment on some of their associated problems.

But, first, whom should the developer regard as the client – the individual manager, the boss, or the company as a whole? Establishing the answer to this apparently innocuous question is a good place to start. A case example brings out the issues.

IDENTIFYING THE CLIENT

CASE EXAMPLE: WHOM DOES THE TRAINER SERVE?

A training officer who ran supervisors' courses was faced with a general manager who wanted some extra places so that more of his supervisors could attend. The trainer suggested to his own boss that he had good reason to believe that the general manager's problems might not lie with his supervisors' lack of training. He therefore proposed that he should respond to the request by visiting the general manager and be prepared to discuss the department's supervisory performance problems. To do this, he would go armed with a diagnostic mental kitbag that went beyond that normally carried by trainers.

But his boss, the training manager, turned the idea down flat. There were other departments for this kind of problem, such as Work Study, Operational Research, Internal Consulting, etc. Furthermore, the local departmental personnel manager didn't want head office trainers coming onto his 'turf'. The training manager's view was 'We are (only) a training department after all; that is all that is expected of us. We are able to maintain a harmonious relationship with our customers in line departments only by giving them what they understand and ask for, not by threatening to scratch beneath their organizations' veneer and risk finding examples of inadequate leadership, lack of resources, absence of trust, scant information, unsuitable rosters, low calibre recruits, etc.'

In today's parlance, the boss's response was 'go where the client is'. Anything else is not good business: it puts the training assignment at risk. But this raises an interesting question. If we define the client as the person whose interests need to be most closely met, who actually is the trainer's client?

○   The group of students (i.e. the supervisors)?
○   The commissioning manager (i.e. the general manager)?
○   The company as a whole (i.e. represented by its chief executive)?
○   The training officer's boss (i.e. the training manager)?

It is tempting to assume that by being willing to challenge the general manager about his *real* requirements, the training officer is best serving the needs of the ultimate client – the company. This conclusion also satisfies the question 'Who pays the training officer's wages?'

Sadly, it is not possible to make practical use of that grand definition of the client. One usually comes unstuck if one tries. The only way to elevate the client to 'the company' in the short term is to refer the dispute to a higher level of management. In the long term, the solution is to reposition the training department, raise its profile, change its reporting level, give it wider terms of reference and change other people's expectations of its role and mission, something we examined in the opening chapter.

Another key client issue is whose confidences do you need to keep – individual learners or their boss? It will usually be the person who has identified the problem and can be said to 'own' it. Later on, we shall examine two interventions – action learning and process consulting – where the answers to these questions can be different.

WHOSE AGENDA IS IT?

Management problems with individuals and groups which need to be solved by developers (as opposed to general skills development programmes) can spring from either a concern held by the company about those individuals (i.e. top down), or concerns held by those individuals themselves (i.e. bottom up).

Company-driven agendas may be either macro, affecting whole departments or even the organization as a whole, or they may be micro, affecting a small group or a single manager. Individual-driven agendas, on the other hand, will by comparison always be micro level in scale. With these, while the company may be quite happy with the individual's performance, it will be aware of the individual's wishes and perhaps be willing to fund development action.

Depending on the scale of intervention needed, assistance may come from a world-class firm of consultants, or an in-company personnel manager, or from somewhere in between. Interventions may be activated from anywhere on the manager development/organization development continuum. When finished, developers may either leave people with enhanced skills or some formula or other potential means with which to solve the identified problem or unidentified future ones as and when they arise, or they may leave the organization with its stated problems directly solved. The developer may therefore focus on either capability or performance.

CASE EXAMPLE: WHOSE AGENDA IS IT?

I was invited by the managing director of a medium-sized transport company to look into problems in the company's Marketing Department. It was no secret that other departmental heads were expressing dissatisfaction with that department's performance. At the same time there was a degree of unhappiness being voiced by the department's three managers themselves, whom we shall call Bob, Anne and Sue. All three were well aware they were collectively performing below par because of internal conflict, especially between Bob and Anne. They had tried to sort it out among themselves but had come to the conclusion they could not do so without external help, which they asked their MD to commission and to which he readily agreed. Whilst driven by both top-down and bottom-up concern, this was clearly a case where the company could set the agenda and where the MD would clearly be my client. In the simplest of terms, what he asked me to do was see if the managers' responsibilities could be redefined in how they related to different market sectors, how they utilized support staffs and systems, and how they were represented in various forums. This was intended to remove some of the structural causes of poor communication and relationships.

When I started to dig deeper it became clear that Sue's problems were rather different. Like the others, Sue was concerned at the department's inner turmoil and low reputation, though she was not at the heart of the angst. She was highly capable and well regarded by the MD and outside the department. External criticism had not been aimed at her. On the other hand, she was deeply unhappy and felt very exposed and stressed. Following an earlier reorganization, Sue had found herself reporting directly to the MD, whereas previously she had reported to a marketing general manager who had since left and not been replaced. The MD trusted Sue and expected her to take decisions which would previously have been taken by the general manager. But Sue wanted a lot of day-to-day support which the MD was unable to give, though he understood and sympathized with her predicament. The MD's attitude towards me was 'was there anything I could do for Sue to meet her needs?'. Unlike Bob and Anne, I was being invited to regard Sue as a personal client to counsel and coach.

The small problem which faced Sue is of the practical and personal kind that often surfaces in action learning programmes, which we look at in Chapter 5. Developers would normally regard the individual as their client in a case like Sue's, but they have to watch out for agendas in which a sponsoring boss has a vested and legitimate interest, and they may need to perform a juggling act. In the case mentioned above, Bob and Anne thought it reasonable for me to present my findings first to them, and they were keen that I should do so, while I was clear that I would first need to check out my recommendations with the MD.

Many clients are quite specific on this aspect, but in these times of democratic management styles and empowerment, some clients are happy to 'go with the group'. In the case referred to, this was indeed how it transpired. After presenting my findings to the MD, he asked for a repeat performance to the group, following which his decision would be influenced by their reaction.

In terms of addressing capability versus performance, with Bob and Anne it was the latter; some organization changes made cooperation less of a problem. In Sue's case, I gave her a formula (openly shared with the MD) for better managing her meetings with the boss.

CONFLICT OF LOYALTIES

Sometimes trainers appear to believe that their mission is exclusively to serve the learners to the point where they jointly conspire against 'the management' who are being criticized behind their backs. Many trainers do not like to be considered part of the management team, particularly if they mainly operate at the level of individual training. But this posture of neutrality is misguided. If we assume that the prime reason behind any training is ultimately to suit the company's needs and not (just) the individual's, this means that training is *de facto* a tool of management. And it follows that trainers are part of the business's management team.

EXTERNAL TRAINERS AND DEVELOPERS

The issue of who is the client is also faced by external consultants and providers of learning products. With open learning programmes, a small manifestation of this dilemma is that some providers put all their effort and expertise into meeting the learners' needs (e.g. excellent workbooks and tutoring), yet neglect to respond quickly to calls from the training manager. That may, of course, be accidental rather than conscious – practice rather than policy. In any case, these services are not mutually exclusive, and good suppliers will try to attend equally to both.

Consultants will try to be as specific as they can about who is their client, especially in their own minds. According to how this is answered, advice and services will be tailored to find appeal. An example will illustrate this.

CASE EXAMPLE: THE CONSULTANT DEFINES THE CLIENT

A heavily centralized company was concerned at how bureaucratically its finance department was run. It hired two sets of consultants to look at this problem. The first consultancy's strength lay in organization strategy. It viewed the company chairman as its client, spoke mainly with users and recommended solutions which appealed to the managers who were the consumers of the finance department's service. It recommended substantial decentralization of the department's resources and severe trimming of its overt and covert power.

The other consultancy had its expertise in finance systems and viewed the finance director as its client. It recommended changes that enhanced the department's control and brought about efficiency improvements through the better use of computer systems.

Both sets of action might have met the brief for less bureaucracy. Neither was necessarily wrong. But they were based on different philosophies and were predisposed to quite different solutions, not least because of who was defined as the client and who was listened to most.

Only where coordination from the top is loose may consultants be allowed this degree of scope to define for themselves, or at least influence, the issue of whom to serve. Usually, they have little choice about who calls the shots. But clients themselves – if sufficiently aware and open-minded – do have this choice. The problem is that clients have a vested interest in not acknowledging that there is an option. It is natural for each one of them to want to grasp the role of client in order to have full control over the consultants and their subsequent recommendations.

THE CLIENT IS A RELATIONSHIP

Difficult though it may be, it can be healthy for consultants to avoid thinking of 'Who is the client?' as an either/or question. Regarding the issue this way implies that the person not identified as the client is put at a disadvantage. A novel way of thinking about who is the client is to ask where you can make your greatest contribution, or who will appreciate most what you have to offer. Viewed like that, the answer is probably the *gap* between the people being served. In other words, your client is to be found in the interstices and relationships (or the lack of them) *between* the people, or the departments, with which you are dealing! (The earlier mentioned case of Sue and her MD was just such an instance.)

Training programmes often achieve this result as a by-product. Whilst they may not directly target relationships, there is plenty of evidence to suggest that well-managed learning can nevertheless have a significant effect on improving boss–subordinate relationships. The design of the support system should actively recognize this potential benefit. Indeed, it may have a more powerful effect on improving performance than skills training itself.

There is in any case often an inherent conflict between the interests of the enterprise and the individual and their respective development, as Jonathan Gosling and David Ashton point out in *Management Learning*:

> directors of courses find themselves in the midst of this conflict … when, on the one hand, they assert a traditional professional dedication to the development of each student, but, on the other hand, reassure sponsors that their delegates will make continuing contributions to the corporation. In effect, such reassurances indicate that there will be no change in the dominant dependent relationship.[2]

Of course, behind the back of the corporate client, we know that the learning may well affect the dominant relationship, indeed might be said to have failed if it did not. As these authors point out, full-time programmes 'are often used as a means for individuals to step back from careers and reconsider their membership of corporate entities'.

If readers find themselves in the position of commissioning consultants or developers, they should at least recognize the options, the consequences and the dynamics before jumping to the convenient conclusion that they themselves should and will in reality be regarded unambiguously as the (sole) client.

ACTIVITY 3.1

How clear is your own understanding and that of other parties of who is and who is not regarded as the client? What tensions and conflicts do you experience in discharging the various responsibilities to your multiple stakeholders: the company as a whole, your boss, individual learners, your profession, and yourself?

APPRAISAL-BASED DIAGNOSIS

One place where a manager's training needs traditionally are discussed is in the annual appraisal interview. There is usually substantial scope here for improvement; it often involves no more than choosing some attractive-sounding off-the-job courses. The typical quality of discussion does not help the cause of training (even less the cause of learning). Some of the problems are listed below:

○　　Usually the discussion not only equates training with courses (half-way understandable), but also equates development with courses.
○　　Since appraisal is often conducted largely as a backward-looking activity (the last year's work), training too may be seen retrospectively, righting wrongs in hindsight, rather than as a forward planning activity.
○　　It takes the emphasis off continual learning and detracts from more imaginative ways of improving performance.
○　　It is centred on the individual (i.e. *manager* development), and may therefore overlook opportunities for wider *management* development – at the team level or the company level.

But if well conducted, there are many possible developmental actions which can result from an appraisal discussion. If, for the moment, we assume that we are only investigating ways to improve performance by raising individual managers' ability levels, learning opportunities may include the following:

○　　On-the-job guidance and coaching.
○　　Access to appropriate learning/educational/informative material.
○　　Traditional educational studies.
○　　Off-the-job training courses.
○　　Open learning programmes.

The following imaginative developmental action – experiential learning opportunities – might also be included:

○　　Undertaking a special project.
○　　Participation in a taskforce.
○　　Enlarging work responsibilities.
○　　Changing the work arrangements.
○　　Temporary job swaps with colleagues.
○　　Internal and external secondments.
○　　A work shadowing opportunity.
○　　Private counselling on personal matters.
○　　A complete change of role.

Involvement in taskforces and projects can be a particularly powerful and directly relevant development tool, since these devices are the main means by which organization change is planned and brought about.

ACTIVITY 3.2

When your appraisal scheme is used to diagnose individual managers' training and development needs and opportunities, how broad and imaginative are the outcomes? To what extent are individual managers encouraged to identify their own needs on a continuous basis?

THE PROBLEM MANAGER

Clients are often faced with an individual manager or supervisor whom they consider a problem, in the sense of being a 'real pain'. Occasionally this may be an objective performance problem. More likely it will be a personality issue – on one side or the other, or a matter of interpersonal chemistry for both of them. It may be perceived to be a problem just for the boss; alternatively both may feel a need to address it. The issue may be rational and discussible; or it might be painful, heated or embarrassing, or all of these. The definition will probably not be mutually agreed. Indeed, the person may be completely unaware of the perceived problem, because handling delicate issues can be traumatic, and bosses tend to shy away from discussing them openly and in an adult manner.

Either way, the client hopes to change the behaviour of the manager to make it more acceptable, or at least feels compelled to try before considering more drastic action. Clients often imagine (hope?) that training will provide a solution, though the problem usually has nothing at all to do with capability. It is frequently a case of could-do-but-won't.

Clients rarely see themselves as part of the problem or question their own definition of the problem. Their dialogue with the manager is often woefully inadequate, and often follows a long history of inadequate performance feedback.

In these circumstances, clients themselves and their advisers need some searching questions to negotiate the diagnostic maze and emerge at the right exit. Figure 3.1 contains a list of suggested questions.

FIGURE 3.1 INDIVIDUAL PERFORMANCE PROBLEMS: KEY DIAGNOSTIC QUESTIONS

1. Are you completely clear about what performance you want from the person compared with what you are currently getting?

2. Why and how much does the difference really matter? Does it matter objectively for the department/company, or just for you personally?

3. How far are you prepared to commit energy or resources to solving it, or press the issue to resolution if it is disputatious? Are you open to compromise? What would you be prepared to settle for?

4. If you disagree with the person, what reasons have you for supporting your own view, other than hierarchical authority? How reasonable are you being?

5. Why should it matter to the person to perform in the manner you require? What will be the consequences if he/she does or does not? Does the person understand and believe these consequences?

6. Does the person have a full knowledge of what you want? Does he/she show an understanding of why it matters to you, and share your concern?

7. Is the person already capable of doing what you want? Has he/she done it in the past?

8. If not, is he/she able to learn?

9. If the person did learn, is it then likely that he/she would then perform in the way you want?

10. What would be needed to support the change?

11. Are either of you predisposed to pretend that the matter can be solved by training, when you inwardly know that the issue is not really about capability at all, but neither is prepared to admit it?

12. Might the issue really be about:
    - Different perceptions of what is needed?
    - Differently perceived priorities?
    - Organization obstacles?
    - Inadequate resources?
    - Unclear requirements?
    - Conflicting stakeholder interests and expectations?
    - Task likes and dislikes?
    - Long-established norms?
    - Fear of mistakes?
    - Wilful disregard?
    - Interpersonal relationships?
    - The kind of behaviour that goes rewarded and unrewarded?
    - You?

JOB–PERSON MATCHING USING COMPETENCIES

One way of inferring training needs indirectly is via competency-based **job–person matching** techniques. The process is explained in *Competency Based Human Resource Management* by Alain Mitrani *et al*. of the Hay Group, leading exponents of this method.[3]

Expressed very simply, the process for measuring managers' potential begins by examining job descriptions to find job requirement criteria. This stage identifies skills, situation–specific criteria (such as freedom to act) and necessary competencies. The competencies are described in terms of behaviours that distinguish outstanding performers from the rest, referring to a dictionary of competencies. These are then aggregated to describe the requirements that each job needs and which job-holders should meet. The criteria are then rated on a scale of importance by interviewing the job-holders' superiors. Panels of superiors then consider managers' personal profiles against the relevant job requirement profiles.

As well as potential assessment, the process, with suitable variants, may also be used for succession planning, recruitment and development. Where there is a gap, training or development may sometimes provide a partial answer.

There are two kinds of competency, that which concentrates on functional outputs from role performance (usually spelt 'competences') and that which consists of personal qualities which are inputs to job performance (sometimes spelt 'competencies').[4]

The Hay methodology is concerned with the latter variety, so with this approach to job–person matching we are talking about personal competencies including generic skills, motives and traits. They might include, for example, initiative, self-confidence, achievement orientation, the ability to direct others, interpersonal sensitivity, group management skills and innovation. As the Hay authors point out:

> The organisation of the future will be built around people. There will be much less emphasis on jobs as the building blocks of organisations. This means that increased attention will be focused on people's competence. If we are using people as the building blocks of the organisation, then what they bring to the job, in other words their competence, becomes crucial.

These competencies are thoroughly researched and developed, and draw on a large international database. However, you need to remember that the final selection of critical competencies for the particular client project inevitably takes subjective judgement, as does the subsequent rating and assessment of job-holders. So it is less scientific than it seems. But the job–person matching process does at least provide bosses with a much-needed competence vocabulary to assist with structured thinking. Thus the process makes a valiant attempt at closing the subjectivity gap, which would otherwise be wide open and irrational.

EXTRANEOUS COMPETENCIES

Applied wisely, the technique should make no pretence at providing all the answers. Practitioners of the technique should acknowledge that there are some less tangible aspects, for example, when making appointments, that are bound to be additional to the competency process. They have always existed and will continue. Take the matter of trust, for example.

Trust is not usually considered to be a competency. But a relationship of trust between a boss and subordinate is probably the most crucial factor in enabling that subordinate manager to function. Even if the manager does not perform well by any objective yardstick, it is likely to be trust which keeps him or her in place, not an outsider's objective measure of competency presented to the boss as an indication of match against the job description. Being trusted actually involves many things:

O   Being trusted to maintain a confidence.
O   Having trusted abilities.

O   Being trusted to share the same aims.
O   Displaying trusted judgement.
O   Being trusted to give honest feedback.
O   Having trustworthy motives and ambitions.
O   Being trusted to deliver what the boss wants on time.

A better word than trust is possibly faith. And faith lies in the *relationship*, part of the personal chemistry between people in a good boss–subordinate partnership. The problem with trust, therefore, is that it is not so much about *job–person match* as about *boss–person match*. Change the boss, and the trust may vanish. But does the job remain the same? Or can we say that the job is effectively redefined by the new boss, since a crucial aspect of the job is to get on with the new boss?

The last item in the above list (being trusted to deliver the goods) comprises a mix of reliability and loyalty. It goes beyond achievement orientation – an important and frequently quoted competency. That should not be taken to mean that loyalty is a prerequisite competence. Loyalty can be stultifying for the company. Loyalty to whom, to what? It raises a host of questions which hark back to who should be regarded as the true client.

BALANCING COMPETENCIES IN TEAMS

'Achievement orientation' itself can be a problem. (It is sometimes called 'results orientation' or 'bias for action'.) I have seen some very effective managers who are not achievement-oriented. As part of a team they have been an invaluable resource; they can often be a source of wise counsel to others, and they may be good at generating ideas. While often highly intelligent, they may have strongly introverted personalities and may not be natural drivers. In a company which decides that all its managers must be action-oriented, these managers may be the first casualties of any downturn.

Techniques which aim to measure the quality of fit between managers and a single model of desired company competencies run the risk of building clones. This is precisely the opposite of research findings of what is needed to comprise a balanced team. Dr Meredith Belbin has probably done more than any other to develop a language and rationale for developing teams on this hypothesis.[5] His 'plant' (or ideas person) may be valued in a small *ad hoc* project group, but be regarded as out of place or as a troublemaker in a wider departmental team.

Writing on the theme of *Nobody's Perfect – But a Team Can Be*,[6] Antony Jay reminds us that we are doomed to search in vain for the ideal manager:

> All of us know in our hearts that the ideal individual for a given job cannot be found. He cannot be found because he cannot exist. Any attempt to list the qualities of a good manager demonstrates why he cannot exist: far too many of the qualities are mutually exclusive. He must be highly intelligent and he must not be too clever. He must be highly forceful and he must be sensitive to people's feelings. He must be dynamic and he must be patient. He must be a fluent communicator and be a good listener. He must be decisive and he must be reflective; and so on.

UNITARY OR PLURAL MODEL OF MANAGEMENT

Because all these skills seem desirable, we naïvely want them in each manager but, of course, we can't have them. Yet in the tug of war between the unitary and pluralistic schools of management, the former generally seem to catch the treasurer's eye. As with so many attractive fads that appear to direct us towards the end of the rainbow, we cannot bring ourselves to reject the idea.

The competence route to improved management has to be closely monitored for evidence of this flawed thinking to circumvent the risk of sacrificing those who appear not to fit someone's idea of the ideal model manager. Lists of competencies which have only a small core of required competencies and wide flexibility about further desirable competencies would clearly reduce the risk. But, as a general rule, the concept works to the disadvantage of individualistic managers who may make a very useful, albeit 'eccentric' contribution to the organization.

Some developers hold an alternative view. They say that pigeonholing people within such team typologies as Belbin's runs the risk of condemning them by typecasting. These developers argue that managers should be encouraged to break out of their niches and to broaden their appeal and range of possible contributions. A behavioural label around someone's neck may push them towards greater specialization or cause them to give up on developing chairmanship skills, for example.

Organizations with traditional 'power' and 'role' cultures are most likely to favour the unitary approach, while 'achievement' and 'support' cultures will generally be more flexible and tolerant in this respect.

Some of the concerns about developing identikit managers exist also with the use of functional or output competences, though arguably less so. Practitioners of output competences claim that their model says little about the *process* by which managers achieve results; it is therefore claimed that managers can be very different from each other at the level of 'how'.

At the most senior level in this output-based approach, the competence model is actually designed for the collective senior management team, not for one individual manager. However, when it comes to applying this model to assess, select and develop individual senior managers, this admirable intention is fraught with potential practical problems, as I have discussed in *Developing Managerial Competence*.[4]

KEY TIPS

❖   Resist pressure to adopt too firm a corporate mould into which all your managers are expected to fit.

❖   Ensure 'misfit' managers are not discharged without a careful evaluation of their unique contributions.

ASSUMPTIONS ABOUT JOB–PERSON MATCHING

There are several dubious assumptions in the way the usual job–person matching process is often applied:

- ○   If you ask people and their bosses for their views about what they do and why they do it, they will give a well-considered view.
- ○   Job descriptions are a reliable indication of what a job consists of.
- ○   Two people doing the same job would make the same comments about the job.
- ○   Interviewees' views will hold steady as long as their position continues.
- ○   The jobs and the organization will remain relatively static.
- ○   The interaction with the interviewer is of no consequence (in terms of corrupting the data) and does not shape the outcome.

Some long-serving personnel practitioners whose experience and reputation lies in the application of techniques may happily go along with the majority of the assumptions listed above. Others, I suspect and hope, will want to challenge them. For example, the reliance on job descriptions appears to sit uncomfortably alongside 'There will be much less emphasis on jobs as the building blocks of organizations.'

DIAGNOSTICIAN DYNAMICS

The last point in the above list is qualitatively different from the others. It makes the often-overlooked point that the identification of a subject's competency is compounded by the relationship with the diagnostician. This is inevitable; some say desirable. One regular interviewer who uses this technique boasts, 'I'm a really tough interviewer.' This implies of course, that there are less tough interviewers. They presumably achieve different outcomes. Since the answers are subjective, we can't say whether being really tough produces a better or worse result.

KEY TIP

❖   Keep a sharp look out for signs of predisposed personal biases and subjectivity.

This factor of dynamics reminds us that competence lies in the eyes of the beholder. It highlights the futility and falsehood of presenting the outcomes of any such analysis in a way which smacks of excessive science. Of course, the cynics will point out that some clients will be more impressed and more likely to buy the service if it appears highly scientific.

THE DANGER OF SPURIOUS ACCURACY

Computerization of the technique has added to the scientific feel of the process. The wizardly ability to calculate numbers to several decimal points has pushed it into fairyland, as far as I am concerned. Certain types of unsophisticated client, plus those with a personnel-as-science orientation, may accept the kind of conclusion sometimes presented as the outcome of such diagnoses, e.g. 'He has an XYZ competency gap of 8.32.' I don't. In one instance I saw a result which stated that Executive L scored 3.19 (out of 5), and Executive E scored 2.76. The average over eleven executives was 2.80. Executive L's future was safe, but Executive E's was in doubt. The four executives with a score of 2.20 were removed from their jobs. The risks are so obvious they hardly need spelling out. But this spurious accuracy fools some people into taking the conclusions at face value.

KEY TIP

❖   Only use technology-based techniques of needs analysis to support personal judgement and common sense.

COPING WITH COMPETENCY

In the example just quoted, not only are the executives' scores subjective, but also the choice of the initial list of competencies. This whole subject of competencies and their use by the so-called 'competence movement' (CM) is still in its infancy and somewhat complex and controversial. My book *Developing Managerial Competence*[4] contains a thorough examination of the competence approach as applied to managers and explains and offers advice on the following:

O   Whether companies should attempt to generate their own lists of company-specific competences.
O   The particular kind of personal competencies which are used in job–person matching techniques.
O   The use of different types of competences for development versus assessment.
O   The analytical process by which competences are derived.
O   The interacting nature of competences.
O   Competence versus performance.
O   The part played by consciousness.
O   Various ethical concerns.

ONLY WORDS

A problem for the competence movement is that studies of the language of competency show that people have quite different views as to what meaning lies behind a given term. Wendy Hirsh and Stephen Bevan in 'Managerial Competences and Skill Languages' point to the variety of interpretations users put on such apparently well-understood items as communication, flexibility, self-confidence, persuasion, influence, reliability, creativity, balance, and – the most problematical of all – leadership.[7] To be fair to competency practitioners, they do their best to overcome this problem with their dictionaries of definitions.

Let's take another common and troublesome competency, negotiating skills. A manager may hone these skills to perfection and score highly, yet misapply them to protect his department's 'turf', putting his own career goals and his own department's goals ahead of the goals of the company as a whole. What is needed in this case is actually less negotiation and more cooperation. So it is important to be clear about what reveals a skills need, and what actually says more about motives, traits and self-concepts.

What we have identified in this negotiation case is clearly not a training need. The real need is for the manager's boss to apply the recognition/reward and punishment system appropriately to influence the manager's actual application of the skill. This example serves to remind us of the opening words in the book's Preface; that alongside 'can do' we need to take more account of 'chooses to do' and 'is allowed to do'.

KEY TIP

❖   Only use a competency list if you can guarantee wide agreement on how terms like 'leadership' will be interpreted and applied.

OTHER ORGANIZATION BOXES

We need to move outside the individual competency box altogether if we are to reach beyond individually centred competency and optimize corporate competency. The *rewards and recognition* box is potentially one of the most powerful boxes in the organization model. Yet this broader kind of needs analysis rarely finds a place in what's on offer from developers. Many continue to emphasize individual skills and personal competencies, and thus make little contribution to total management performance. In the next chapter we shall look at ways of diagnosing the wider range of organization needs.

ACTIVITY 3.3

Are the various means for individual needs analysis being used in ways that are open to factors and influences which lie outside individuals' performance in the wider organization?

WORKING WITH OTHER CULTURES

Those working internationally should recognize that cultural difference plays a part in these analyses. Let's take some instances. Being a 'manager' will not be understood as a concept or a role in some of the less-developed countries, but will mean having a particular designation. In these countries, to be a 'director' means one is not a 'manager'. Whereas in the UK, for example, being a manager is usually interpreted generically as having responsibility for achieving results through others. A director is therefore a manager.

Another potentially corrupting factor with such techniques can be the respondent's wish to please the interviewer rather than establish the truth – a norm in some cultures.

The more remote the culture, the more difficult it is for consultants to stand in the other party's cultural shoes. It is all too easy to make wholly false assumptions. Take this case:

CASE EXAMPLE: CULTURE DIMENSIONS IN JOB–PERSON MATCHING

One company embarked on such an analysis beginning top-down with its chief executive, then reviewing its directors, with no apparent thought or commitment about what it would do with the outcome. 'Ah,' the developers say, 'some directors are coming up for replacement and this technique is intended to help.'

The problem is that this is not how most companies choose their top management, and it most certainly wasn't in this case. Here was an overseas nationalized company where directors are appointed because of their connections, often family connections, with prominent government officials.

This was an instance of developers' rational minds (both the computerized system's designers and its practitioners) making the mistake of believing that organizations behave equally rationally. This is a real problem for outsiders, who may have difficulty appreciating the nature and degree of non-rationality in an organization – not understanding the real holders of power, the politics and the social systems that determine how decisions are taken.

KEY TIP

❖   If using a competence model, watch out for cross-cultural misunderstandings over the terms and the value attached to the managerial concepts.

As a commentator on job–person matching, perhaps I have been a shade hard. For all its problems, the job–person matching process might actually help senior managers make up their minds. For example, they may have had a feeling all along about Executives L versus E, but either they couldn't put their finger on it, or they couldn't summon up the courage to act on it. Now they have the evidence and the wherewithal.

Competency analysis clearly provides a useful vocabulary for the client which would otherwise be missing. It therefore has an educative effect which might find application in a number of unforeseen ways over the longer term. Most important is to use it with your eyes and mind open; let it assist your judgement, not dominate it.

Also recognize that its most important value to clients might lie in allowing them to blame the consultant!

REFERENCES

1. Martyn Sloman (1994) *A Handbook for Training Strategy*, Aldershot: Gower, pp. 83–105.
2. Jonathan Gosling and David Ashton (1994) 'Action Learning and Academic Qualifications', *Management Learning*, **25** (2), pp. 263–74.
3. Alain Mitrani, Murray Dalziel and David Fitt (eds) (1992) *Competency Based Human Resource Management: Value-Driven Strategies for Recruitment, Development and Reward*, London: Kogan Page, pp. 18, 28, 85–94.
4. William Tate (1995) *Developing Managerial Competence: A Critical Guide to Methods and Materials*, Aldershot: Gower.
5. Meredith Belbin (1993) *Team Roles at Work*, Oxford: Butterworth-Heinemann.
6. Anthony Jay (1980) 'Nobody's Perfect – But a Team Can Be!', *Observer Magazine*, 20 April.
7. Wendy Hirsh and Stephen Bevan (1991) 'Managerial Competences and Skill Languages', in Mick Silver (ed.) *Competent to Manage – Approaches to Management Training and Development*, London: Routledge, pp. 83–100.

4
DIAGNOSING
ORGANIZATIONAL NEEDS

OVERVIEW

This chapter puts forward some ways of diagnosing the full range of development needs, taking full account of the organization context.

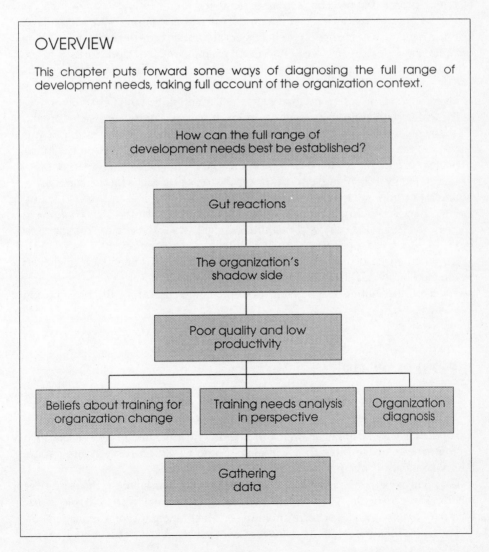

INTRODUCTION

Managers need help with learning at two levels. The first level is with their own personal ability – through training, education and wider forms of development activity such as career moves. This individual orientation of managers' learning addresses their personal needs, usually independently of their colleagues, aside from the local context, and often without regard to the organization's problems. It is well accepted and widely practised, despite these obvious limitations, and it is relatively well understood.

But all too often this is the only concern of developers and development. There is, however, another contextual level, that of helping managers – individually and collectively – move with (and more importantly at senior levels 'move') the business and its organization. This is more difficult and is comparatively neglected.

Developers also have an interest in a third level, that of fostering organization-level learning, renewal and change. Here managers are not directly the target or working material of the developers' interventions. An example might include looking at the extent to which a company makes sound use of standing committees as part of its decision-making processes. This particular focus for development diagnosis and remedial action is discussed in Chapter 9 'The Fall and Rise of the Organization'.

These different levels of managers' learning should be intertwined, seamless and mutually reinforcing, but they are often considered separately. For example, it is commonplace to find newly promoted supervisors studying an open learning package or attending a training course on the role of supervision. It is less common for the company to examine seriously its future corporate needs for the supervisory role and consider what that implies for supervisors' training and development. Indeed, I know of a large company's training department which is busily training engineering supervisors using a bought-in package, whilst the engineering director is retiring swaths of supervisors as part of a delayering operation.

This chapter discusses needs analysis in its various forms and at various levels beyond the individual manager, expanding and placing development in a wider performance-permitting and performance-enhancing context for the organization as a whole.

THE GUT RESPONSE

Ask any manager what his or her company should do most to become more profitable, and it is probable that only a few would put 'train the managers' at the top of their list. Some might answer with a comment about the business itself, such as 'improve its image through advertising'. Some would probably suggest some internal organization action or change.

Ask them what concerns them, as the Institute of Management did, and they mention 'lack of training', 'not having the right skills' and 'ability to fulfil role' *at the bottom of the list*.[1] What concerns them most is incompetent senior management. (To be fair to their bosses, if the managers' own subordinates were asked the same question, they might make the same criticism of their own middle management. It is always the level above that's perceived to be the problem!)

Training might or might not provide the answer to the problem with their 'incompetent' senior management masters, but it is not likely to be the first solution to spring to the respondents' minds, nor is it for the senior managers themselves.

Yet ask a chief executive how best to improve the bottom line, and the chances are that he or she may well put training higher up the list than the managers themselves would – a positive score for the government's propaganda machine. But the chief executive would not necessarily mean management training – let alone management development. Indeed, his or her answer may well be a gut reaction. Training has been politicized: training is the politically correct answer. Politicians of all parties who try to outbid each other in crudely calling for more training *per se* as the solution to Britain's economic woes do us no service whatsoever. (This is quite different from some of the well-considered and highly specific initiatives emanating from the Employment Department's Training, Enterprise and Education Directorate.)

Superficial observations about training arise for a number of reasons. Training suffers from (enjoys!) being an easy diversion, particularly when it's someone else who needs it. Training is easy to understand – or at least it seems so from the outside. It is easy to spend money on because of the feel-good factor. And you know what you're buying.

The upshot is that consultants who offer to train clients' staff find buyers more easily than do consultants who offer to help clients understand their organization problems. Putting your finger on other kinds of management and organization shortcomings and obstacles to performance requires more analytical skill and courage. It is also often uncomfortably 'close to home' for the client.

What many of the respondent managers would really like to suggest to improve their company is to get rid of Fred the Production Director, or whoever or whatever. We can all name someone or something which we believe prevents us from doing better. Getting rid of Fred may be as trite an answer as 'put up our wages'. Fred might simply be a hard taskmaster and therefore unpopular, yet he might be good for the company. On the other hand, Fred might constitute a genuine organizational obstacle (with apologies to readers called Fred – no slur intended!).

We tend to suggest training as a solution given the slightest excuse, but are more loath to admit openly to real obstacles – especially if they are people. There seems no limit to the amount of effort we will expend to avoid dealing with them. As a culture we prefer to throw money at people problems while keeping our fingers crossed, rather than confront them directly and honestly. We even send people on courses to remove the problem for a while.

THE ORGANIZATION'S SHADOW SIDE

Ask any manager whether he or she is enabled to deliver actual performance to his or her full potential, and the answer is invariably no. We traditionally like to blame the employees for low productivity, but they are in chains – chains fashioned out of

rules, job boundaries, territorial disputes, protocol, and other organization imposi-
tions, plus conflicts and rivalries between departments, bosses not on speaking
terms, and all manner of organization craziness.

This is the result of office politics, ambition, power struggles, greed, fear, insecurity, rivalries, personal friendships and so on, which Gerard Egan labels the
organization's 'shadow side'.[2]

CASE EXAMPLES: INSECURE BEHAVIOUR

1. The head of the derivatives business in the Barings Bank collapse is said
    to have told his board to mind its own business, that he could handle
    Singapore, and he didn't want amateurs messing it up.

2. A senior HR official asked a newly recruited HR manager to run a team-
    building workshop which he had himself run in the past. His instructions
    were that he was not to do it too well as he didn't wish to hear sub-
    sequently that he did it better than the boss.

Exchanges such as these are commonplace, especially in arguments over 'territory'
in which managers want to prove they need neither help nor supervision. But
shadow-side behaviour is not always negative in appearance or damaging in effect.
Egan describes such behaviour generally as 'arational', since some aspects of the
shadow, such as friendships, may be the means by which employees make a bad
organization structure work in practice. This dichotomy between the rational and
non-rational manifestations of organizational life is displayed in Figure 4.1. The
rational dimensions are generally more concerned with managing 'what' issues,
and the non-rational ones with uncontrolled 'who' issues.

FIGURE 4.1   THE RATIONAL AND NON-RATIONAL FACE OF ORGANIZATIONS

Rational

- competence
- mission
- goals
- codes of practice
- organization charts
- job descriptions
- people's titles
- published policies
- legal statutes and requirements
- company rules and regulations
- committees

Non-Rational

- departmental rivalries
- personal jealousies
- office politics
- territorial disputes
- ambition
- greed and self-interest
- fear and insecurity
- power struggles
- personal friendships
- bosses not on speaking terms
- in-groups and out-groups

Many employees are weighed down by tall hierarchies, bureaucratic rules and requirements, confused accountabilities, static careers, unimaginative work roles, negative performance frameworks, and feedback which concentrates on what they get wrong, not on what they get right, let alone how they might improve.

In their various ways these are organizational impediments to improvement. Tackling them is not necessarily an alternative to training but may be additional to it. Whilst training may enhance personal capability, the organization's capacity to perform is limited if obstacles such as these remain in the way of its application.

That said, it has to be admitted that dealing with this kind of blockage and handicap can be exceedingly difficult, especially when it is deeply embedded in the organization's culture. But that does not excuse failure to try to recognize it and own up to it (render it discussible). Holding up a mirror is a good place to start. In other words, we first have to see what is happening inside the organization. We may then begin to understand it, openly acknowledge it and begin to discuss it. Only then do we stand a chance of proposing a well-targeted intervention.

CASE EXAMPLE: THE WHITEMOOR PRISON BREAKOUT

1994 saw the escape of five highly dangerous IRA prisoners and a Mafia gang leader from Whitemoor Prison, adding to the hundred-plus at large at any one time. How could this breakout happen, and how could it and others like it be prevented in future?

The prison already had sophisticated cameras which could cover the full perimeter. It had arrangements for visitors to pass through metal detector portals. It scanned their belongings so they could be viewed on a monitor. It tape-recorded prisoners' phone calls. It trained officers to conduct thorough 'rub-down' body searches. It had a Board of Visitors to regularly inspect and report their findings to the governor and prison service management.

In the light of the subsequent inquiry, the Home Secretary announced the following additional action:

1. Introduce a more systematic method of recording intelligence and security information on staff.
2. Issue high-security unit staff with personal alarms.
3. Reinforce the walls and fences.

Along with the inevitable calls for more training came the equally predictable memos to officers reminding them of their duties and responsibilities. The memo from the Director-General called for the following action:

- Ensure that all ladders are stored securely.
- Ensure that all tools are accounted for daily.
- Ensure that loose items that could be stacked against the perimeter fence to aid climbing are either fixed or located in an area where they cannot be effectively used.
- Use ground and fence patrols to prevent escapes as frequently as resources allow.
- Search effectively cells, prisoners, visitors and items entering the establishment.

This is all highly rational and good common sense. But does it reach the heart of the problem?

We learn that one or more cameras were left static as a matter of conscious practice (if not explicit policy), leaving a blindspot by the perimeter fence. Why? Because some of the better-connected prisoners complained that it was an invasion of privacy! We learn that the cassette tapes were turned over to erase and re-record over the previous conversation and were not played back. The principal Mafia convict was allowed to talk in Italian, and none of the officers could understand what he was saying. The metal detector had been installed near pipes and had to have its sensitivity reduced to avoid false alarms, so it no longer detected visitors' metal objects. The officer who should have been watching the X-ray monitor had to stand at the end of the conveyor belt to take the items off because there was no one else to do it. The inmates made curtains to put over the hobbies room windows so that officers couldn't see them making escape ladders. Body searches were not carried out because it upset the high-security prisoners. Their possessions were so numerous that they could not practicably be searched; some of their adjacent cells were requisitioned as extra 'wardrobes'. Prisoners pushed the visiting-room's doors shut when friends called, and the officers felt reluctant to open them. Written edicts were ignored, as were the concerned reports submitted by the Board of Visitors. Officers who could have been watching prisoners were out getting their shopping, buying the wealthier inmates Cromer crabs, fresh salmon, and rare spices. The prison management was deeply implicated in the mess, and that's being polite about it!

The analysis and response was as predictable as it was misguided. There is nothing revelatory from the Director-General in his memo. It's already understood; it's simply not happening. The Home Secretary wanted to be seen to be taking action (spending money) in terms his constituency could understand. But it missed the target. The Home Secretary and his management team were looking for rational answers to little-understood irrational problems. What happens in most organizations most of the time is not at all rational. To get to the truth you need to turn a few stones over and examine the organization's darker, shadow-side.

What lay behind these symptoms of organizational insanity that were fairly apparent to all but the blind? The ingredients of this long-running prison farce included an inevitable power struggle; the trading of favours between staff and inmates; a process of manipulating and conditioning officers to put them off their guard; a dose of corruption; management insecurity; a fear of responsibility under the spotlight, especially at the top of the political ladder; party politicking to appeal to the electorate; an inefficient and complex bureaucracy replete with both buck-passing and pulling the rug from under managers in the complex management chain between officers, governors, regional directors, the Director-General heading up the government agency, and numerous ministers and Home Office civil servants.

Managers' performance went unmanaged, not least because responsibility could never be pinned firmly on any one person. That is not to say that, consistent with this blame culture, fingers were not pointed at individuals, especially at the governor. But he was the wrong target. As is frequently the case, it was the interstices which really needed attention. It was the gaping chasms in the complex web of relationships which most needed the developer's glue. When the Director-General refers to a successful meeting with a group of governors as evidence of 'good industrial relations', you know the opposite must be the case. The language of industrial relations applies where there are two opposing sides trying to reach agreement from the position of inherent differences, not to a unified management team sharing goals and trying to pull in the same direction. Language always provides a powerful clue for developers to understand what is going on.

Managing the shadow side means undertaking an honest diagnosis and then deciding where to focus your energy and put your problem-solving resources. Start by listing the rational and shadow factors in the system. In this case they would look something like Figure 4.2.

FIGURE 4.2   ANALYSIS OF RATIONAL AND SHADOW FACTORS AT WHITEMOOR PRISON

Rational Factors	Shadow Factors
Governor announces new vision, including public statement that Special Security Unit is 100 per cent escape proof.	
A Board of Visitors monitors and reports.	The Board of Visitors' reports are ignored.
Written edicts and exhortations by Governor.	Instructions ignored in practice.
Heavy expenditure on equipment. Cameras installed which can swivel 360 degrees.	Cameras sometimes turned off. Cameras left static, creating a blind spot, because of 'invasion of privacy'.
Policy of regular searches.	Volume of possessions out of control (extra cells used as wardrobes, and huge containers in yard).
Phone calls are tape recorded.	Tapes not played back. Mafia convict allowed to converse in Italian; no one can understand him. Worldwide phone calls (at public expense).

Rational Factors (cont.)	Shadow Factors (cont.)
Incoming deliveries to prisoners by visitors monitored by security screen on conveyor belt.	One officer at end of conveyor belt taking things off; no one to watch the monitor screen.
Visitors pass through metal detector portal.	Sensitivity of metal detector portal turned down because underground pipes close by.
Officers trained in rub-downs (body searches).	Visitors not body-searched, because inmates threaten violence.
Visitors meet prisoners in special room with officer to observe through open door.	Prisoners push the door closed and officers dare not reopen it.
Policy of providing local employment for young unemployed persons.	Naïve and inexperienced young officers put in charge of high-risk category prisoners. Officers remain in contact with same prisoners for long periods of service.
Claimed official policy of tough regime.	Applied practice of appeasement and concessions. Widespread intimidation. Conditioning of officers. Psychological textbooks in cells. Wreaths sent to officers' homes. Bribery and corruption rife.
	Prisoners issued with hacksaw blades to use in the hobbies room. Curtains drawn over window of hobbies room where escape equipment made.
	Staff act as lackeys for inmates, doing shopping.
	Officers overruled by Governor. Governor overruled by Home Office. Regional directors blame all problems on the governors. Director-General speaks of good 'industrial relations' with governors.

KEY TIPS

❖ Describe what is happening by listing the rational and shadow factors in the system.

❖ Try to explain and understand what underlies the apparent features of organizational behaviour.

❖ Decide where to concentrate your energy and where to commit your problem-solving resources.

ACTIVITY 4.1

How strong is your organization's non-rational, shadow side? What are its main features? How well are developers able to recognize it and take account of it?

POOR QUALITY AND LOW PRODUCTIVITY

In the specific field of quality, the guru Dr W. Edwards Deming recognized that it is the system which is largely responsible for poor quality, not the individual. He estimated that individuals' ability to make a difference to quality was no more than 15 per cent. In my own estimation, this figure is also a fair estimate of our general power to deliver our potential; in other words, we could achieve several times more by way of results for our employers if we were only allowed to.

The quickest route to improving productivity is therefore to remove system obstacles. This is usually more productive than increasing the forces trying to overcome them or compensate for them. And that, sadly, is what much training is – a roundabout way of trying to fix the wrong problem or avoid facing up to it.

We tend to question the individual's performance before questioning the department's performance. We should reverse this order. Very often departments are not even performing the most useful role, and therefore individuals are being asked to do the wrong tasks. It is time to broaden our goal and perspective from the development needs of the individual manager to the needs of the wider organization.

Developers can help by openly acknowledging these truths and sprinkling a liberal dose of realism and context on their offerings. The purpose here is not to debunk individual and conventional development training – far from it. But what we badly need is to sharpen its cutting edge, point it at the right target, give it a sense of proportion and place it in a realistic context.

KEY TIPS

❖   Work down from the department's performance towards the individual manager.

❖   Ensure that managers have useful work to do before examining whether they are doing it right.

ACTIVITY 4.2

In any key areas where you are currently developing managers' performance capability, try to identify any substantial organizational obstacles which should first be removed.

TRAINING NEEDS ANALYSIS IN PERSPECTIVE

The following example will illustrate an all-too-familiar shortcoming in conventional training needs analysis when applied at organization level. The problems arise from compartmentalization of training and from too narrow specialist expertise. This training needs analysis concerned a few thousand security staff.

CASE EXAMPLE: TRAINING NEEDS ANALYSIS

The 'presenting problem' was:

> (the department) is concerned that the standards achieved by those responsible for XYZ security is not as high as it should be.

Therefore, it was argued (perhaps rightly) that the staff and supervisors needed training and the first task was to spell out the necessary competences. There were five key questions:

- What tasks are performed?
- What knowledge is required?
- What skills are needed?
- What are the appropriate performance measures?
- How are they measured?

Whether or not the heart of solving the problem was to be found in training (or rather in re-specifying its need), one might reasonably assume the staff would at least gain from it. That is not in question. The problem is that once a client has jumped to this conclusion, he or she then circumscribes the problem and problem-solver. If you hire a training company (or even a training needs analysis company) you can predict what you'll be told. Comfortably, your training contractor won't challenge your basic premise, and you'll be able to report that you took some action to improve the standards. Very likely, there will be some improvement. But will it be optimal? Probably not.

The contractors tendering to undertake the above analysis had substantial expertise in the area of TNA and they were well able to meet the client's brief. What they could not do was help the client understand and question the limitations of the brief, be open to non-training data that came their way, or advise on possible non-training outcomes.

To be fair, in this particular case the client may have already gone through that wider diagnostic process with other advisers having expertise in the non-training aspects. Or he may have felt able to make those wider connections for himself rather than share the sensitive ramifications with a training contractor. But it is common for factors inherent in the setting up of the analytical process to foreclose options from the outset.

With antennae up, I raised a few very gentle pre-contract questions, encouraging a systems-wide view, hoping to achieve integration of the total standards-raising effort. For example, I asked:

- What feedback can we obtain from customers?
- How well do others, such as the police and equipment suppliers, collaborate with the security staff and what do these stakeholders suggest to improve standards?
- Since this requires international collaboration and effort, what is

happening about harmonizing the different standards and practices within Europe?

- Do other countries' similar security staff have the same needs? How are they tackling them? Have they undertaken competency analyses? What can we learn from them?

These organization-level questions were additional to more predictable ones:

- How well motivated are the staff?
- How well are they communicated with?

The questions I asked were not welcome and could not be accommodated. The client had decided in advance that we needed to interview the security staff only for their own perception of their work and training needs, and similarly managers for their own perspectives. Needless to say, I took no further part in the exercise.

Training needs analysis is often used to identify individuals' learning needs, and this can be a useful activity, highlighting areas for personal training to address the gap between an identified present state and a desired end state. Nowadays it is often conducted against a competence model, and it is increasingly carried out by self-analysis. It does have inherent weaknesses:

O   It lacks objectivity, being driven by personal preference.

O   It is predisposed to available 'solutions', especially by what training is already available.

O   It is rarely linked thoughtfully to its local context.

O   It treats the individual in isolation of interaction with others.

O   It has a habit of ignoring the organization's real problems.

O   It tends to be regarded disproportionately compared with other organizational factors.

Because of these inherent shortcomings, training generated in this way is not particularly efficient or effective, and is not of strategic importance in terms of the business's prosperity and survival.

Systematic and formal **training needs analysis** (TNA) or **gap analysis** can also refer to a work-group's needs. When conducted at this level, the process may be valid where it concerns something specific which is known to have changed (e.g. a new piece of equipment or procedure) and therefore leads to a need for mass re-skilling.

However, training needs analysis conducted at the level of the work-group in connection with a general organizational problem with low performance standards is so prior-circumscribed that I would like to ban it! It should be replaced with Performance Needs Analysis. In the words of an Industrial Society spokesman, 'Perhaps TNA is better termed needs analysis.'[3] Yet there are still many companies with the need, say, to raise the standard of customer service, who will call for a simple (simplistic?) TNA. (As we all know, some even skip this stage altogether and say they need some training courses for their customer-contact staff – probably because they're not being friendly enough!)

The Industrial Society spokesman goes on to observe (correctly) that 'It's more than training alone', and stresses (correctly) that training programmes must be set in the context of business strategy. But even from this more enlightened perspective there appears to be scope for confusion between analysing needs (which may show a need for some other action in place of training) and jumping to 'programmes' as part of the solution.

The reason for this common mistake is that needs analysis is usually *training-led* and *trainer-led*. The process consciously looks for solutions of one particular kind and closes the eyes and mind to other solutions – let alone other problems. Yet interventions other than training are probably more powerful levers for bringing about improvement for the organization. The only useful kind of analysis at the organizational level of performance problems is one that leaves all the options open while a wide range of relevant data is being gathered and examined.

KEY TIPS

❖   Ask whether the aim behind the needs analysis is to help managers with themselves, or whether it is to help them develop the organization and business.

❖   If the company is generally concerned with low performance, look at management and organization systems first, before analysing individual performance and capability issues.

GATHERING DATA

The data gathered will comprise both hard and soft kinds. Some examples are listed in Figure 4.3.

FIGURE 4.3 EXAMPLES OF HARD AND SOFT DATA
            GATHERING

Hard Data

- Top management's business plans; e.g. to change the product
- The results from customer research surveys
- The changing business, social, political and legal environment
- Organizational plans to change roles, restructure, etc.

Soft Data

- Managers' opinions
- Front-line staff's opinions
- Attitudes and feelings
- Experiences
- Complaints
- Ideas
- Morale

The data can be garnered using
- interviews
- focus groups
- surveys
- direct observation

Trainers may usefully take part in that data-gathering process, especially if they are likely to be involved subsequently in conducting some training. But don't be talked into letting them conduct a training needs analysis while someone else handles the organization analysis; the two areas of interest cannot be separated until it is time to begin discussing possible solutions. Instead of being training-led, the process should be training-responsive. Training should be an output from diagnosis, not an input to it.

The problem is not with a presumed need for frequent updating of the population's skills via training. Nor is it with interviewing the potential 'trainees' as part of the analytical process. But it overlooks a number of opportunities for the following:

1.   Interviews which are open to any data which might have a bearing on improving performance standards (structure, leadership, resources, communications, staff levels, equipment, relationships, systems, policies, procedures, etc.).
2.   Data from additional sources and directions of enquiry which might be relevant to the problem, which can generate 'context' for change-oriented, management-based (rather than only manager-based) learning and action.
3.   Complementary solutions which allow training to reinforce other interventions, and be reinforced by them.

Putting training in its own closed box forecloses on these wider needs and opportunities. That is the problem. Worse still is putting training needs analysis into its own compartment. As well as having specialists in this narrow field of activity, this segmentation practice is replicated inside some large companies. I know one company which has four training centres, one of which undertakes all the training needs analysis. The claimed benefits from developing extra expertise are more than offset, in my opinion, by the likelihood that the recommended solutions will be as detached as the process and its people.

Even where training is preordained to be the only intervention, training effectiveness itself is dependent on a number of factors in the learner's environment. According to Len Holmes, writing in *Training and Development*, these factors include the following:

O   Organizational culture.
O   Organizational climate for change.
O   Organizational structure.
O   Management support.
O   Management involvement in advance of, during and after training.
O   Career structure within occupational area.
O   Learning styles of trainees.
O   Other personal characteristics, including age, experience, previous education and training.[4]

For this reason too, trainers need an organization level of awareness if they are to conduct training effectively.

FIGURE 4.4 BELIEFS ABOUT TRAINING FOR ORGANIZATION CHANGE

1. **Organization change should not be 'training-led'; training's role is to support change.**
   Training often fails because:
   - it is planned as an independent 'intervention';
   - too much is expected of it;
   - other things are not done at the same time;
   - there is inadequate understanding of the organization issues and context.

2. **Real change comes about only as a result of a number of reinforcing initiatives.**
   Training is often one of these.

3. **Training works in particular areas of change.**
   These areas are:
   - staff's understanding of their roles and relationships;   ⎫ as
   - what the company expects of them differently in future;   ⎬ part of
   - new knowledge, skills and practices needed;   *managing*
   - empowering and generating enthusiasm for change   *change*
     and high performance.   ⎭

4. **Performance is affected by other factors more than by training.**
   Other types of initiative are therefore also needed. These tackle problems with:
   - policies, rules, restrictions and procedures which constrain performance;
   - how much authority and discretion staff have to use their initiative and judgement;
   - quality and quantity of resources (all kinds);
   - staff levels and quality;
   - rewards and recognition for good (or poor) performance;
   - management and leadership quality and vertical relationships;
   - organization structure;
   - relationships between departments and support from other departments.

5. **Any training should be grounded in the real-life problems of the business in context.**
   It should not be remote, generic, and deal only in abstract concepts.

6. **Training and any other initiatives need the support of each successive level of management.**
   Otherwise no one will feel empowered to act differently.

7. **Any changes expected as a result of training must be reinforced by the recognition system.**
   That doesn't necessarily mean financial rewards, though it may do.

8. **Consultants and trainers need to understand and take account of the climate and culture – both to make use of them and to improve them.**

9. **People's motivation, either to support or oppose training, needs to be understood by trainers, as do the pressures on the business as a whole to change.**

10. **Trainers need to be seen to be able to talk from experience of the company and its products, in order to be credible, and be able to make use of relevant material in context.**

FIGURE 4.5 'PROMETHEUS' STRATEGIC CHANGE DIAGNOSTIC MODEL

UNDERSTANDING → *IDENTIFYING* → *SPECIFYING* → *RECOMMENDING* → *DECIDING* → *DESIGNING* → *IMPLEMENTING* → *MONITORING*

DATA GATHERING in	FIELDS OF ENQUIRY to establish	DEFINED CONCLUSIONS leading to	POSSIBLE INTERVENTIONS
by: • Individual interviews of members of management	Business: mission & goals, customer-service product, business strategy, plans, etc.	Where now, and where wanting to get to. Causes and how bad the problems are.	Define goals, standards. Set up monitoring process.
• Focus groups • Customer research	Organization: structure, the key players, how it functions, roles, relationships, resources, etc.	Which levers to pull. Obstacles in the way to be removed.	Changes to managers and staff discretion, roles and practices.
• Company plans, documents, announcements, etc.	Organization: culture, climate and 'shadow' analysis	What is achievable? How much, for whom, by what, by when? How to capitalize on what is in place, and support available.	Performance management system
• Possible surveys (if needed at later stage)	Staff attitudes and opinions, morale, understanding of the company's expectations	How system changes can be kept in place. How personal change can be supported and rewarded.	Compensation system
	Quality of supervision and leadership	Disciples and champions to work jointly on the programme. Etc.	Training/ development, design and delivery • for staff • managers/ supervisors • support staffs
	Current standards and actual performance levels		Changes to policies, rules, regulations and systems.
	Other related initiatives, e.g. evaluation of past training effort		Structure
			Communications programme Etc.

(The right-hand column is headed vertically by the word: R E C O M M E N D A T I O N S)

KEY TIPS

❖   Don't let needs analysis be training-led; consider training only as a possible response.

❖   Stay open to a wide variety of data from many sources.

ACTIVITY 4.3

What are the implications for present trainers' and developers' roles, expectations and skills to take full account of a wide range of potential inputs to important diagnoses in connection with planned development activities?

BELIEFS ABOUT TRAINING FOR ORGANIZATION CHANGE

Where training is to be part of a company's change strategy, it is important that those involved in the interventions as internal or external management/organization/human resource consultants, specialists and trainers, and those on the client side, share a common set of beliefs. These beliefs are about what training is and is not able to contribute, and how its contribution should be optimized. Figure 4.4 shows my own set of beliefs.

ORGANIZATION DIAGNOSIS MODEL

A generic diagnostic model which I use in my own consulting practice is shown in Figure 4.5.

REFERENCES

1. *Management Today* (1993) 'The Mixed-up Manager', October.
2. Gerard Egan (1993) *Adding Value – A Systematic Guide to Business-Driven Management and Leadership*, San Francisco: Jossey-Bass, pp. 88–132, 140–6, 164–7.
3. Paul Fisher (1993) 'How to Mind the Gap', *The Guardian*, 3 March.
4. Len Holmes (1990) 'Trainer Competences: Turning the Clock Back?', *Training and Development*, April.

PART THREE
INTERVENTIONS, METHODS AND ACTIONS

❖

5

CHOOSING DEVELOPMENT INTERVENTIONS

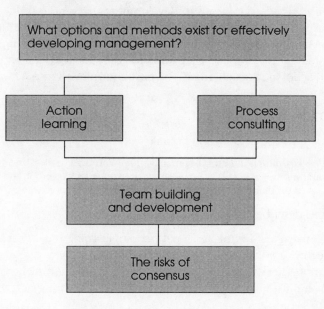

OVERVIEW

This chapter discusses some developers' intervention methods, considerations and actions. They have been chosen because they have a direct impact on business effectiveness.

What options and methods exist for effectively developing management?

Action learning

Process consulting

Team building and development

The risks of consensus

INTRODUCTION

As we saw at the start of this book, much development action that takes place in organizations has, at best, only an indirect connection with the real business at the company's sharp-end. It's designed that way for all sorts of reasons, mostly practical. But there are exceptions, where the learning material and process are part and parcel of the learner's here-and-now world of work. We shall make a cursory examination of a couple of these direct intervention methods: *action learning* and *process consulting*. We shall examine how well placed your organization is to avail itself of these approaches. If your appetite is whetted, there are many sources of information and help available to delve further into these individual methods.

These approaches are often employed in connection with team issues and therefore we shall make a critical pass at this ever-popular subject for developers. This should be fertile ground, yet their seeds rarely germinate. Why not? We also need to understand the limits to teamworking, why the route isn't always a one-way track.

USING ACTION LEARNING

> There is no learning without action
> and no (sober and deliberate) action without learning.[1]

There are recognized approaches to development that aim to tackle live issues – whether business- or organization-related problems – in a structured learning environment and which capitalize on managers' experience. Blending *theory with practice* or *learning with action* are ways to consider it. The assumption is that learning and action need each other. The best known method is Action Learning.

WHAT IS ACTION LEARNING?

According to Mike Pedler and John Boutall:

> Action Learning is a method of management and organisation development. Over several months, people working in small groups tackle important organisational issues or problems and learn from their attempts to change things.[1]

Alan Mumford describes the core features:

O   For managers and professional people, learning means learning to take effective action.

O   Learning needs to be expressed through actions on real work problems which must involve implementation as well as analysis and recommendation.

O   Learning is a social process in which individuals learn with and from each other.[2]

Now, you might say, this is what managers are paid to do all the time. Not so. In practice, managers lack the right kind of environment in which to learn as much as they might from their experience. Both the manager and the company suffer. The winner? The quick fix. Hierarchical reporting structures, cross-functional boundaries and short-term goals all work against long-term collective learning, as do individually centred appraisal and reward systems, coupled with the normal social and political pressures at work. Consequently, this means that many of an organization's more intractable problems are never solved, and managers fail to learn lasting lessons.

Action learning takes managers out of that routine, pressurized, results-oriented context. It helps them share their experience with like-minded others who will offer them support, challenge them, test their assumptions, and help them reflect on their problem solving – both learning and doing – in an open, confidentially secure and privileged setting.

Learning takes place at three levels:

1.   About the problem being tackled, whether organizational or about managing.
2.   About oneself.
3.   About the process of learning ('learning to learn').

FACILITATING ACTION LEARNING

Action learning takes some skill to set up. It is important to put together a group of people who will gel and contract to work together and observe certain important guidelines. They need to agree, for example, on what kind of self-disclosure will not go beyond the group's confines.

Action learning group meetings themselves take more skill to facilitate. Trained facilitators need to be able to ask the following kind of questions:

O   Why did everyone ignore Mark's question?
O   Who is helping you most at the moment in the group?
O   Perhaps it would be helpful to turn that comment into a question.
O   How do you feel about what's going on?
O   Have we been honest in challenging each other?

MORE A PHILOSOPHY THAN A TRAINING TECHNIQUE

This kind of group discussion doesn't turn action learning into a training technique. Its premise is incredibly simple, as stated at the outset. This explains why it has been around, in one way or another, for as long as humankind has had to learn from its actions to be able to solve the next problem. Professor Reg Revans, action learning's long-time advocate, has been practising it and writing about it for over 25 years.

The particular relevance of action learning to this book is that its sheer obviousness at once shows up the foolishness behind the many false divides with which we usually arrange learning. Action learning strikes a fine balance between on-the-job and off-the-job, between the individual's needs and those of the organization, and between manager development and organization development. These are core themes for this book; they will recur in later chapters. Action learning is further sympathetic to the book's values in that it also has moral origins based on humanistic assumptions about the kind of workplace people have a right to expect and about the quality of their working life.

WHY ISN'T THERE MORE ACTION LEARNING?

Action learning concerns managing significant (though not substantial) change for oneself and for one's company. The kind of problem which managers bring to their learning groups (often called 'sets') is most likely to be those they have most difficulty with, those outside their normal capability to resolve. These often have to do with other people, other departments, bosses, practices and policies, and with the wealth of obstacles, politics and dysfunctional practices which we love to hate.

However infuriating they may be, these problems are fascinating to talk about. And without them we lose some of our excuses for our own inaction. But given the courage to find the root of problems and solve them – even fairly small problems – it means challenging norms and vested interests. It means risk! 'Opening a can of worms!' as one participant expressed it. This requires support.

One of the paradoxes in training is that those who most need it are usually those who least recognize it. At the organization level, this paradox translates into 'those organization cultures which could most benefit from action learning are those that will offer it least support'.

TACKLING THE NON-RATIONAL

The basic action learning model is a rational one, and most managers by their upbringing are inclined to examine and discuss their problems through a rational lens, mentioning what they *perceive* about their experience rather than what they *feel* about it. But, as we mentioned in Chapter 4, 'Diagnosing Organizational Needs', organizations are anything but rational places in which to work. Most managers' problems have a significant psychological, emotional and political component. This may be more than a mere obstacle to performance; while apparently complicating otherwise rational discussion, it may well hold the key to solving the real problem.

If this level of interference with rationality is not bad enough, the action learning set itself presents its members with similar irrational dynamics and social power relations, as pointed out by Russ Vince and Linda Martin:

> the expression of powerful feelings like anger; the risk of speaking or not speaking; the risk of leading or of staying out. Individuals struggle with the consequences of their risk within a group, such as other people's reaction, or their own emotion at having aired something long suppressed.[3]

The solution to this range of psychological problems is to create an expectation in the set that the facilitator will prompt discussion at both the rational and non-rational level. This means that the group members will be expected to be honest with themselves, and to explore and reflect on, learn about and learn from the psychological dimensions; and naturally be frank with the other members of the set. This legitimizes bringing onto the agenda issues concerning the members' own emotional and political experiences at work. It aims to prevent a sub-optimal, task-oriented approach to problem solving.

This wider description of the action learning process goes beyond Revans' purely 'scientific method'. As such, it not only enhances learning about the issues in hand, but also operates at the level of learning to learn.

CONDITIONS FOR ACTION LEARNING

To quote Pedler and Boutall, the conditions for action learning require that:

> Participants have to feel permitted (or even encouraged) to address potentially difficult and sensitive organisational and managerial issues. Action Learning involves a questioning approach to problem-solving. Participants need to be unafraid to pose difficult questions, and to arrive at original and potentially controversial answers.
>
> Senior managers should demonstrate their openness to new ideas and invite participants to pose difficult questions. They will need to deal constructively with ideas and proposals which arise, recognising that they may be different from, or better than, their own preferred solutions!
>
> The problems will need to be put into context with other issues around the organisation. Problems seldom have neat boundaries, but will often overlap and be dependent upon other factors within the organisation. Hence participants will often find themselves exploring areas outside their original brief, involving others within the organisation – and thereby raising questions elsewhere![1]

This implies that considerable energy is required to embark on action learning, and that those with power in the organization have positively to welcome it. Pedler and Boutall offer a test of 'organizational fitness' to embark on action learning, and this is reproduced as an Appendix to this chapter.

The potential benefits to be obtained from action learning hardly need stating and occur at three levels:

1.   The individual's personal development.
2.   The individual's managerial performance.
3.   The organization's capacity and capability.

USING PROCESS CONSULTING

The term 'process consulting' is used generically to cover assignments where the consultant provides facilitation skill with the process rather than expert skill with the subject matter. This type of consulting can be applied specifically in a development context. The service can be provided by either internal or external consultants who possess these particular skills.

As managers seek to tackle protracted problems in their everyday pressured business environment, they often struggle to find their way through the morass of data and the complexity of the dynamics. They lack the opportunity to hang onto a structured logic (assuming they had one) to apply to the situation. And they lack the opportunity to stand back and reflect on what is happening. Thus they fail to learn from it and improve next time. Process consulting can fill this gap, with a facilitator working with either an individual or regular work-group in their normal job situation, rather than with a specially composed group off-site.

Process consulting bridges the on- or off-the-job learning environment. While it *de facto* takes place on-the-job, process consulting has an off-the-job feel to it. Managers' much vaunted *learning from experience* is quite inefficient on its own without some imposed structure and outside help. Mumford says that what is true about learning from experience is that,

All managers do actually learn from performing real jobs and real tasks, but their capacity to recognise opportunities, to know what they are learning and how they are learning it varies considerably.[4]

John Gill and Sue Whittle, writing in the *Journal of Management Studies*, describe a process of facilitation on the job which helps managers understand what is happening 'by offering feedback, interpretation and insights'.[5]

PROCESS CONSULTING AND ACTION LEARNING

Process consulting can be thought of as a close relation of action learning. Learning and action in the form of problem solving remain the twin objectives. Unlike action learning, process consulting does not attribute learning to all-important social interaction, one of the criticisms of Revans' work. As Mumford points out, we all have our own preferred learning style, and just as this inclines us more or less towards open learning, outdoor learning, book learning, case studies, action learning, etc., our need for social interaction varies too.

There is a further difference. In process consulting a group's boss identifies a problem, usually with a group's performance or dynamics, and will therefore expect to be regarded as the principal client. In action learning sets individual members identify their own problems and bring them to their groups, and they therefore expect developers to regard them as individual clients.

PROCESS CONSULTING AND HELPING

Edgar Schein describes process consulting as a 'general philosophy of helping'.[6] He arrived at his model after failing to bring about the change he expected by providing straightforward team facilitation skills. He offered feedback to dysfunctional groups and invited them to examine the consequences of their behaviour. As he says,

> Their response was always one of interest. Members were grateful to have their behaviour pointed out, and they expressed regret and some shame at what they themselves could easily see was 'bad'. They complimented me on my perceptiveness, and then continued to do exactly what they had been doing. In other words, nothing changed.

Schein realized he was making some false assumptions and poor choices about how best to help:

> I was assuming that I knew how the group should operate better than the group did itself. I was importing a model of effective group action from my training experience into a work setting. I was also imposing a set of humanistic values pertaining to how people should communicate, how they should not publicly embarrass each other, and how they should reach consensus on decisions.
>
> I was missing a crucial point – the group had an agenda more important than all the above considerations. That agenda was driving and stabilizing their group processes. Specifically, the agenda was to resolve critical strategic issues around choices of technology and products in an industry where no-one really knew what would and what would not work, and where the academic tradition – that ideas had to be fought out in order to be tested and validated – prevailed. I was busy trying to civilize

the group, while the group was searching for the truth in a life and death struggle against its competitors. I was imposing my expertise about groups on a group trying to solve a problem far more important than how to be an effective group.

His conclusion about what constitutes successful process consultation depended upon the insight that, '*I could not be helpful until I gave up my own notion of what the group should be* and began to pay attention to what the group was *actually trying to do*.' He realized that he had 'to intervene in the *real* process of the group, its task process'.

TASK VERSUS PROCESS

Ian Cunningham, Chairman of the Centre for the Study of Change, criticizes those 'who, in order to remain process focused, avoid addressing issues around the strategic focus of the team and the tasks it has to carry out'.[7] When developers become involved in live groups, they generally make the mistake of believing their interventions should be limited to the interpersonal transactions and dynamics. Cunningham forcefully argues that 'assistance has to move beyond crass over-simplified distinctions (such as task vs. process)'. A distinction which has real meaning for developers may not be understood or be seen as useful in the eyes of the team members. The risk lies not so much in how developers arrive at their own private analysis of what is going on, but in how they seek to explain and make use of it in a task-related context.

At times like this, developers may have to subordinate publicly their private insights and work overtly with the wisdom in the group. The pressure to 'go where the client is' is a frequent dilemma and source of tension, if not of conscience, for developers. This manifests itself when, all too often, clients are more interested in a quick fix than a long-term cure. Apart from congenital short-termism, they don't understand what the long-term cure approach would look like, quickly come to realize that it will cost more, and start to fear that it will upturn stones and find hidden 'nasties'. The only advice is to tread cautiously in trying to pull clients in the direction which developers feel they know is best.

GAMES AND INSTRUMENTS

The problem is not helped by a market flooded with games, which has led to stereotypical expectations of what developers' fare looks like. Clients either would like help with their task problem or they expect a generic abstract package. The purely process developer who rejects both and wants to work with the live group runs the risk of falling between two stools.

Some of the games are most ingenious and great fun, but it is questionable how much real and lasting change they bring about. The consultant Bruce Nixon criticizes the typical fare of developers' courses:

> To talk in generalities or work on anonymous case studies and role plays is far safer than to work on one's own actual difficulties or opportunities and to make commitments to change. Yet the risk must be taken if there is to be a worthwhile pay-off. The practitioner must create the conditions in which that risk will be taken.[8]

Developers can also make the mistake of over-using psychometric instruments, tests and models which have a language of their own that can seem obscure and lack utility for laymen. Use with caution.

It is salutary for developers to be reminded of the fact that managers' interest in learning is very much secondary to producing work results, and that the workplace itself is a rich learning environment if used imaginatively.

KEY TIP

❖   Go where the client is.

ACTIVITY 5.1

What current organization problems might best be tackled by the approaches described here? Would your organization culture support this type of intervention?

TEAM BUILDING AND DEVELOPMENT

Action learning and process consulting are closely identified with teamworking. This question of team building and development suffers from more woolly and wishful thinking than most. Clients who are faced with a poorly functioning team or team member are too often enticed to buy-in a solution, rather than search within the group of players, themselves included, to understand exactly what is happening and what the boss can do about it. Too often packaged training is the intervention of first resort.

There is also a tendency to think of teams (with a little t) rather than Teams (with a big T). Most team-building effort is aimed at improving individual contributions in low-level intact groups, rather than at improving teamwork between departments and functional units.

Yet teams, at one organization level or another, are the main clue to corporate competence. What can be done and what should be done?

CHANGING THE APPRAISAL SCHEME

One possible intervention to improve teamworking is to change the way the formal recognition system handles teams and team behaviour. This means re-examining the management appraisal system (assuming there is one) and any rewards driven by it. This includes the following:

O   Re-assess the management practices built into the appraisal scheme.
O   Review the kinds of personal and team objectives that managers are set.
O   Investigate what feedback is given and how it is given.
O   Review what kind of behaviour is rewarded.

O   Examine financial incentives and rewards used to endorse or promote either self-centred or teamly behaviour.

Rewards may take a number of forms:

O   Promotion.
O   Leadership of a project.
O   Overt public recognition.
O   Compensation, especially performance-related pay (PRP), which may affect salary increases or lump-sum bonuses.

In the next chapter, 'Managing Performance', we look in some depth at various aspects of performance management and appraisal, including how to encourage and incentivize teamwork.

SOUL-SEARCHING QUESTIONS

Making changes to the appraisal and reward system in favour of more teamly behaviour, at the expense of individualistic behaviour, can help considerably, but it won't be enough on its own. Neither will sending recalcitrant managers on one of the many off-the-job team-building courses advertised. Managers can't simply be trained to be good team players. Skill is but a fraction of the problem. It equates a manager's dysfunctional behaviour to a client's broken-down car: 'Please take it away from me and return when fixed.' Unlike a car, 'faults' with a manager's performance cannot be diagnosed independently of colleagues, not least the boss. With a car we are trying to extenuate an asset's depreciation; with managers we are trying to enhance an appreciating one. (Paradoxically, accountants treat the car as the asset, while the manager is a cost.) A manager has a soul and values; a car doesn't. Many skills-based solutions are more analogous to toning muscles than souls. What we should first be paying developers to do is to seek answers from the client to some soul-searching questions. My own list is contained in Figure 5.1.

FIGURE 5.1 IMPROVING TEAMWORK: SOUL-SEARCHING QUESTIONS

1. Who do you want to behave more like a team?
2. Why do you want these people (or this person) to behave in a more 'teamly' way?
3. How is the absence of good teamworking currently manifesting itself?
4. If you had the kind of teamwork you want, what would be happening that isn't now?
5. Is this a genuine teamwork issue or is it really a problem to be faced with a difficult person?
6. Is this a single problem faced by all members, or are there varying aspects of the problem with different members?

7. What is the team members' understanding of the behaviour you are looking for?

8. At the moment, how is good team behaviour rewarded?

9. At the moment, how is poor team behaviour punished?

10. What is blocking the path to improved teamwork?

11. What is the nature of your own involvement in the team?

12. What effect is your own behaviour having on the team's behaviour?

13. What enmities exist in the team which any amount of team training won't overcome?

14. What understanding do you have of other interpersonal dynamics in the team such as rivalries, jealousies, ambitions, anxieties, inhibitions, sexual motives, attitudes towards you?

15. How strong a barrier are the current norms of teamworking, both of this team and in the wider company's management style and culture?

16. How can you signal a clear break with past norms that are getting in the way?

Answers to the questions in Figure 5.1 should begin to provide developers with an initial analysis before going on to seek data from others. The solution might ultimately lie in one or more of several areas, including modelling, goal setting, appraisal and compensation, training, and even banging heads together! More likely the best answer will involve a number of mutually reinforcing responses. This targeted approach is more likely to realize a benefit than putting everyone through a team-building exercise.

CHANGING TEAM MEMBERS

Action might include changing one or more of the team members. This may be messy, but it may have a more powerful effect than all the other actions put together. If well-handled and communicated, it can send a very strong signal down the organization about the kind of management behaviour which is valued by the boss. But this has to be consistent with the perceived organization culture, the organization's established values, beliefs and norms, which have a strong effect on the way managers generally behave.

THE BOSS IS PART OF THE PROBLEM

Bosses have a habit of stepping to one side and discussing their team's performance as though it has a dynamic which is independent of the part they themselves play. But the style exhibited above and especially at the very top of the organization is very powerful. Some chief executives run their directors by divide-and-rule, and only interact with them on a one-to-one basis regarding their departmental function. The directors will not then behave as a team – either in the sense of feeling empathy with colleagues, or in terms of feeling a collective responsibility for the business as a whole.

THE HUMAN ZOO

Large organizations are rarely havens of peace and tranquillity, resembling the anonymous city more than the village idyll. At their worst they are a bear pit. As a norm, they resemble the anthropologist's 'human zoo', with loyalty given to tribes small enough for people to be able to know and with which they can form an identity. The rest are strangers, for which the coping mechanism is a blank stare. Developers, being more than mere zoo-keepers feeding and tending the sores, try to improve conditions for the inmates. They search for the middle ground, wherein lies a vital community with sufficient tension and controlled competition to avoid complacency and to provide stimulation and growth.

Therefore there needs to be limits to ever more teamwork and friendly co-operation. We have to guard against the client who desires more teamwork because he or she wants yes-men or lacks the personal ability to handle a degree of conflict.

KEY TIPS

❖   Before considering members' skills, resolve any other issues, e.g. member-ship of the team.

❖   If bosses say they have a problem with the team, include the boss in the problem equation.

THE RISKS OF CONSENSUS

In *Managerial Courage*, Harvey Hornstein[9] comments on the questionable trend in organizations towards greater use of teams, committees, taskforces, *ad-hoc* groups, etc., citing Abraham Zaleznik's 1977 celebrated article in *Harvard Business Review*, 'Managers and Leaders: Are They Different?'[10] Zaleznik observed that 'Business has established a new power ethic that favours collective over individual leadership, the cult of the group over that of personality.' The trend worries Hornstein:

> Groups have a capacity for producing a special, perniciously subtle tyranny. The ascendance of the social ethic, the priority being placed on both maintaining harmony and working through social consensus, and the swelling endorsement of teams as a means of getting work done, all augur poorly for individual acts of managerial courage and organization regeneration.

Individual acts are not always ones of courage. Indeed, many such acts are not virtuous or to be admired in any way. Even courage has its downside; Robert Maxwell frequently displayed courage, but it was driven by an unacceptable level of self-interest and with a cavalier disregard to the risk of damaging others. While team pressure may indeed serve to constrain individuals, this may augur either poorly or well for the organization's health, depending upon the person's naturally unrestrained inclinations, motives and behaviour.

It is also questionable whether the exercise of leadership has shifted significantly in favour of group action in the intervening period. It might further be argued that forces other than social pressure exercised through team colleagues (e.g. media attention and fear of legal redress) also militate increasingly against high-profile individual acts of leadership. Yet there can be no doubt that many voices are calling for improved teamwork. But these calls are not aimed exclusively at leadership; they apply to the managerial hierarchy in general. And they are increasingly likely to be driven by concerns to improve collective learning than the quality of decisions, two consequences of teamworking which may either be mutually supportive or work against each other.

Peter Senge, one of the foremost authorities on the idea of the *learning organization*, sees the team as the principal learning unit within an organization.[11] But he observes that teams can suffer from the lowest common denominator syndrome as they seek to avoid internal conflict and take weak decisions that result from compromise. And Gerard Egan points out that 'management teams afflicted with "group think" not only do not learn but also make decisions that have devastating consequences.'[12]

Jerry Harvey is famous for inventing the Abilene paradox, where everyone agrees to go somewhere that no one wants to go. He believes that 'people feel that unless they continually agree with others in a group, the group will decide they are not team players and will take steps to get rid of them'. But, as he says:

> confrontation does not inevitably involve conflict. Confrontation is simply the process of discovering the nature of the underlying reality of organizational situations … I also find that most organization members know what the nature of that organizational reality is, but frequently hesitate to state it or assume that they share it with others.[13]

This reminds me of a painful episode in my own career, where my boss (a high-scoring *adapter-dealer*) frequently counselled me to make compromise my number one priority, whereas I had regarded compromise as a tactic of my last resort. My proposals were always first considered against the criterion of 'had I sought everyone's point of view, and did they agree?' The inherent merit of my proposals was certainly not paramount, and indeed often not even discussed at all.

The laws of cybernetics state that an organism needs contention to keep itself vital; disagreement should lead to a higher-quality solution. This was always true in nature, but continues to grow in business. The need for a fixed managerial framework for bosses to give orders and monitor compliance has long gone. As we saw earlier when discussing the merits of educating managers to question rather than training them to comply, progress comes to those who instinctively challenge established practice and are prepared to contest the organization's norms.

The handmaiden of consensus is passivity, i.e. gutless managers – something developers need to guard strongly against. In Chapter 8, 'Linking Development to Organization Performance', we shall return to this closely related theme of what leaders really need (but rarely want) of their managers as good *followers*. The dire consequences of a lack of independent challenge from below is exposed in some well-publicized cases.

INTERNAL COMPETITION

It is commonly said that companies suffer from too much internal competition, with a resulting lack of aggression aimed at external business competitors. Therefore, it is assumed that this imbalance should be addressed by fostering more collaborative internal working relationships, i.e. teamly attitudes.

But internal competition is not necessarily wholly negative. One of the numerous British Airways reorganizations deliberately left fuzzy departmental boundaries and presented opportunities for pairs of departments to believe that they had overlapping responsibilities. Put simply, the idea was that they would fight it out, and the best would survive. An organization (it is argued) might have to progress through this phase before it can have the products and the spirit to take on the external enemy.

Put more elegantly by Egan:

> The work that is divided up must be brought back together again in order to deliver the company's products and services to customers, so interunit teamwork or 'fit' is essential. Split and fit leads naturally to tension. A degree of restless tension in an organization stimulates learning and keeps the firm from complacency.[12]

One of the National Freight Corporation's divisions decided to encourage internal competition as an interim strategy because it believed the same behaviour would then be replicated externally. This may carry a risk of leaving some long-term damage; you can probably provoke internal conflict more easily than you can turn it off. But it serves to make the point that while some forms of internal competition are destructive, others may constitute constructive conflict – an organizational virtue. Internal competition can be directed in a number of directions: over 'turf' – unhealthy, over resources and jobs – natural, over ideas – an asset.

The National Freight example raises the incidental question of what kinds of managerial personalities can be expected to direct their competitive instincts wholly in one direction. There is an assumption here that the two different personality focuses can exist in the one personality. But those who are highly collaborative internally may lack externally aimed aggression. Unfortunately, this is not the place to discuss that theoretical dilemma, nor whether such external competitor aggression is necessary or desirable – another assumption.

The lesson for developers is quite simply the need to think through what their companies need in terms of cultural and climatic development at a given phase in their own development, and what this implies for managers – their selection, development, compensation and appraisal – to develop the right kind of balanced teamwork.

KEY TIP

❖   Moderate excessive cooperation with constructive challenge and tension.

ACTIVITY 5.2

How good is the balance in your company between healthy and constructive conflict on the one hand, and friendly, cooperative and supportive relationships on the other? Where are there currently strong imbalances in one direction or the other that need attention?

REFERENCES

1. Mike Pedler and John Boutall (1992) *Action Learning for Change – A Resource Book for Managers and other Professionals*, National Health Services Training Division, p. 7.
2. Alan Mumford (1992) 'New Ideas on Action Learning', in *Approaches to Action Learning*, University of Keele: Mercia Publications.
3. Russ Vince and Linda Martin (1993) 'Inside Action Learning: An Exploration of the Psychology and Politics of the Action Learning Model', *Management Education and Development*, London: Association for Management Education and Development, **24** (3).
4. Alan Mumford (1990) 'The Individual and Learning Opportunities', *Industrial and Commercial Training*, **22** (1).
5. John Gill and Sue Whittle (1992) 'Management by Panacea: Accounting for Transience', *Journal of Management Studies*, **30** (2), March.
6. Edgar Schein (1990) 'A General Philosophy of Helping: Process Consultation', *Sloan Management Review*, Spring.
7. Ian Cunningham (1994) 'Against Team Building', *Organisations & People*, Association for Management Education and Development, London: Kogan Page, **1** (1), January.
8. Bruce Nixon (1984) 'In Search of Excellent Management Development', *Industrial and Commercial Training*, July/August.
9. Harvey Hornstein (1986) *Managerial Courage: Revitalizing Your Company Without Sacrificing Your Job*, New York: John Wiley and Sons Inc., pp. 103–4.
10. Abraham Zaleznik (1992) 'Managers and Leaders: Are They Different?', *Harvard Business Review*, March–April, p. 126.
11. Peter Senge (1990) *The Fifth Discipline: The Art & Practice of The Learning Organization*, London: Century Business.
12. Gerard Egan (1993) *Adding Value – A Systematic Guide to Business-Driven Management and Leadership*, San Francisco: Jossey-Bass, pp. 194, 200.
13. Jerry Harvey (1974) 'The Abilene Paradox: The Management of Agreement', *Organizational Dynamics*, New York: American Management Association, Summer, p. 4.

APPENDIX: ORGANIZATIONAL FITNESS QUESTIONNAIRE FOR ACTION LEARNING[1]

The following resource suggests some helpful questions which you might consider before embarking on Action Learning. By ranking each item on a scale of 1–5 (1 = low, 5 = high) you may highlight those areas in which the organisation may be weak, and hence in which effort needs to be focused.

No organisation is likely to score all 5's or all 1's, and in any case the ratings are subjective rather than absolute. Action Learning cannot be used to rectify major deficiencies in your organisation, but can be helpful in supporting development and growth. (You may take a strategic decision to begin Action Learning in the part of the organisation likely to be most supportive.)

Another way to use the resource is to get your team colleagues (or others in the organisation) to complete the questionnaire and then compare rankings. This may reveal how different people perceive the same organisation and may help to generate understanding of how the organisation functions.

An organisation which can:

O   expose itself to a good questioning approach
O   encourage people within it to question the status quo responsibly
O   encourage people to generate new and innovative ideas with a personal commitment to implement them

is likely to be one which is fit, both in the sense of being healthy and being ready for Action Learning.

1. Purpose/direction ☐

Is there some shared clarity about what the organisation is in business for? Do people within the organisation have a sense of its purpose and direction – its values, i.e. what is acceptable/legitimate about what we do and how we do it?

2. Individuality ☐

Does the organisation value individuality and seek to harness and encourage individual development and interests? (Or is individuality seen as a threat – people must conform!?) Can senior managers acknowledge that they do not always have all the answers? Can they cope with difficult questions about their decisions?

3. Corporacy ☐

Is there a shared sense of interdependence between the various parts of the organisation, so that 'the whole is greater than the sum of the parts'? Do managers look for win-win solutions and assess the impact of their actions on other parts of the organisation? (Or do they compete regardless of the consequences?)

4. Flexibility ☐

Is the organisation flexible? (Or is it excessively hierarchical?) Can it be innovative in the way solutions and ideas are generated across internal boundaries? Does the organisation enable and encourage people to take risks? Can and does it respond to new situations quickly and effectively, employing new methods and combinations of skill and experience?

5. Communication

Do open systems of communication exist which ensure that issues and concerns can be shared and aired? Do managers actively seek to find out the views of staff and accept criticism constructively? Do systems exist to allow staff to 'whistle blow' if they see something wrong?

6. Conflict

Does the organisation manage conflict? (Or is it suppressed or avoided?) Do people have the opportunity to put their point of view, knowing that it will be listened to and taken into account, and are decisions taken overtly and communicated? (Or are all difficult issues relegated to working parties without clear objectives or timescales?)

7. Reward systems

Do reward systems attempt to recognise achievement and contribution? (Or are they based solely on seniority?) Does the organisation find ways of rewarding people in other than pay and rations, e.g. training and development? Does the organisation celebrate achievement and give clear messages about what constitutes success?

8. Organisational learning

Is the organisation able to stand back and review its actions and preview the challenges ahead? Does it learn from previous failures and successes, what worked and what didn't? (Or does it always stumble and offer knee-jerk reactions to new situations?) Does it have systems to get feedback on its performance?

9. Environmentally friendly

Does the organisation continually monitor its performance and its relationships with the outside world? Can it anticipate changes in the environment and position itself accordingly? Does it seek to understand how others outside perceive it?

[1] The 'organizational fitness' advice and the questionnaire are reproduced with the kind permission of Mike Pedler and John Boutall, and the National Health Service Training Division.

6

MANAGING PERFORMANCE

OVERVIEW

This chapter examines performance management systems for managers, as a general management development intervention, as an aid to highlighting individual managers' development needs, and as a means of reinforcing teamwork.

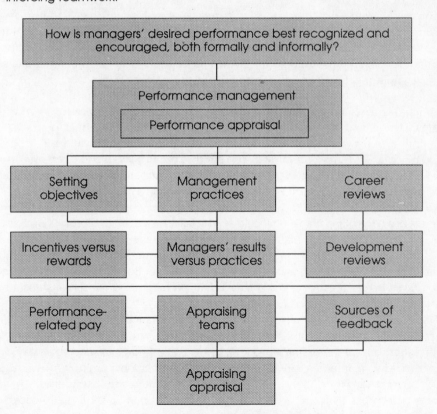

INTRODUCTION

I n this chapter we consider how to derive the best from performance management practices generally and from appraisal systems in particular. This means taking a view on the relative importance of managers' achieved results versus their everyday work behaviour. It also means being able to manage monetary rewards and incentives in order to have a desired effect on individual and team performance.

The subject is of interest to developers at two levels. At the lower level is the part of the process concerned with encouraging dialogues which identify individual managers' needs and plan how to develop their abilities. But, at a higher level, if we accept that management development is more than manager development, then performance management should look beyond the individual too. The performance management process should therefore also be about appraising and developing management's general performance capability and delivery, including such matters as obstacles and opportunities beyond individuals' personal control.

Performance management can also be seen to take place at both an informal and formal level; the spontaneous managing of performance year round, as well as regular though infrequent appraisal (say, quarterly or annually).

It is the formal aspect which attracts most criticism and is the most problematical. But it is arguably the informal and ongoing aspect which is most under-used. Thus, it is ironic that detractors of formal appraisal argue that if they manage performance well on a continuous basis, then infrequent and formal appraisal becomes superfluous. If practice followed theory, then there would undoubtedly be some sense in that argument. This would be more true for intimate units, and more applicable for Level 1 in Figure 1.1 (i.e. the individual manager) (see p. 7).

The late and highly respected W. Edwards Deming was one of performance appraisal's best-known critics. He claimed that results have more to do with the organization and its systems than with the individual. Individual performance appraisal, in his view, was therefore the wrong target and was invidious.

The critics of formal appraisal also claim that the process is too often associated with a backward-looking evaluation of performance, and neglects development. The word 'appraisal' certainly sounds judgemental, which doesn't help to allay these fears. Viewed from the developer's perspective, appraisal carries heavy overtones of a controlling managerial culture, not far removed from Theory X principles. The very existence of evaluative appraisal could be taken to imply that individuals will deliver to their maximum only if they are set fixed objectives by the boss and have their achievement against these fully monitored. But appraisal does not need to be viewed so negatively. Well managed, it can help develop relationships, build shared goals and extend commitment.

Here, I intend to be wholly positive about performance appraisal, using the term synonymously with the more neutral-sounding 'performance review' to mean the formal process of discussing all-round performance (individual and collective) in a constructive manner, and including both job- and personal-oriented planning for the year ahead, with whatever follow-on development action that implies.

Many companies try to achieve a mix of both formal and informal processes, partly through a justified lack of faith in the average line reviewer's ability and commitment to performance management unless forced into it by a formal annual mechanism, and partly to achieve direct links to pay awards. We shall begin by briefly looking at informal, ongoing processes.

MANAGING GOOD AND POOR PERFORMERS

Aside from any need to link assessment to pay, there is no doubt that matters concerned with individuals' performance – good or bad – are best handled as and when the need arises. And any spontaneous action may additionally benefit from formal reinforcement during annual appraisal.

Many line managers find it extremely difficult to manage either good or bad performers. You may find the checklist in Figure 6.1 useful as guidance.

FIGURE 6.1 ONGOING PERFORMANCE MANAGEMENT OF GOOD AND POOR PERFORMERS

General

1. Make clear what you expect, both generally and as short-term objectives.
2. Specify both results you expect to be delivered and working methods and behaviour.
3. Give frequent informal feedback – both positive 'strokes' and constructive criticism.
4. Differentiate widely in performance ratings, both *between* performers and *within* individuals' performance.
5. Use labels such as 'unsatisfactory' – 'excellent' to rate and encourage discrete *aspects* of performance rather than *total* performance.
6. Differentiate clearly in rewards between those who perform as required and those who do not.
7. Set an example by modelling good behaviour yourself.

Consistently good performers

1. Give them lots of positive feedback.
2. Display trust.
3. Involve them.
4. Make sure they are employed in interesting jobs.
5. Offer them leadership responsibilities.
6. Give them prominence and publicity.
7. Favour them with development opportunities.
8. Reward them with stimulating and challenging projects.

Consistently poor performers

1. Be sure you have correctly isolated the cause of poor performance, and that it's not you.
2. Give them unambiguous feedback, but in an acceptable and constructive form.
3. Try to anticipate likely opportunities for mistakes to occur and give formative feedback in advance.
4. Make sure your appraisal ratings reflect your true assessment.
5. Be specific about what improvement is needed.

6. Develop a joint plan for improvement.
7. Be clear about the consequences of making an improvement or not.
8. Remove persistent poor performers from positions of influence to minimize their impact.
9. Identify and develop possible successors.
10. Use organizational change to create opportunities to move people.

FORMAL PERFORMANCE APPRAISAL

Companies struggle to find the right formula for their management appraisal schemes. The reason? There is no single right answer. And why not? The simple explanation is because of incompatible aims. On the one hand, companies want their schemes to look back at past effort and evaluate it. On the other hand, they want them to look forward and plan and develop future performance. Therefore the appraisal discussion and documentation comprises the following four elements:

Evaluating the past year:
(looking backwards)

1. What was achieved compared with that expected (i.e. the results).
2. How abilities and expertise were applied (i.e. the means).

Planning the year ahead:
(looking forwards)

3. How capability can be developed and applied.
4. Setting objectives and improvement targets.

An evaluative discussion about results is not conducive to an open and honest discussion about personal needs, growth and risk-taking. And rewarding short-term achievement sits uncomfortably alongside longer-term development. For good measure, companies often add some form of scoring past performance, and these days they are likely to throw in money too – performance-related pay (PRP), or 'eat what you kill' to devotees. It is said that over the last five years, the average British manager's performance pay element has increased from 10 per cent to 40 per cent. This is a further complication and pressure.

Companies often feel that in formal schemes they are faced with a choice of aims and have to decide how to balance them. They may favour, even entirely forgo, one purpose at the expense of the other. Or they may split the judgemental part of the process away from the development part, so that they can take place at different times in different atmospheres. Discussion about one's future career may be another component or may be linked with discussion about developing present job performance.

In particular, PRP schemes attract great interest and scrutiny from those being appraised, not least because opportunities for some mean risks for others. On balance, it is usually easier for people to find fault with appraisal schemes rather than to see their virtues. The subsequent poor internal PR, along with the complexity and mixed purpose, eventually defeat most appraisal schemes to a greater or lesser degree. They are rarely acclaimed.

EFFECT ON MOTIVATION

Frequent attempts are made to conduct scientific studies of appraisal schemes, particularly those with a pay-for-performance component which drives variable salary increases, lump-sum bonuses, or both. The results of such formal studies usually paint a depressing picture. But what are their success criteria? Whether such schemes are successful or not depends on what you are hoping to derive from them. The studies invariably conclude that the schemes 'are failing to motivate'. That is almost certainly true. But is that the point?

Frederick Herzberg long ago taught us that money doesn't motivate. It is its absence which demotivates. Why then should we expect performance-related pay schemes to be excepted from what Herzberg, and our own experience, tells us?

MONEY AS A MEANS OR AN END

Some disagree with Herzberg, and claim from their own experience that money motivates them – especially those who do well out of it and want to retain their high differentials. What they probably mean is that money *fascinates* them, so they are very conscious of it in their own employment. They personally think of money as an end, rather than as a means to that end.

This confusion between means and ends at the individual level is also mirrored at company level. There are those who believe that a company's ultimate purpose is to make a profit, and those who believe (more wisely in my view) that the company needs to make a profit in order to be able to achieve its purposes. Money only acquires value when it's spent or otherwise used.

Making a profit is a necessary fact of existence. It is the essential requirement, as food is to life. But once companies are able to ensure that they survive and prosper, what do they then offer that no one else can? To find their *raison d'être*, they must ask, 'What impact does this have on the community?' and 'What value do we add to the wider world?'[1] As the Chief Executive of Häagen-Dazs put it, 'We are not in business to make a profit. We are in business to make the world's best ice cream. We happen to believe that will be very profitable.'

I find the Häagen-Dazs view attractive. Not only does it put profit into perspective as a means, consequence and yardstick, it also expresses a unique motive for the company in place of the usual generic one. However, considered at the philosophical level, it should be possible to articulate a common purpose behind all commercial business, and the best formula seems to be 'to maximize long-term owner value'. As Tom Lloyd, author *The Nice Company*, points out, such a financial-sounding objective can be met in practice only by being simultaneously concerned with 'distributive justice and ordinary decency'.[2] History shows that unethical and self-interested, money-centred practice is to the long-term detriment of a business.

MANAGEMENT PRACTICES

Management practices are the means by which managers achieve their end results. One company I was involved with recently took the decision to review the factors formally appraised in its performance appraisal scheme for its managers, i.e. its management practices. The Personnel Department had previously suggested that it was time to add 'creativity and innovation', but the MD had ruled this out at the time on the grounds that 'it would cause trouble'!

There is probably little need to say that this company was starting from a very low performance base. Individual effort was hardly recognizable, and the top management was equally deficient. Revisions to the performance management scheme was only one of a number of necessary interventions being carried out.

After discussion, we decided this was the right time to encourage creativity and innovation in managers through the express highlighting of these factors in their PRP scheme. Much more was added simultaneously in order to encourage other behaviour. (The chosen factors are described in Appendix A at the end of this chapter.) It was also felt appropriate to couple the appraisal of managerial practices with a system of rewards for the achievement of results against objectives.

ACTIVITY 6.1

Think about your evolving culture and management style. Is your company clear about what management practices and behaviour it would like to encourage?

SETTING OBJECTIVES

Objectives and targets for the period ahead can take several forms and cover many facets. Conventional wisdom says they should be measurable. That partly depends on whether achievement against the objectives is to be quantified for reward purposes. It is also a matter of trust and reflects the management style and organization culture. Similar considerations determine how formalized they are.

TYPES OF OBJECTIVE

Business/operational objectives

Some companies cascade their company Mission and Goals statement down to individual departments in order to generate more tangible objectives against which achievement can be measured and rewarded. These amount to standing accountabilities and may lead on to their equivalent for individual managers within those departments.

Objectives are also often set as part of cascaded annual business planning processes. Department heads are required, with the help of corporate planners, to commit themselves bilaterally to a departmental annual plan, complete with quality and quantity targets that accord with and contribute towards corporate revenue and cost targets. This is undoubtedly a useful process, but it can generate only one kind of departmental objective, one which is business/operational in nature.

The problem with this cascading method is that it tends to generate targets to be met largely within the present system's capability and norms. The trick is to complement this planning process with three other kinds of objectives which focus on change, development and means.

Change objectives

The purpose of these objectives is to introduce change. They will rarely be volunteered by the departmental head. They usually need some outside pressure, from the boss, peers, competitors, etc.

Development objectives

The purpose of these objectives is to concentrate attention, effort and resources on ways of developing the present capability of the manager, the manager's individual subordinates, the manager's team, the manager's organization, and the manager's relationships with other teams, departments, boss, customers, etc.

Means objectives

Any departmental objectives which aim to contribute to the company's mission or business plan will emphasize end results. But companies also have an interest in *how* their managers go about their work as well as *what* they achieve. This kind of objective allows us to complement the bottom-line with a focus on the means (i.e. management behaviours or practices) by which those results are obtained.

The annual performance appraisal is a good forum in which to establish these separate kinds of commitments. Figure 6.2 contains a sample of the range of possible objectives.

KEY TIPS

❖ Distinguish between the various kinds of objective. Have some of each where appropriate.

❖ It is the important which is worth measuring; not what is worth measuring that is important.

SHARED OBJECTIVES

It goes without saying that, wherever possible, managers' objectives should be mutually agreed between the job-holder and boss. To achieve this commitment, it is now very common for subordinate managers to be asked to take the initiative and propose appropriate objectives for joint discussion. But those managers who are most able to identify and initiate meaningful objectives for themselves to be discussed with the boss are those least in need of the objective-setting approach to management. Bosses therefore need to tailor their handling of the process to fit the degree of initiative which they can expect from individual managers. Managers likewise need to be sensitive to the style of leadership they are being offered.

FIGURE 6.2　MANAGERS' PERFORMANCE APPRAISAL: POSSIBLE OBJECTIVES

- **Raising standards**
  Make sure that no more than ...
  Increase the rate at which ...

- **Hitting targets**
  Contain increases in costs to no more than ...
  Achieve a throughput rate of ...

- **Special projects**
  Join the ... taskforce.
  Carry out a review of ...

- **Introducing change**
  Reorganize the ... section to achieve ... by ...
  Implement the recommendations of ...

- **Management of the organization's processes**
  Build bridges with the X group by including them in ...
  Develop a means of getting feedback from internal customers.

- **Self-development**
  Obtain the ... qualification.
  Find out how to ...

- **Subordinate development**
  Expand three of your junior managers' portfolios.
  Let ... attend the regular monthly meetings in your place.

This raises an important point about the organization's leadership style and culture. Many textbooks argue that it should be sufficient for a leader to set a clear direction and then expect responsible managers to be able to sort out for themselves the implications for the management of their part of the business. Classical objective-setting implies a more hands-on role for the boss than that ideal.

Whether initiated from below or above, the important aspect of mutuality is only one level at which objectives might be said to be 'shared'. The three possible levels of sharing are as follows:

1. Shared in the sense of **agreed**. That is, discussed and agreed between the boss and subordinate manager.
2. Shared in the sense of **joint**. All section heads in a department may share some common objectives, agreed with the departmental head.
3. Shared in the sense of **communicated**. All members of a team may know the other team members' objectives.

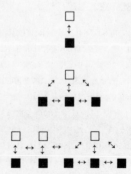

ACTIVITY 6.2

Examine your own objectives and see how they match against the various categories. Where could you make use of other types of objective?

MANAGERS' RESULTS VERSUS PRACTICES

Should top management be more interested in appraising means or ends – the management practices or the results managers achieve? Can they have it both ways? Indeed, why should management practices matter at all as long as the managers achieve the right results? This is obviously a crucial performance question, not least for the design of any management performance appraisal scheme.

In one large international company's scheme, managers' achievement of results against pre-set objectives accounts for up to 60 per cent of their evaluation for their performance pay. The demonstration of approved management practices accounts for the remaining 40 per cent. This represents a recent change from the previous 50/50 arrangement. It implies a planned shift of concern towards results with less regard for the consistency of management style.

It is interesting to speculate on the signals sent down an organization by overt changes to the values and rewards associated with results versus management practices. It is also doubtful whether the full impact which the shift in emphasis is hoped to have on the management culture has been thoroughly considered in advance, and the risks carefully weighed.

However, it could be argued that once the desired management practices have been defined and managers have been trained over a few years so that the new culture based on them is firmly in place, it is reasonable for the company to take those new behaviours for granted. If so, it should then be possible in theory to shift the emphasis safely towards results. Does it work like this in practice?

Since a greater emphasis on results is *de facto* part of a new results-oriented culture, and given the conditioning power of the reward system supporting it, it is likely that the previously trained management practices will attract personal re-questioning or even abandonment by managers in order to meet the specific end results being sought. It would be surprising if this was not so. The achievement of results does not just involve personal *effort*; it also requires personal *methods* which are results-oriented. Both can be affected by system opportunities and incentives.

Shifting the emphasis towards results is not to be contemplated lightly; it *will* affect behaviour. But how? And can we rely on appraised and rewarded management practices as a bulwark against unethical or otherwise undesirable behaviour?

RISKS IN EMPHASIZING RESULTS

One instance of the ends-versus-means processes getting out of kilter concerned some British Airways managers who it was said took it upon themselves to attack their sales targets by dubious means. (I will discuss this well-publicized case in more depth later.) More recently – as I mentioned in the Preface – the financial services sector has suffered considerable public embarrassment with some of its members' performance, where bottom-line results received more attention than wholesome and customer-friendly practices. The industry watchdog Lautro claimed that as many as four out of every five sales of personal pension plans was faulty and based on wrong advice to customers. Norwich Union was fined £65 000 for misleading advertising and £325 000 for failing to train staff properly. Eight hundred of their salespeople were suspended from duty and ordered to undergo 'retraining'. Likewise, Nationwide had to pull 1300 staff off the streets. The Prudential came in for review, and Barclays Life ordered retraining of its sales staff.

But is this fair? It points the finger at the individual employees. They can hardly be held responsible for their organization's culture, even the industry culture. Nor will training help if the reward system is not overhauled at the same time. Here is another instance where the dark art of training is held to possess magical powers, at once blamed for past mistakes while naïvely heralded as saviour. This may flatter training, but it is an unreasonable burden.

It also reflects an undue emphasis by the industry's regulators and critics on individual competence, and therefore almost inevitably on training as the solution. This happens because training is a highly visible and tangible variable in the organization system. Action can be ordered quickly. The bosses can be seen to be taking action. But the performance of individual employees is a symptom, not a cause. And the training lever is not the most powerful one on which to pull. We need to look deeper. The trouble is that problems of culture are more difficult to analyse, understand, articulate and remedy.

HIERARCHICAL IMPLICATIONS

Besides the risks highlighted in these cases, there is another good reason for questioning the wisdom of placing too great an emphasis on results. Increasingly, managerial work is becoming more specialized, complex and impossible for bosses to control and understand. The hierarchy has to take on trust the performance of managers reporting to it. So the idea of top-down setting of precise objectives to be achieved is increasingly out of place.

Peter Drucker points out that a key competence will be subordinate managers' ability to identify the contribution which they can make in the forthcoming period, and to make sure that it is accepted and understood by those around them: bottom-up management, not top-down.[3]

It is now common for bosses to ask their subordinate managers to draft their own objectives, as we said earlier. But this should only preface subsequent discussion and shared commitment. I know one chief executive who opted out from the dialogue. Whenever directors asked him to discuss and agree objectives, his reply would be, 'Don't worry, you'll soon know if you're not doing the right things!' While the objective-setting process may be delegated, the ultimate content in terms of its degree of challenge to the job-holder and in its validity both to the job and more especially the company should not be. Otherwise delegation approaches abdication.

The problem in this particular example was that the directors felt a need for agreed annual objectives, for a number of reasons. First, Personnel kept insisting that the chain in the cascading process had to start right at the top and should not be broken. But, as we saw earlier, this is only a serious problem with certain kinds of business objective. Second, Personnel also insisted on a good example being set from the top to encourage other managers to take the whole appraisal process seriously. Third, and probably most significant here, the directors knew that what the chief executive meant by his particular kind of feedback ('you'll soon know ...') could mean loss of their jobs; agreed objectives might have made it easier to read the boss's mind.

Well managed, the bottom-up approach to objective-setting appears highly virtuous in organizations which are trying to become more 'empowering'. But it needs careful handling. The best intentions can be misconstrued as a lack of leadership, interest or commitment to the objective-setting process. Where the individual manager is self-confident and prefers a boss who doesn't interfere too much, this approach may be well received and be effective. Other managers who are newer to their jobs, and are generally less experienced or confident, may prefer the boss to take more of a lead. Bosses therefore need to give careful and individual thought to where they place themselves on the continuum which has 'interferes' at one end and 'keeps out of the way' at the other.

MANAGING CLIMATE AND VALUES, NOT PEOPLE

Where subordinate managers are competent and trustworthy, their bosses should not so much *manage* their subordinates, but manage their climate and environment, leaving the managers to work out for themselves how best to capitalize on their skills, goodwill and energy, within a clear understanding of the company's chosen direction.

To give managers licence within a framework that comprises the company's direction coupled with a favourable environment is not to say 'we want these results and it's up to you to work out how to deliver them'. The former signals a trusting leadership style and carries low risk. The latter sounds like authoritarian abdication and entails high risk.

There are now signs in business of what may be a shift away from results and towards greater interest in management practices, and indeed in the values that underpin them. The Personnel Director of the computer firm Unisys is quoted in *Personnel Today* under the headline 'Computer Firm Shifts Emphasis from Results to Behaviour', as saying, 'We are now looking at how people perform their jobs rather than what they actually achieve.'[4] The behavioural assessments include whether behaviour is 'team-centred, customer-dedicated, innovative, creative, motivated and accountable'. The Unisys plan follows moves by the company's American parent to change the culture of the company in the 1990s.

NatWest Life Assurance takes the view that 'Most companies look at performance in terms of what people have achieved, but we felt it was important to measure and reward inputs, not just outcomes.'[5] The John Lewis Partnership grades employees on personal qualities such as their ability to get on with people.

Moves like these could well signal a break with the 1980s bottom-line culture. Compensation specialists are increasingly pointing to the need for a more balanced approach whereby hard financial measures are complemented by softer behaviour. The softness may appear as value statements to drive management behaviour and practices. British Telecom publishes the following character set:

1. We put our customers first.
2. We are professional.
3. We respect each other.
4. We work as one team.
5. We are committed to continuous improvement.

Thus you can affect managerial style in two ways: by emphasizing and rewarding new management practices, or by downplaying these and emphasizing specific results. The management practices route to change is more likely to provide the company with control over the change process, whereas emphasizing results can lose control.

ACTIVITY 6.3

Review how your management performance appraisal scheme currently emphasizes end results versus their means of achievement. Are those components thoughtfully and well balanced? What effect are they having on managers' and corporate performance?

INCENTIVES VERSUS REWARDS

Just as we confuse means with ends, so we confuse rewards with incentives. Rewards look back. Incentives look forwards. You can undoubtedly reward managers for past effort. You can do this either with their foreknowledge or as a surprise. This memory of past rewards or the lure of forward promises may motivate managers to apply greater effort, but you cannot be certain about this.

In any case, what precisely do we mean by *motivate*? Do we mean 'make them feel appreciated' (rewards), or do we mean 'make them feel inspired' (incentives)? There is often woolly thinking here.

Paradoxically, rewarding managers unexpectedly for past effort will probably motivate them more than if they felt they were entitled to it. Yet, by definition, the surprise reward cannot have been an incentive behind that effort, which will have been given without expectation of the reward. The surprise reward may incidentally also act as an incentive for the next year's effort; yet if and when that reward comes, it may be less motivating the second time around since it will have been due and expected! So the pay-off from such a scheme may decline over the years as the benefits to individual managers become increasingly taken for granted.

For some groups, highly specific or large incentives may be motivating in the sense of encouraging more effort. They may also encourage different practices, shortcuts, bending rules – which can sometimes be beneficial. But they might also encourage unethical practices, short-termism or poor teamwork, and can be highly stressful. As we have seen in the case of Barings Bank, the lure of annual personal bonuses as high as £2 million can prompt uncontrolled risk-taking, especially as the year-end date for bonus calculation approaches, and when the sums at that point are negative. The problem is that such incentives as these are a one-way bet: the employee can't lose, but the employer can.

BUYING UNHAPPINESS

Football pools coupons and the National Lottery should carry a health warning. Scooping the jackpot has ruined many normal lives. Whether or not you believe the adage 'money is the root of all evil', as a generalization, Herzberg's dictum holds true. It is very difficult to give money away and make people genuinely happy. This is not the same as saying we don't want more of it! We all want to win the pools or the lottery.

Why is dispensing money through appraisal schemes so difficult?

O   From a backwards perspective, either the managers expected more, or they don't know if they are happy until they find out what other managers got!

O   From a forwards perspective, the managers are the way they are. Habit, comfort and confidence all contribute to inertia. Incentives can't make silk purses out of sows' ears, as the saying goes. Managers may also feel that their appraisal will be conducted idiosyncratically, however objective their appraiser tries to be.

WHY DO IT?

The motivational effect is very questionable. But should motivating managers be the prime purpose? We can probably make them happy in easier ways. There may, however, be other good reasons for using performance-related pay appraisal schemes. I can think of three good reasons:

1.   To differentiate managers' pay as part of managing turnover – sending signals to those whom we would like most to keep, and to those whom we would mind least if they left, encouraging them to look outside. (In practice, the effect of differential pay is limited: the better managers are encouraged to feel more marketable and may simply move on for even higher salaries. And the poor performers probably can't get another job anyway.)

2.   To be intrinsically fair to the good performers compared with their less-deserving colleagues. Now cynics say life isn't supposed to be fair! But a manager who sees an undeserving colleague equally well compensated *feels* it's unfair, and this is demotivating.

3.   Most important of all, to stop managers being able to complain, 'What's the point of doing a good job round here? It doesn't make any difference!'

In the fashion of Herzberg's so-called hygiene factors, one of the reasons for having such a scheme is to stop people being *demotivated*.

PERFORMANCE-RELATED PAY

As the above shows, there can be some good arguments for differentiating pay according to performance for otherwise similar job responsibilities. I introduced such a scheme for computer programmers in a company needing to gain control over its 30 per cent per annum labour turnover among this group. But as we have seen, there is often some very confused thinking. Not least, this is found where PRP is applied disproportionately within the senior management group.

One company with which I have worked has just cut its directors' salaries by 50 per cent, but at the same time has substituted scope for earning more by performance bonuses. While some pundits, such as Tom Peters, would applaud that, others are increasingly sounding the alarm bells.

PRP can be logically justified. Those who contribute most towards meeting the business's goals on behalf of its owners should receive the greatest reward from them. PRP is not the only element in achieving this equitable distribution, but the balance is compromised without it. The problems with PRP arise not so much from the philosophy as with the practice – both in making a continued success of schemes, as well as using PRP as an instrument of change.

To continue with the example of top management incentives, one can readily see the point of introducing a substantial element of PRP as a conscious and necessary attempt to change a management culture where directors earn high salaries in complete security of employment without having to perform well. But that is not the case in the example quoted above. This company already has a high-performing culture, where directors have a substantial element of PRP, have no job security and already have to 'perform or else'. It is therefore hard to see justifiable reasons for hiking the PRP component even further, other than the fact that schemes eventually lose their impact and decay, needing re-gearing from time to time.

PROBLEMS IN RAISING PRP

There are several potential problems with an intervention of this kind:

O   It encourages short-term results – usually those which can be achieved within a year.

O   It concentrates on tangibles, but there are many achievements which are not measurable.

O   It usually encourages individual performance and fosters internal competition, rather than helping colleagues perform well as a collaborative management team. (Schemes can be designed to contain a group element, e.g. the company's financial result.)

O   It usually rewards results at the expense of ethically acceptable methods.
O   It carries signals for the rest of the population about the company's values. Among these might be the adverse highlighting of widely different compensation treatment for the bosses from the rest of the employees.
O   It produces diminishing returns over time, raising the question of where do you go from here.
O   It emphasizes present achievement rather than personal development.

On balance, if well designed and well managed, PRP schemes probably make a positive contribution – at least initially. I add this qualification because, like every-thing else, they suffer from entropy, that is, they tend to deteriorate as they progress through their natural life cycle and inevitably lose their effectiveness. The need for them as a means of differentiating rewards is arguably increasing as rewarding people through promotion becomes more difficult as a consequence of flatter hierarchies. But if you don't feel you need to include a performance pay element, and especially if you can avoid mechanistically scoring past performance, you have a better chance of making the developmental aspect of appraisal more successful.

Ultimately performance does matter and does need to be appraised, in one manner or another, formally or informally, and by one person or another. You can't avoid it.

APPRAISING TEAMS

Most appraisal schemes centre heavily on the individual. Once an unchallenged feature of virtually all appraisal schemes, this individual orientation is now increasingly being questioned. Some developers even regard it as a damaging flaw, believing that it encourages personally oriented behaviour which runs counter to the well-being and the full functioning of the group.

THE EFFECT OF CULTURE

In western culture there is some inevitability about this traditional individual orientation. In individualist societies people are bound to be concerned primarily with how their own individual performance is perceived, ahead of improving the performance of the group as a whole. Cultural values and conditioning apart, it is also logically individual managers who ultimately have to make their own unique contributions since that is all they can directly influence, and this fact has to be acknowledged. So as well as working from the company's standpoint, an appraisal scheme has to appear relevant from the individual's viewpoint. In particular, the more any PRP scheme dilutes the emphasis on the individual, the less fair it may appear to be and the less motivating.

This problem is particularly likely to be true in the two most extreme examples of individualistic cultures, the UK and the USA, which encourage individualism and competition from birth through school life into employment. The problem in collectivist societies is rather different, a fact which brings complications as work-forces become more multi-cultural and firms more international.

The question of culture affects dimensions other than purely the individual-istic–collectivist one. The masculine–feminine cultural dimension (i.e. competitive vs. nurturing continuum) is another. A new Dutch chief executive appointed to run a UK liquid petroleum gas bottling company could not understand why his directors always seemed to be looking for reasons to disagree with each other. Similarly, inherent societal values about how much untrammelled power a boss should reasonably be expected to hold is another factor in teams, as it is in the mechanics of appraisal itself.

TEAM FACTORS

To the extent that appraisal schemes highlight individuals' performance and seek to foster and incentivize it, they tend to do so at the expense of collaborative team effort. Indeed managers may be most successful in their employer's eyes and as measured by tangible consequences if they put their own personal goals higher than the group's goals. Such individually biased schemes may inadvertently encourage managers to claim credit for others' efforts, including their own sub-ordinates. Yet this is clearly not what the company really wants or needs.

The thoughtful design of appraisal schemes can ameliorate this damaging individual effect. The management practices identified, the way results are measured, how feedback is given, and what kinds of objective are set for the forth-coming period, all help generate expectations of either an individual or group emphasis. The effect is most powerful where there is a direct and highly geared link between performance and rewards.

Where it is inappropriate or impractical to develop from scratch a wholly team-based approach to appraisal, then an alternative is to build some of the values of team-type behaviour into the individual appraisal mechanics. This might include, for example, the appraisal of interdepartmental cooperation, with feedback sought from such sources. The way work is organized (especially projects and taskforces) should also be used to foster flexible and cooperative relationships, based on shared higher-level company goals.

Though much more difficult than wholly individual appraisal, some degree of team-based appraisal and rewards is fast becoming the conventional wisdom and best HR practice. The idea looks like lasting until it either becomes practically unworkable, or until the emphasis on rewarding high performance financially, or even the concentration on results itself, goes into terminal decline. This could happen in a serious way only if the values and higher-order principles within the learning organization take hold, something that will be discussed in Chapter 11.

TEAM REWARDS

Several companies now have appraisal schemes that include team objectives rather than, or in addition to, individual ones. Similarly, there are now systems of team rewards of one kind or another, including cash bonuses.

Appealing to the team is usually additional to appealing directly to individual members. A balance between managing the individual's performance and the group's is all important. A single company-wide bonus is sometimes to be found on its own, but as a general rule, team rewards should be in addition to individual rewards, certainly for managers. This protects high-flyers and it works against free-loaders.

Charles Handy, writing in *The Empty Raincoat*, can foresee the time when the manager's total compensation will comprise four elements.[6] Besides the salary component based on job size (perhaps only 50 per cent of take-home pay) will be three personal elements:

Salary:		50%	
Bonuses:	individual contribution	10%	(personal)
	total company surplus	20%	(big team)
	value of departmental work	20%	(local team)
		50%	

Many companies already have the first three components in place. It is the last one (i.e. the local team) that is the most difficult to define. How can we determine where a departmental team begins and ends? This is far from easy. To answer this, it is helpful to think of the various organizational and working arrangements and circumstances as lying on a continuum. These give rise to different kinds of team scheme.

Intra-group

At one end of the scale lies the intact work-group, all members of which are working towards the same result, usually on a permanent basis, though they could be seconded together for a full-time project instead. At shopfloor level a frequently discussed example is manufacture assembly, as with cars. In this kind of arrangement, the members are fully interdependent, and may even have scope to make their own working arrangements. They view themselves as part of the team, have substantial face-to-face contact and require close and frequent *coordination*. This is the key word. The group will function only in this spirit and manner. Individualistic behaviour is anathema to the group.

Given this arrangement, goal setting, measurement of results, and incentives and rewards are, by definition, best pitched at group level. The individual performance element is much less important in these terms and may even be discounted altogether.

Inter-group

At the other end of the scale the company is merely looking for less selfish behaviour and more cooperation across boundaries and between functions in what remains primarily an individually based work structure and culture. Cooperation replaces coordination. This is where most managers' jobs fit in.

Here, the heart of the goal-setting process, appraisal and rewards remain weighted towards the individual level, but performance may be moderated by a group element – perhaps goals and rewards. There may be significant individually based salary increases for the manager, plus cash or equivalent bonuses based on personal contribution, and the person's perceived contribution to the group(s) to which the manager belongs.

Between these two extremes are various shades of teamwork, including short-term teams. An example would be a team formed to manage a business acquisition. Partnerships are another variant.

For a group to justify the 'team' label and be managed and rewarded collectively, they need to satisfy a number of criteria:

1.   Do they view themselves as part of a team?
2.   Do they enjoy significant face-to-face interaction?
3.   Do their tasks require close and frequent coordination, or a degree of cooperation?

If so, it is still necessary that the organization culture emphasizes the virtues of group-centred behaviour. And it requires the appropriate behaviour and results to be capable of measurement. That leaves plenty of scope for design of the most suitable ways to reward teams and encourage good team behaviour. This is a specialist field, needing experts to advise on how best to structure the goal-setting, measuring and reward system. There is considerable skill in deciding what kind of payment should be made, its size, frequency, allocation, etc. One such specialist consultancy is the Hay Group.

One type of scheme that is gaining ground across a wide range of team contexts is *gain sharing*. The concept is simple. A group, such as a department, is given a collective target to hit, e.g. achieving savings worth £x. Coupled with this target is an agreement that all members of that department will enjoy a given percentage of those savings shared equally among the team's members.

While the idea is simple, the practice is not. Group goal-setting, appraisal and reward schemes are not without considerable difficulty. The simpler the scheme (such as the gain-sharing one described), the easier it is to make it work and have it understood and recognized as being fair, and it may act as an incentive.

The main problem remains defining the team. Managers are usually members of several teams, though many are probably not recognized formally as such, they don't appear on organization charts, and they cut across functional boundaries. This complication is compounded by the increasing fluidity in organizations, with *ad hoc* projects and taskforces, part-time involvement and external contributions. You can see the growing problem when you couple this with fast-changing work priorities which interfere with the idea of a fixed target to be measured and evaluated at the end of a period perhaps as long as a financial year.

ACTIVITY 6.4

How do your current appraisal scheme and your recognition and reward system for managers affect team behaviour?

WHERE TO REVIEW CAREERS

The sharing of ideas about managers' ambitions, hopes and fears about their future career may be embraced within a formal performance appraisal scheme. Alternatively, a sharp distinction is sometimes drawn between potential and performance. I am not going to discuss the content of career management here. That is the theme of the next chapter. My only immediate interest is the structural one – where does the activity best fit?

If a single appraisal scheme is used to manage evaluation of performance and development in the present job, then I personally favour hiving off longer-term career discussion to another forum. In this case it can be linked with wider career management systems and considerations of succession planning and job rotation. If the total development aspect of appraisal is separated from the evaluative aspect, then development can embrace both current and future job considerations. But there are no hard and fast rules. It is a case of what the company can cope with and make a success of.

The problem to guard against in a unified scheme is the temptation (on both sides) to seek refuge in talking generally about career aspirations, and to fail to face up to short-term performance issues.

DEVELOPMENT REVIEWS

Often only one small section of appraisal is thought of as development. But a wide discussion can take place in a developmental frame of mind, rather than a judge-mental or a managing/controlling one. Think of performance appraisal not simply as the boss appraising the subordinate's performance, but as the two of them jointly appraising how well the collective management team is performing.

The scheme I introduced for the rather unsophisticated client mentioned earlier in this chapter included documentation for personal development needs and plans. This is designed to tie development action plans in closely with the behaviour areas being valued, evaluated and rewarded. There are many possible ways of designing this type of documentation. Appendix B at the end of this chapter shows the format used in the scheme to which I refer.

FEEDBACK SOURCES

SELF-APPRAISAL

Team-based pay and appraisal is one recent development; another interesting initiative struggling to take root is that of self-appraisal. The problem is that it is at odds with the power/results orientation found in many organization cultures. Self-appraisal implies a shift towards a more development-centred culture, with con-siderable devolved power, responsibility and trust. It also entails a broadening of the idea of who your customers are, only one of whom is your boss. Thus appraisees are encouraged to obtain what is called '360-degree feedback' from a variety of stakeholders.

UPWARD FEEDBACK

The content and handling of the feedback can span the following range.

Narrow, one-way and sensitive

A specially structured format can be provided for telling the boss(es) certain facts and perceptions which wouldn't normally be acceptable. This feedback often comes from a large employee group to the management group. But it is sometimes sought from the level immediately below.

Broad, responsive and deep

Alternatively, the feedback process can take the form of a structured two-way dialogue based on the subordinate's views. Issues may be sensitive or may simply be too long term or philosophical to fit with typical day-to-day dialogues. This feedback can be initiated by the boss asking thought-provoking questions in writing before the performance review. The broader dialogue which ensues may then give space for more sensitive oral feedback.

The MD of Rank Xerox asks for feedback twice a year from his 15 subordinates. Max De Pree, Chairman and Chief Executive of Herman Miller Inc. asks his subordinates highly crafted written questions in advance, which are followed up in the live interview.[7]

CAREFULLY CRAFTED QUESTIONS

There is considerable skill in formulating good questions and listening to the answers. Using appraisal for telling and controlling is easier but less developmental. Of course, the character and competence of the boss will determine the actual nature and depth of the discussion, as well as the extent to which it is either largely one way or a genuine sharing. As, too, will the seniority of the managers and how credibly they are regarded.

I have provided a handful of written and oral questions in Figure 6.3 to illustrate the idea. These are taken and edited from *Leadership is an Art* (by courtesy of Arrow Business Books).[7]

Note that how any discussion and conclusions are captured – formally or informally – will vary from one setting to another. Bear in mind that paperwork, especially pre-printed appraisal forms, will generally be less appropriate at the higher levels.

STRUCTURED EMPLOYEE FEEDBACK

Obtaining honest feedback is not easy. It first requires the building of a confident and trusting climate in which people feel safe. In the right climate it can be argued

---

FIGURE 6.3 MANAGERS' PERFORMANCE APPRAISAL: SAMPLE QUESTIONS

The boss's role

1. How can I personally have more time to focus on such matters as strategy, our value system, participation, continuity, and team building?
2. What key goals do you have as a leader of the company and in which you feel I can be of help and support?
3. What are a few of the things you expect most and need most from me?
4. If you were in my shoes, what one key area or matter would you concentrate on?

The manager's career

5. What do you want to do (to be)? What are you planning to do about it?
6. How do you see yourself personally, professionally and organizationally?
7. Does the company need you? Do you need the company?

The manager's contribution

8. In what significant areas of the company do you believe you can make a contribution but feel you cannot get a hearing?
9. In the past year, from the perspective of integrity, what has most affected you personally, professionally, and organizationally?

The manager's subordinates

10. What will you do in the coming year to develop your three highest-potential persons? Who are they?

The business

11. What are your thoughts on our competition? Where do we need to respond to it and what should be our response?

The management of the organization

12. What examples of budding synergy do you see in your area and how can we capitalize on them?
13. What signals of impending entropy do you see in the company? What are you doing about it?

---

that formal and occasional performance appraisal devices like this should become unnecessary, and be replaced by ongoing open, two-way dialogue, as we said at the start. The CEO of Intel tells his managers, 'If you have not challenged your boss in the last two weeks, you're not doing your job.'

An alternative approach for top managements is to obtain company-wide input under a number of headings in a questionnaire survey. The scope of data may be broad as in general climate surveys, or may emphasize management style:

O   It may concern the management group or individual managers.
O   It may be directly linked to annual appraisals or be a separate exercise.
O   It may be mandatory for the managers or voluntary.

Allied Dunbar's scheme is voluntary, anonymous and linked with appraisal, but there is a general belief that schemes should progress towards open feedback as part of the development of a more open culture.

W.H. Smith Retail uses an approach linked to an annual appraisal of management style, dealing with aspects such as delegation, approachability, decisiveness and honesty. The data is gathered anonymously and processed by an outside agency. This approach is supported by research which shows that the biggest single influence on employees' perceptions of a company is the attitude of their individual managers.

The danger with mass anonymous data is that the results may be difficult to pinpoint and are liable to be misrepresented. One Board received heavy feedback on 'management style' after considerable bad press about anti-competitive behaviour. It chose to interpret this as a problem with individual managers rather than the organization's uncompromising and combative culture.

APPRAISING APPRAISAL

As well as plans for developing individual managers, you may want a plan for how your appraisal scheme itself can develop over time. One should hope that as inter-personal skills, confidence and trust develop, the appraisal process will become better able to handle discussion at the level of how well the company's management as a whole is succeeding and can do better – in other words, management development more than manager development.

Whatever scheme you have, you need to consider some questions about purpose and population. What are you trying to achieve? How are you trying to change and develop the organization? For example, do you want to encourage results, promote learning or risk taking? Do you wish to strengthen or dilute the power of the hierarchy, cement approved management practices, foster greater individual effort or more collaborative teamwork? Or is your scheme simply aimed at mere individual skill development?

ACTIVITY 6.5

Review your management appraisal scheme. How well is it balancing the differing aims? Where is it achieving most benefit? Where does it need strengthening? What else could it achieve?

My purpose has been to present ways of making a practical reality of some high-flown concepts. So, by way of contrasting relief, let me end this chapter with a tongue-in-cheek performance appraisal suggestion.

Mahatma Gandhi once wrote that there were seven sins in the world:

1.   Wealth without work.
2.   Pleasure without conscience.

3. Knowledge without character.
4. Commerce without morality.
5. Science without humanity.
6. Worship without sacrifice.
7. Politics without principle.

As De Pree says, 'Performance considered in light of those seven sins would be a well-reviewed performance indeed.'[7]

REFERENCES

1. Mike Pedler, John Burgoyne and Tom Boydell (1991) *The Learning Company – A Strategy for Sustainable Development*, Maidenhead: McGraw-Hill, pp. 162–3.
2. Tom Lloyd (1994) 'Through the Moral Maze', *Management Today*, August (book review).
3. *Harvard Business Review* (1993) 'The Post-Capitalist Executive: An Interview with Peter F. Drucker', May–June.
4. *Personnel Today* (1994) 'Unisys Links Rises to Personal Skills', 8–21 March.
5. *Personnel Management Plus* (1994) 'Paying the Price for Performance', June.
6. Charles Handy (1994) *The Empty Raincoat*, London: Hutchinson.
7. Max De Pree (1994) *Leadership is an Art*, London: Business Books, pp. 117–20.

APPENDIX A: EXAMPLE OF MANAGEMENT PRACTICES IN AN APPRAISAL SCHEME

1. Standards

Treats others affected by own work as though they were customers. Continually raises work standards. Monitors and takes responsibility for own work level and standard. Works with others to deliver a high standard joint result.

2. Planning and organizing

Involves relevant people in plans. Sets and reviews objectives. Organizes activities and timescales to achieve objectives on schedule. Monitors performance measures and quality standards. Thinks ahead and produces timely contingency plans.

3. Use of time and resources

Makes best use of time available at work. Treats time as a valuable resource. Respects others' work commitments and deadlines. Seeks acceptable shortcuts. Recognizes the need to make best use of material and financial resources.

4. Judgement and decision making

Analyses alternatives and concentrates on relevant data. Assesses implications for profit, costs and customer (internal and external) acceptability. Faces up to tough decisions. Takes calculated risks. Makes sound decisions under pressure. Displays fairness without favouritism.

5. Commitment and urgency

Shows a sense of urgency and energy to achieve results. Perseveres against resistance. Takes self-responsibility for getting tasks done and shows initiative rather than waiting for instructions. Shows resourcefulness to get round obstacles. Responds well under pressure. Meets deadlines.

6. Flexibility and innovation

Adapts to changing demands. Quickly acquires new knowledge when needed. Challenges existing approaches. Recognizes when there is a need to change. Generates practical and creative ideas. Encourages the implementation of new ways.

7. Communicating and influencing

Supports and cooperates with other departments. Presents in a convincing and informative manner. Encourages others to think and to share their ideas. Listens and displays open-mindedness. Asserts own opinions clearly and firmly. Regularly and frequently briefs staff.

8. Leading and motivating

Provides clear direction. Delegates effectively. Develops subordinates. Gives honest, accurate and timely feedback. Seeks and creates opportunities for team-working. Provides subordinates with guidance and support. Recognizes achievement. Keeps commitments.

9. Strategic and business awareness

Keeps abreast of customer needs and priorities. Demonstrates wide understanding of company activities outside own department area. Identifies opportunities and how to exploit them. Translates mission, goals and strategies into action plans.

APPENDIX B: SAMPLE FORMAT FOR DEVELOPMENT PLANNING IN PERFORMANCE APPRAISAL

The following section of an appraisal document developed for a client should be seen in conjunction with the Management Practices set out in Appendix A. They are taken from the same appraisal scheme (shown without their associated rating advice).

The full documentation comprises:

PART A: EVALUATION OF PERFORMANCE
Section 1: Achievement of Results Against Objectives
Section 2: How Results were Achieved by Good Management Practices

PART B: PLANNING NEXT YEAR'S PERFORMANCE
Section 3: Development of Personal Capability
Section 4: Setting Next Year's Objectives

SECTION 3: DEVELOPMENT OF PERSONAL CAPABILITY

This part of the appraisal allows for an open and shared exchange of views about how the appraisee's capability may be further developed in a positive way appropriate to the job. It is about identifying current strengths and showing recognition for them. It is also about identifying further needs and planning ways of meeting them. The responses available to meet identified needs might include:

- enlarging work responsibilities
- undertaking a special project
- involvement in taskforce activities
- reorganizing the work arrangements
- on-the-job guidance and coaching
- access to appropriate learning material
- a short off-the-job training course
- educational studies
- a temporary secondment outside the company
- a complete change of role

The appraisee should be encouraged to propose appropriate learning opportunities and development action. Wherever possible, decisions should be jointly agreed.

Now please discuss the appraisee's capability against the Management Practices in the previous section. Then consider the need for additional personal skills (e.g. IT literacy). Record outcomes from your discussion below. You may wish to formalize any key ones as objectives for the coming year.

Major strengths

Areas for further development

Personal development plan

How to make most use of strengths:

Action to be taken for each need identified:

By whom:

Preferred timing:

Any resources or assistance required from others:

7

REFOCUSING CAREER MANAGEMENT

OVERVIEW

This chapter closely examines current career management activity and finds much of it clever but misdirected, rigid and narrowly focused. It concludes with a proposed role statement for the function.

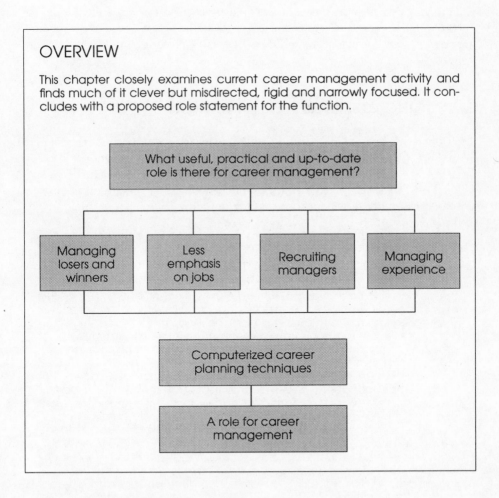

INTRODUCTION

C areer management activity in most large companies is overly concerned with the body of managers who are already there and are likely to remain so. It is insufficiently engaged with two other constituencies: those who need to be recruited, and those who may be about to depart – voluntarily and involuntarily.

This chapter condemns the preoccupation of developers with managing the careers of the patently successful while at the same time turning a blind eye to the armies of unknown soldiers allowed to flounder in the muddy fields of outplacement consultants' offices.

We then investigate how best to manage the subject of managers' experience – not a matter of choice, yet much underrated and underexploited in organizations.

In this chapter we also suggest that sophisticated computerized techniques for recording career plans are easily abused, replacing common sense and a genuine care and respect for managers and their careers. Such tools should be used with caution.

MANAGING LOSERS AS WELL AS WINNERS

Developers are, by and large, positive and humanistic people who are motivated to help their charges. While this is both laudable and satisfying, it ignores much of what is actually happening in companies today. Managers are leaving in droves, not of their own free will, but as a result of much publicized pressure on manpower costs, delayering fashions and outsourcing flexibility. Here's an example of one company's practice.

CASE EXAMPLE: COORDINATING LEFT AND RIGHT HANDS

The demarcation of development in a company contributed to a limited expectation of what the developers could help with. It blocked their involvement in macro-manpower planning and, most importantly, with exiting decisions. Their only involvement in these areas was by way of providing outplacement guidance, an undoubtedly worthwhile activity, but not a strategic role.

While one part of the personnel department continued apace with leading-edge management development programmes, another part of the department was acquiescing in crudely pushing managerial talent and invaluable experience out of the door as fast as it could, based on non-development criteria such as minimizing the cost of severance to the pension fund.

No one seemed to notice. It was as though the right hand didn't know what the left hand was doing. But it did: communication was not the issue. The problem was that the two hands thought they belonged to different bodies. One was thought to be healthy and concerned with tomorrow; the other was considered unhealthy and belonged to yesterday. Development believed it was only part of the former.

The result in this case was poor economics, poor public relations, low morale and severe scepticism about the company's claim to career management.

Quite apart from the moral issues, the process of separating the sheep from the goats usually has little rationale to commend it. Many of the managers written off as yesterday's people can easily become tomorrow's in an appreciative environment. There is ample data available to support the belief that managers who leave prematurely have above average competence and initiative. What usually happens is that they fall out of favour – not so much with their company as with their boss. The criteria are rarely rigorous in definition let alone in application, and auditing by disinterested parties is non-existent. This applies just as much to those who want to take the money and run but shouldn't be allowed to, as it does to those shed against their will. The numbers game that is played out is often a highly inter-personal one, exacerbated by obsessions with headcount.

PERMANENT SHAKE UP

Many companies' top managements are becoming rather attracted to the idea of the permanent shake up. Perhaps they see the same kind of benefit as Tom Peters who believes, 'Churn is success – creative destruction. Progress is made by elimina-tion (mostly inferior jobs) and creation (valuable jobs).'[1] Their initial motivation to shed managers is usually cost-driven and more about efficiency than effectiveness. It may well masquerade as Business Process Re-engineering (sometimes known as Big Personnel Reduction).

While there must be natural limits to potential economies – and there are some signs of slowing down – the attack on middle management hierarchies is unlikely to be a short-lived phenomenon.

Charles Handy, London Business School's visiting professor, expressed the problem well:

> Inside the goldfish bowl we have half the number of managers, paid twice as much and expected to be three times as productive, while outside the highly-trained and once highly-regarded talents of the other half are running to waste. In terms of Britain's corporate and economic health it is not a sustainable balance.[2]

DEVELOPMENT'S ROLE

Developers must accept that they cannot simply stem the tide of exiting managers, nor is it their role to do so. They can, however, help bring a humanistic, talent-driven and strategic perspective to this reality. And they can ensure that retention of talent enjoys as much attention as developing it.

Management developers must therefore have a seat at the table where decisions are taken on manpower, structure and costs. The euphemistic 'letting go' of managerial talent should very much be developers' business, as is its motivation and its potential linkage with genuine managerial effectiveness interventions. Without this input, we shall continue to experience the haemorrhaging of talent while bemoaning the lack of it.

KEY TIPS

❖   Include developers in decisions on organizational restructurings.

❖   Include developers in decisions on which managers to 'let go'.

❖   Link the release of managers to other structural changes and benefits.

❖   Make 'stem the bleeding talent' the number one career management role.

ACTIVITY 7.1

Re-examine the career management processes, the parties' roles, the release criteria, and the long-term organizational (not simply cost) benefits, associated with releasing experienced managers. How can development's influence be felt more?

LESS EMPHASIS ON JOBS

The days of a fairly fixed step-ladder which one could hope to climb steadily throughout a long career with one employer are gone. Therefore, what has to be managed are assignments rather than jobs. CVs will increasingly emphasize what was achieved, more than what positions were held.

This shifts responsibility for career planning towards individual managers and away from the company. Managers need to know themselves, their values, their strengths, their competencies, and to be able to manage their own career moves as unforeseen opportunities present themselves.

CASE EXAMPLE: CHANGING CAREER MANAGEMENT'S ROLE

A heavily centralized company practised a career management role consisting of the following:

● The personnel department had a veto over directors' ability to promote managers.
● Detailed plans to prepare managers were made on an annual basis.
● All the planning was done by the company.
● Plans assumed a static organization.
● Management appointments were made on a provisional basis for six months.
● Vacated slots could only be filled after the new appointments had eventually been confirmed.

As the consultant, I advised changes which meant the following:

● More power for the line directors to choose their managers, with personnel's *advice*.

- More spontaneity and ability to react to unforeseen needs and events.
- Detailed career management effort centred on a smaller number of senior jobs and managers.
- More emphasis on aspirations and career development than on career plans.
- Individual managers share responsibility for their own career planning.

RECRUITING MANAGERS

Managing succession is concerned less with who should be considered for what job when it falls vacant, and more with whether the company will have the managerial talent it will need for its future. The planning activity is an insurance policy, an insurance against the company's having to cope with new work demands simply on the basis of who is already there, even if they are less than ideal. That means auditing current talent against anticipated needs, and then plugging the gaps.

The gaps might be closed by developing existing managers and also by management trainee schemes, but the response also includes the direct recruitment of experienced senior line managers. This activity should include the development department and not simply be left to the line to work with the selection department. Placing responsibility for psychological assessment services under Development rather than Selection helps with this question of involvement.

MANAGING EXPERIENCE

Most managers remain in their jobs too long and grow stale. After approximately three years it is difficult for managers to continue to bring a sense of excitement and fresh ideas to the job. It is part of the role of developers to argue the case for proactive career moves – even disturbing those who are comfortable where they are – without waiting for vacancies. This is no criticism of individuals; it is just that talent – whatever its level – frequently needs a change of environment to produce the best out of it.

Where developers are permitted such a role in their companies, it is sometimes narrowly concentrated on a high-flyers agenda. This is too narrow a focus; the process should be broadened to include *all* managers above an agreed level. Those who are competent but stagnating, those who have plateaued, as well as those with more potential and the ineffective, should all be possible candidates for enforced career moves. All should find a place on the career management agenda. The benefit is as much the new opportunity created for change in the area they leave behind, as it is the development of experience and rejuvenation for themselves.

It is not merely sufficient to argue the case for a particular career move. There will always be good reasons against, for example, a close colleague who is relatively new, an important impending piece of work, or the boss simply can't face the disrupting effect of a new subordinate; it's comfortable as things are. But the effect of acceding to the arguments is to achieve too little individual movement and too little total change.

SHORT TENURE

The process should be stood on its head: the case should have to be argued why managers should be allowed to remain in their job after three years' tenure, or five years' at most. In other words, there should be a predisposition towards job rotation at this kind of frequency unless there are good reasons for leaving managers where they are.

This kind of management development action broadens the type of organizational learning that takes place and does much to break down sectional territorial attitudes and behaviour. Writing in *Management Today*, Gerard Egan tells the story of one company's new chief executive who needed quickly to break down some territorial boundaries:

> He sat his directors in a predetermined order at a round table. In front of each was a title plate indicating the function he headed. After emphasizing the importance of interunit teamwork and how important it was for everyone at that table to take a general management rather than a head-of-unit view of the business, he asked each to pass the title plate in front of him to the right. In one stroke each of these executives headed a different function. The cost of each learning a new business or function, he reasoned, would be much less than the cost of challenging each of the empires they had created.[3]

Frequent rotation is particularly important for those in more senior and generalist positions which call for leadership. John Harvey-Jones, ex-chairman of ICI, recognized this when he courageously refused his board's five-year contract and volunteered to give them the option of terminating it after three years if he was seen to be running out of ideas. Such wisdom sets a fine example. It is time to move when you may be viewed as part of the problem rather than part of the solution.

In some companies, short tenure is accepted at the very top of the company but not lower down. In other cases, the person at the top might remain ten years or more. Both stances are wrong, but the second is worse.

To set the right example, those working in the development function themselves should also fall under this system and be moved on from time to time before they become too comfortable, complacent and predictable.

As an alternative to permanent job moves, placing individuals on temporary or part-time assignments, projects or taskforces, has a similar energizing effect. (Chapter 6 contains a discussion on a range of options for learning through job experience.)

KEY TIPS

❖   Move people before they are perceived as part of the problem, rather than the solution.

❖   Use moves inside the personnel and development functions to set an example.

❖   Make a habit of switching general managers' portfolios.

ACTIVITY 7.2

Establish how long your managers tend to remain in a fixed post unless proactively moved, and set a target for the upper limit (to be applied judiciously) for managers' job tenure. Where could you use some imaginative career moves to break the organization's norms?

LEARNING FROM EXPERIENCE

The trick for developers is to find ways of ensuring that the experience is a learning one in a planned rather than accidental sense. Job experience provides a rich learning environment, but it is all too easy to have the experience and still fail to see or take the opportunity to learn fully from it. There are devices available to developers which can be used to structure and fully capitalize on the learning opportunity. Here are a few to consider.

KEY TIPS

❖   Develop managers' ability to reflect on experience through journaling techniques.

❖   Draw up 'learning contracts' (as used increasingly for programmes of formal study) between managers moved for career development reasons and their bosses.

❖   Build in fixed review times, off-site, with someone senior in the development function.

❖   Make permanent mentors available for newly moved managers.

RETHINKING CAREER PATHS

Increasingly these experience changes will not fit the traditional onward-and-upward career path. As organizations become less top heavy, more decentralized, leaner and more project-based, the conventional career aspirations of regular promotions with a single employer are for most of us no longer realistic. As Kerr Inkson, Professor of Management Studies at the University of Auckland, puts it:

> Perhaps we need to develop a new orientation, a new psychology of aspiration that fits better with the harsher, more competitive conditions. Rather than assuming each new job is ours until we choose to leave it, we should assume it is temporary until it proves permanent. Rather than assuming a lifetime of corporate

ascent, we should seek a lifetime of interesting experiences. Rather than planning personal development in relation to a defined coherent career path, we should perhaps ensure we remain flexible, and develop skills and abilities in relation to the best map we can draw of society's future rather than follow an extrapolation of our own past.[4]

KEY TIP

❖   Provide new job experiences for personal learning and growth as an alternative reward to traditional promotion.

ACTIVITY 7.3

Examine how the message of career progression is currently carried in the organization's culture, and how different kinds of reward structures can be signalled in future.

PERSONAL TRANSFERABLE SKILLS

The message for managers is clear. They should seek what help they can – including from their employer – to maintain their marketability via the acquisition of transferable skills. Wise employers will also recognize the benefit of this, because a more mobile management workforce is less resistant to change and less expensive to change. Those companies with a national sense of responsibility and a broad view of who their stakeholders are, seem more likely to be disposed to developing their managers with an eye to the next career.

There are many open learning packages from companies like Lifeskills International designed to help managers in this way, that is, with themselves. Subjects include Learning to Learn, Develop Your Own Career, Self-Awareness, Managing Personal Stress, Gaining Power and Influence, in addition to more obvious external skills such as Problem Solving, Decision Making and Delegating.

'Learning to learn' is a topical theme because it opens the door to so much else. But it is more an attitude of mind than a skill and can't be thought of as just another course; it's not as simple as that. Carl Rogers was saying as long ago as 1969:

> The most useful learning in the modern world is the learning of the process of learning, a continuous openness to experience and incorporation into oneself of the process of change.[5]

The United States culture (largely as a result of the wholesale provision of university education in the GI Bill of Rights following the return of troops after the Second World War) has embraced this openness to learning much more than the UK culture has. But this may be changing for the better in the UK. Certainly, the ready availability of modules of the kind indicated is doing much to fuel the *continuous development* culture needed.

KEY TIPS

❖ Value increased marketability for managers' careers with multiple employers.

❖ Make self-development packages readily available to increase transferable skills.

USE OF CAREER PLANNING TECHNIQUES

Many companies practise sophisticated career planning processes. These consist of detailed plans listing current jobs and potential successors, high-flyer lists, and ideal progression paths, which more recently have made much use of computer models. The surface impression is often most favourable. Yet, in spite of all the action, it often seems difficult to manage managers' careers in this way and at the same time make their subjects feel cared for. Alongside all the rhetoric and the systems there is perceived arbitrariness about who gets what job, with mixed messages about worth, and a general feeling of expendability. There are at least three problems here.

Detached from reality

First, the systems used by career planners are generally developed separately from the user organization's culture. And they are often purchased by developers on the basis of wishful thinking about the managerial culture rather than with honest regard to it. The systems have intellectual appeal but lack a good fit with the organizational reality. To take a common example, often one finds that when a vacancy *does* materialize, the director chooses someone not identified in the company's succession plan. Organizations do not behave as rationally as planners like to believe.

Mismatching values

Second, and closely related to the first point, there may be a mismatch in values, quite probably between those in Personnel and those line managers who ultimately take the big decisions on managers' appointments. These differences should not surprise us; indeed, it would be surprising if different values were *not* present. The problem is that developers may be felt to overuse systems and processes as transparent compensation for the lack of perceived corporate concern for the genuine nurturing of talent. On the other hand, if Personnel cannot appeal to its masters' hearts, it may be an appropriate strategy to use systems which will appeal to their heads.

Systems cannot keep pace

Third, the pace of change is such that clever and detailed plans are unlikely to bear fruit. When the time comes to fill a crucial vacancy at least one of the variables will have changed. For example, the need will be different from that previously envisaged; there will be a different boss who will value candidates differently; there will be new players in the frame. This is before even considering more drastic change, such as a reduction in the number of managers' jobs, reorganization, relocation or merger.

Career planners and managers themselves often make the mistake of believing their purpose is to narrow down options with ever greater specificity, whereas it is to open them up. Another mistake is to assume that the heart of the process lies in the plans rather than in the planning. The plans are almost worthless, but the discussion which gives rise to them may have considerable value.

One of my client companies' personnel departments asked its chief executive to stop his frequent restructurings for a few months so that its career planners could redraw all their organization charts and regain control over their succession plans. Wisely, he refused to listen. They still don't understand why!

KEY TIPS

❖   Think long and hard about your managerial culture and circumstances before buying computerized career-management systems, especially for succession planning.

❖   Make sure that any clever techniques are used in a practical way which supports common sense rather than to generate fixed plans.

❖   Invest in keeping your database up to date to ensure continuing credibility, but don't let the tail wag the dog.

❖   Ensure that the system is owned by the line management.

A ROLE FOR CAREER MANAGEMENT

Ingredients for a role statement for career management are set out in Figure 7.1.

FIGURE 7.1 A ROLE FOR CAREER MANAGEMENT

● To ensure that the company is not exposed in key senior jobs and critical functions by a lack of upcoming talent, but to identify where succession generally needs to be planned for and to develop and make available a pool of talent.

● To lead discussion with the top management on the identification of persons with senior management potential and to plan ways of developing that by such means as rotating jobs, secondments, shadowing, special projects, mentoring, etc.

● To make sure that those with ability at senior levels are not allowed to remain in the same job for too long to the point where they become stale, but are forced to move to broaden their experience, re-energize, and create promotion opportunities behind them.

- To be a source of career counselling to managers about their own career development.

- To advise top management on the suitability of candidates for senior positions.

- To ensure that managers with considerable ability and experience are retained in the company as far as possible.

- To represent the developer's point of view in corporate discussions on macro-manpower planning and organization strategy.

This role should be seen as part of development's general mission (discussed in Chapter 1).

ACTIVITY 7.4

You may like to review your current career management role in line with this role statement.

REFERENCES

1. Tom Peters (1993) 'Hard and Fast Rules for a Soft Economy', *The Independent on Sunday*, 29 August.
2. 'The Mixed-up Manager', *Management Today*, October 1993.
3. Gerard Egan (1993) 'The Shadow Side', *Management Today*, September.
4. Kerr Inkson (1993) 'Managerial Careers Facing the New Reality', *Professional Manager*, July.
5. Carl Rogers (1969) *Freedom to Learn*, Columbus, Ohio: Charles E. Merrill.

PART FOUR
WORKING TO DEVELOP THE ORGANIZATION

❖

8

LINKING DEVELOPMENT TO ORGANIZATION PERFORMANCE

OVERVIEW

This chapter shifts the emphasis for analysis and development action from managers' needs to those of the organization's management as a set of systems. The management of the business can only be enhanced if these variables are also understood and managed.

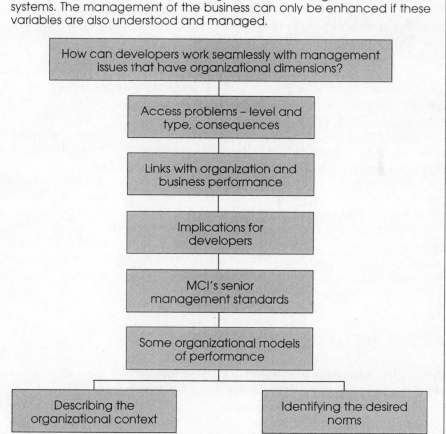

How can developers work seamlessly with management issues that have organizational dimensions?

Access problems – level and type, consequences

Links with organization and business performance

Implications for developers

MCI's senior management standards

Some organizational models of performance

Describing the organizational context

Identifying the desired norms

INTRODUCTION

One of the many flyers that came in my post recently posed the question 'How can business planning, training and development be integrated?' A good question. We need to align training and development with where the company is trying to reach. And we need to integrate training and development with other interventions pulling in the same direction, that is, towards a shared performance improvement objective.

Yet most of the development action that we witness in organizations assumes that the lever to pull to increase *individuals'* performance is individual ability. This is a little worrying because, as we saw earlier, the connection is not as direct as it first appears. More worrying still is that the common assumption remains that the best way to leverage *organizations'* performance is individual ability. Yet individual ability is not (to use the jargon) a *high-leverage variable*.

The training of managers does not hold much potential for organization change when contemplated in isolation. It is not a change strategy. Warner Burke, organization consultant to NASA and a highly committed developer, pointedly argued that training should never be used as a change intervention in its own right.[1] If so, it was bound to fail. The only way to make a success of training was, he continued, to anchor it in a wider organization-level intervention. His case, argued in the American journal *Training and Development*, makes compelling reading, and I have therefore repeated it in abbreviated form in the Appendix to this chapter.

Many developers justify their emphasis on individuals by claiming that improved organizational performance is the sum of many improvements in individuals' abilities. But even if individuals' development is as well coordinated as this requires, it still provides only a partial answer. To understand why and be able to do something about it, we shall delve into the links between interventions which aim to develop managers' skills and those interventions which are pitched at issues concerned with the organization's effectiveness, whatever they might be.

Some developers working in large corporations struggle valiantly to make a strategic contribution which goes well beyond arranging individual development activities. But market, organizational and national pressures tend to push them towards seeing their role in more limited terms. This chapter explores the problems faced by developers who try to (or are obliged by their organization's structure of responsibilities to) separate the development of individual capability from the development of corporate management capability. It offers a model for integrating the full range of development interventions.

ACCESS PROBLEMS FOR DEVELOPERS

Developers' orientation is a function of the various pressures on them, of their understanding of the organization's dynamics (which may be limited), of development's general history and tradition, past practice in their own company, and their own perception of their role. Importantly, it can also be a practical response to the degree of access they have in the client system.

For many developers, access is quite limited, even for those on the company payroll. The position is exacerbated for those employed by outside companies as development consultants, facilitators and product designers, seeking in their various ways to provide assistance to company clients.

This is a worrying trend. It has been estimated that as many as one-fifth of professional middle management levels have vacated in-company positions as a result of delayering, outsourcing and other long-term restructuring trends affecting large businesses.

The access problem shows up in a number of ways.

Generic, not bespoke

The market appears to be bulging with more off-the-shelf products than ever. They look increasingly sophisticated, especially with new technology behind them. National initiatives, while welcome in one way, may encourage the belief in generic solutions and fuel the generic product market. The best the product designers can usually do is to try to bolt on skilful facilitation. Occasionally this is part of the inherent design; some BBC Executive Video seminars provide a good example.

People, not problems

While developers are allowed to handle the company's people, they are rarely trusted with its deep-seated collective management and organizational problems. These problems may not even be adequately understood or capable of articulation by the top management; and the developers may lack the access and therefore the means of helping to explain them.

Training, not careers

Developers may have difficulty in getting close enough to up-coming job-change opportunities or potential project areas, thereby lacking sufficient say in how managers' careers are actively handled. Key players may fail to be managed as a corporate resource. Developers may be left with a role which equates development with training programmes, at the expense of talent retention and utilization, and exploiting job experience for learning and personal growth.

Managers, not directors

Directors see themselves as the clients, not the subjects of their developers. They prefer guest appearance slots in programmes rather than learning overtly themselves. They defend their position by claiming that they learn best from their peers, or they say they would have an inhibiting effect on managers (which may be true), thereby cutting themselves off from learning from inside their organization and from their subordinates.

ACTIVITY 8.1

Consider the levels and issues where you have open access, and those which are no-go areas. Where do you need to extend your brief and develop key client relationships in order to be more effective?

RESULTANT DEFICIENCIES

The limited kind and level of access which the various types of developer have to the system contributes significantly to a number of traditional limitations on the scope of management development:

1. Too much attention on learning through training, and not enough on making use of planned and managed experience as a prime vehicle for learning.
2. The isolation of development learning material for students from real-life current company problems and contexts.
3. A lack of developers' efforts at the top of the organization.
4. An emphasis on *capability* (which assumes opportunities to apply it), rather than ensuring *capacity*, which also includes consideration of all manner of obstacles and their removal.
5. Too much attention given to individual capability rather than direct organizational capability.

Our interest in this chapter is on items 4 and 5.

LINKS WITH ORGANIZATION AND BUSINESS PERFORMANCE

Ultimately, what we are seeking to establish are, first, the real management problems which are amenable to solving, and second, the most powerful and sensible levers to pull in order to bring about the desired improvement in *business* performance through *organizational* performance. That is the bottom-line.

Whilst some developers might find it regrettable, it is naïve to believe that companies deliberately set out to spend money on improving managers' abilities wholly for altruistic ends. Figure 8.1 contains a confession by John Garnett, former Director of the Industrial Society (1962–86) which was first published in *The Independent on Sunday* as part of its series *My Biggest Mistake*.

FIGURE 8.1 'MY BIGGEST MISTAKE'

The point about the need for a convincing business-led policy for developing people was emphasized by John Garnett, who admitted, 'My biggest mistake was trying to sell ideas in relation to my own objectives, rather than the objectives of the people I was selling to.'

He described how his passionate vision about the value of developing people's abilities and potential blinded him during his time as Personnel Manager of the Plastics Division of ICI to the equally important need to relate what he did to the objectives of the business. It led to the loss of his job:

> My work, in the view of the board, was irrelevant and, more seriously, distracting. They were in the business of making profits in plastics, while I seemed to be in the business of developing people, which took their eyes off the main purpose.

> It taught him an unforgettable lesson: unless employee development is seen to be business-led it will fail to convince top management of its value to the business. This can lead to the entire function's demise.

With acknowledgements to J. Garnett and *The Independent on Sunday*

Even if John Garnett's top management *had* been more willing to concentrate on developing individual ability, it might still have missed a trick. Did Garnett's 'passionate vision about developing people's abilities' equally blind him to his responsibilities for working with and developing the organization's capabilities? That is the question. And if he had fulfilled the latter, would his board still have considered it 'irrelevant, and more seriously, distracting'?

The point is that we need to look beyond individual capability at the organization's wider needs. That means building collective management competence and combining this with facilitating management systems in the widest sense. The problem is that some top managers may not want their developers to do this either because it implies a powerful organization rather than a few powerful individuals. Some cases will expose a few of the issues.

CASE EXAMPLES: POWER CONCENTRATED OR DISPERSED

1. I have heard it said that the founder of Lear jets would point to his name on the side of aircraft and claim that this virility symbol meant that he didn't need to listen to his managers. This, it was claimed, might help explain why Lear's market share of the executive jet industry which he started and which generically bears his name is now small compared with other manufacturers.

2. Ken Olson, founder of Digital, held to a set of strategic assumptions until it was too late. His top managers didn't see an acceptable role for themselves in challenging the boss's assumptions. If you examine DEC's senior management development programme, its expressed aim is to develop the managers to 'support' the company's directors! They want big managers, but not too big. What they may get is simply better *group think*, rather than its antidote *fresh think*.

3. In the case of the so-called British Airways 'dirty tricks' campaign, it was alleged that some employees used illicit methods to attract potential passengers away from Virgin Atlantic Airways. In terms of reputation, legal fees and settlements, it is reputed to have cost BA millions of pounds. It is said that some managers interpreted their duties too creatively.

EMPOWERED FOLLOWERS

It is impossible to create new kinds of organizations without creating new kinds of managers. For managers to be able to take risks, be self-starters and be independent problem-solvers, they need to be better leaders in their own areas, but equally they need to be better *followers* of their top management's leadership. This is what empowerment means for managers according to Simon Caulkin, writing in *Management Today*. One of their functions, he says, is 'to keep leadership on the straight and narrow'.[2]

We really need two kinds of follower, or perhaps a new kind of follower. The conventional view of the all-too-familiar managerial follower is represented by Harvey Hornstein, writing about *Managerial Courage: Revitalizing Your Company Without Sacrificing Your Job*:

> Managers who ascend the corporate ladder because they are compromising, cautious, and conforming are followers. They are essential to the successful maintenance of day-to-day organization operation, for they keep the system functioning smoothly, consistently, and predictably. Without these people organizational stability and equilibrium are threatened. They are the best reason to respect the forces of continuity, but they are not leaders.[3]

For Caulkin, this is clearly not enough. We need followers who have the courage to speak out, and Hornstein's can't and won't do that strongly enough for us because, paradoxically, this is a quality of leadership. If managers possess such qualities, they may well already occupy positions of power in their own units, and they can't automatically be assumed to relish having their own views challenged from below.

We are locked into a mental model of leadership which causes the followers to expect those at the top to behave largely the way leaders do. If *we* had struggled for years to climb to the top, wouldn't we also raise the drawbridge round the inner bailey? It suits the leaders, but closed behaviour and concentration of power rarely suits organizations over the long run. So we have to change role perceptions and the effective distribution of power, at the top and below.

Caulkin takes a critical look at the current model of leadership and followership and finds it badly wanting. He states bluntly:

> It is hard to believe that empowered employees would have allowed Robert Maxwell to get away with what he did; or that independent, critically minded managers would have failed to signal to BA's top management the disastrous course it was running with the dirty tricks campaign against Virgin.

Writ small, scenarios such as these are acted out in organization power-plays every day. And it is frequently painful for those with inferior authority as they try to make their point of view heard. Long-term company well-being depends on the successful management of difference, but paradoxically it frequently results in individual acts of self-sacrifice, however much managers try to utilize Hornstein's career survival kit.

CASE EXAMPLE: CONSTRUCTIVE CONFRONTATION

A personnel manager in a new-entrant company to the public telecommunications market had misgivings about where his line director was trying to take the department. He considered that he best added value, as a personnel professional and as a member of the departmental team, by asking his director searching questions which helped to clarify the consequences of proposed action. Recognizing that the questions were difficult and potentially confrontational, the personnel manager used utmost skill to press his points firmly without appearing to oppose the director's natural inclinations and decisions. In spite of the risks, the interpersonal strategy nonetheless worked well with the director and was much appreciated. Then the director was replaced by another who had equally strong business views but who was not prepared to listen or countenance any kind of implied challenge to his authority. As is so often the case, an apparent firmness of leadership masked a weakness of character and meanness of spirit. The personnel manager stuck to his guns, however, and continued to voice doubt whenever it seemed necessary, well aware that his questioning style no longer seemed welcome. One day the director called him into his office and told him that it was clear that he was not being fully supportive and would have to go. He lost his job.

NON-EXECUTIVE DIRECTORS

A structural solution to the corrupting tendency of power in company heads is sometimes sought via the appointment of powerful non-executive directors to boards of publicly quoted companies. There have been several well-publicized cases of chief executives losing their jobs at the hands of secret cabals of non-executive directors. It doesn't seem to work very well. It either seems to have no effect at all, or it is too dramatic, too public and too late. Such chief executives also feel fettered and say that's bad for business risk-taking, but they would, wouldn't they? Ongoing moderation from within the executive ranks of the company seems to me to be at least as vital.

ACTIVITY 8.2

Think about your company's leadership culture. How safely under control is it from rogue behaviour?

IMPLICATIONS FOR DEVELOPERS

Just from these few examples it must be apparent that development has, at the very least, to be concerned with management culture, mission, organization values and ethics, leadership style, climate, appointments, the recognition and reward system, exiting policy and practice, quite apart from developing personal competence. The BA case raises interesting development questions about performance monitoring, appraisal, feedback, and the company's valuing of means versus results, before you even consider the moral and ethical issues involved.

Many would agree that these matters are the very stuff of management development. Then how is it that large companies can and do spend substantial sums on management development and yet remain relatively impotent when it comes to influencing key features of their management culture and style? It is not sufficient to say that management development can't be expected to solve everything. Of course it can't. That is not the point. The point is that most companies' management developers do not start out with any expectation that their efforts *should* be expected to have this kind or degree of influence. Nor do chief executives. It is our low expectation of management development that is worrying.

The business press frequently reports examples where companies' management process has gone badly wrong. But management development usually continues in its own separate world, possibly feeling isolated and impotent in the face of the intimidating culture found in many large companies. That is, assuming it has the vision. It turns a blind eye, not just to what it sees going on, but to what it can't even get to see because of too restricted a role.

One can sympathize with the many developers whose role is closely circumscribed. They have a doubly tough job: they need to become more empowered themselves and gain high-level access in order to be able to practise their role of empowering others. And they can't shirk this duty lightly. But we can also see from the case examples given how difficult this is: leaders don't naturally expose their actions openly or sacrifice power readily to those below. Developers are not their natural allies.

MCI'S SENIOR MANAGEMENT STANDARDS

The case examples show the importance of developing a healthy and safe management climate. It is not sufficient to have a climate which merely avoids shooting the messenger (i.e. the developer); he or she must be positively welcomed whether the messages are palatable or not. This is just one reason why it is not enough for developers to target individuals: they have to work on the climate as well, and indeed the culture, not just for the good of the organization but for their own safety and effectiveness.

In *Developing Managerial Competence*[4] I look at the full four-level set of management standards developed by MCI in its capacity as the government's Lead Body for the occupation of management. But here we are interested only in the top level in that set, the senior management standards,[5] because of what they have to say on the subject of developing the organization.

MCI appears to place an excess of faith in its senior management standards to achieve what we are looking for organizationally. It is true that the standards state (quite rightly) that managers are required, *inter alia*, to 'review and improve the organisation's structures and systems ... and plan how to develop the effectiveness of the management team'. But the fact that some senior manager clients of developers will read of their responsibilities and that some may ask for help is not a guarantee of necessary or appropriate improvement action.

Nor can these clients' own assessment against the standards be relied upon to stimulate the need to act in this area. The standards are (wisely in my view) collective in intent. By definition, this means that the competences should reside within the team but not necessarily in each person. We know from our own experience that chief executives can be very different and there is nothing necessarily wrong with that. We should not expect them all to see eye-to-eye on the need to develop a particular kind of internal climate (or any other organizational intervention). In any case, the standards state only that senior managers (collectively) *should discharge* their responsibility in this area; they don't describe, for example, just what *kind* of climate they should try to create. Robert Maxwell saw the need. He created a climate you could feel. Would he have passed the test?

Base motives apart, some senior managers will claim that their terms of reference are inherently contradictory – that they are paid to reconcile conflicting demands. Some may believe that a threatening internal employment environment maximizes short-term shareholder dividend, yet this kind of climate may be incompatible with treating fairly those employees who are struggling to make the grade and who, if given time and support, may get there. For all their inherent merit, the senior management standards can never hope to prescribe an unambiguous interpretation of desired performance. Expressions such as '… respond to … trading climates' and 'identify … interests of stakeholders' will always be open to multiple interpretations. It also seems reasonable to conclude that part of the developer's role (and indeed that of the human resources department) is to help senior managers interpret their roles in a balanced way, so that an appropriate internal environment (climate and culture) meets the needs of the spread of stakeholders, including employees. It is a short step from that to believe that the climate and culture improvement needed stands a chance only with greater awareness, legitimization and proactivity by highly skilled developers working directly with organization issues.

The above discussion does, of course, beg the question of who sanctions developers' work. Who commissions it? Who evaluates it? Indeed, who is the client? And perhaps an even more important question: how can developers survive working in this area, since they are most needed where they are least welcome? Elsewhere in this book I have done my best to try to answer these vital questions. But here we are interested in developers' roles *vis-à-vis* the senior management standards.

MCI'S PHILOSOPHY

To understand MCI's faith in the power of the senior management standards we need to remind ourselves of MCI's position.

MCI focuses wholly on individual *manager* development (though in common with most other bodies it talks about this as *management* development). Within that area it concentrates most of its effort on defining competence to drive recruitment, assessment and training. This secondary shift occurred when MCI became a Lead Body and was obliged to put its eggs into the 'competence movement' basket.

It tacitly assumes that the cultures of its client organizations conform to the traditional 'power' and 'role' forms, rather than the newer 'achievement' and 'support' types of culture (discussed in Chapter 10) which are characteristic of smaller and faster-moving young businesses. MCI does, however, recognize the importance of small and medium-sized enterprises (SMEs), even though they pose more of a challenge for its products.

Underlying some quite radical and imaginative methods for recognizing competence are a set of traditional values based on rational and hierarchical principles concerned with who and what drives managerial performance. In line with these assumptions, MCI seems to operate to a traditional training model where others know what's best for you and require you to conform, rather than a more empowering development or education model where managers are expected to work out more of this direction for themselves and for their organizations.

Furthermore, MCI is wholly concerned with individual *can-do* competence, albeit assessed in the workplace. Its promotional byline – indeed its byword – is that 'organisations are only as capable as their managers'. Those who accept this argument at face value should not be lured into believing the reverse is equally true. If we take the word 'only' away, we are left with 'organisations are as capable as their managers'. This is akin to saying that the sum of individual competence can deliver corporate competence without the need for additional or parallel interventions with the organization itself.

The problem is that MCI does *indeed* believe and suggest that corporate competence is to be attained in this manner, through the medium of its senior management standards. Attractive though this line of argument is, I must counsel against relying on it, although I should also add that in no way would I wish to discount the dominant contribution which individual managerial competence obviously makes to corporate performance, or MCI's significant and valuable contribution towards defining and raising standards in this important area.

The fact is that MCI's remit does not extend to concern with what organizations do, and need to do, to *utilize* their managerial talent wisely and to the full. It does not see a role in directly encouraging bottom-up *choose-to-do* competence nor facilitating top-down *allowed-to-do* competence. As I explained earlier, these are essential refinements of competence if one is to stand any chance of achieving corporate competence. MCI's given objective (by the National Forum for Management Education and Development) is only concerned with supply-side issues: 'To increase the quantity, quality, relevance and accessibility of management education and development.' This may well account for their lopsided interest, but that still leaves a missing demand-side ingredient in the recipe for corporate success – the organization's own unique flavouring and its own contribution to the party.

Some will counter that my proposition, which appears to endow the organization with an identity and personality of its own, is absurdly anthropomorphic, and that the organization is really nothing more than its people and what its senior managers want it to be. Perhaps those same people would agree with Margaret Thatcher's infamous remark 'there is no such thing as society'. I maintain that the organization *does* have a separate dynamic and is a legitimate target for developers' imagination and proactivity.

MCI's stance is that senior managers are responsible for developing their organizations as well as themselves (which I agree they are); so if these senior managers are chosen, developed and assessed as competent, then, it is argued, the organization's own parallel development will be fully taken care of. All you need to do, it would appear from this, is put your faith in the senior management standards. How many would place bets on that? Valid though these standards are, this route on its own is unlikely to prove sufficient to bring corporate competence, for several reasons:

1.   In working through individual senior managers and working exclusively to their commissioned agendas, the impact of development activity on the organization will be reactive, indirect and require considerable faith and patience. Problems which transcend senior managers' areas of responsibility may not be tackled and effort will be dissipated.

2.   Only where there is a significant take-up of the senior management standards will organizations themselves see significant change. As the 'organization' of the future becomes more diffuse (partnerships, outsourced services, etc.) it won't be possible to achieve the necessary degree of top-down control and conviction across the 'organization' to apply the senior management standards widely enough to bring about organization-wide action.

3.   It assumes no inherent contradictions exist in senior managers' responsibilities, and that they may therefore be relied upon uniformly to interpret their terms of reference with respect to improving the organization in a way with which their colleagues and developers would agree.

4.   It fails to legitimize and promote a proactive role for developers as part of the management team, expected to identify corporate management issues and directly develop management systems and managers' environment.

5.   It places an excess of faith in hierarchical management. To make an organization-wide intervention (e.g. reducing bureaucracy) theoretically requires the chief executive (or possibly the personnel director) to interpret his or her senior management standards positively in this manner and then initiate action.

6.   It works against the development of products (models, advice, codes of conduct, diagnostic, auditing and assessment tools, case material, etc.) for application *directly* on organization management problems, as opposed to products which only help to develop individual managers.

7.   Competence is one of an organization's *rational* factors (like policies and edicts). But the *non-rational* factors need understanding and developing too (e.g. power structures, relationships and climate).

For all these reasons, I believe the value of the senior management standards needs to be seen in the wider context of multi-pronged development.

MODELS FOR ORGANIZATIONAL PERFORMANCE

Once we are organized soundly to deliver management development, we need what Gerard Egan calls some 'shared models' to provide managers with a better understanding of what goes on in organizations and what impacts performance.

EGAN'S MODEL A

There are many ways of representing the inter-connecting boxes which comprise individual and organizational performance. One of Egan's three models, which he calls 'Model A' (the others are B and C), is a Model for Managing Business and Organizational Processes.[6] This takes the form of a template which can be laid over the organization's process and used in a checklist manner to question the component parts and consider how healthy or deficient they are. Or as Egan himself puts it, Model A 'is a pragmatic process managers can use to review the needs of the business and those of the organization that is to serve the business'.

Egan's words remind us of the important and often overlooked distinction between business and organization, mentioned in the opening chapter. Model A is

---

FIGURE 8.2 EGAN'S MODEL A

Master Task (an example)

Establish the kinds of human resource management (HRM) systems that managers can use to develop a committed and productive workforce.

1. **A human assets framework and audit process.** Establish a human assets audit process to take stock of the human resources of the institution.

2. **Incentives and rewards.** Establish the kind of incentive and reward systems that promote both productivity and high-quality work life.

3. **Recruitment.** Hire people who have the working knowledge, skills, and attitudes needed to do the job or who can be cost-effectively trained to do so.

4. **Socialization.** Socialize newcomers into the business and into a culture that supports both strategy and operations and key strategic drivers such as quality and customer service.

5. **Utilization.** Strive to maintain optimal staffing levels and continually try to put the right person in the right job, thereby enhancing both productivity and quality of work life.

6. **Development.** Establish a process of ongoing development based on the needs of the business and the career focus of employees. Explore developmental strategies beyond formal training.

7. **Career paths.** Establish a career path system that contributes to both business outcomes and the quality of work life. Clarify the roles that both employees and managers are to play.

8. **Labour relations.** In non-union institutions, work at fostering the kind of work life that makes a union superfluous; in union institutions, work toward a business-enhancing and worker-enhancing partnership.

9. **Retention and separation.** Establish viable HR retention and separation systems and policies together with guidelines for implementing them.

Reproduced by courtesy of Jossey-Bass

therefore presented in two parts, and it is the second half (organization) which is of relevance in this chapter.

In 'creating an organization that serves the business', Egan's model first comprises a number of *master tasks*.

The organization master tasks

O   Create a structure that serves the business by optimizing information sharing, decision making, and work flow.

O   Establish the kinds of human resource management (HRM) system that managers can use to develop a committed and productive workforce.

O   Establish systems to develop a cadre of knowledgeable and skilled managers to identify and take care of the needs of the business and to provide value-added supervision through coordination, facilitation, and support of others.

O   Develop leaders at every level of the organization to provide institution-enhancing innovation and change.

These master tasks break down into numbered subtasks. It is not possible to do full justice to the model here, but Figure 8.2 shows one of the master tasks in shortened and edited form to give the flavour.

Note that most of the subtasks in Egan's Model A do not involve developing personal competence, but instead are concerned with developing processes, policies, systems, resources, understanding, frameworks, etc. Quoting from his book *Adding Value*, he says, 'What may be needed is a shift in perspective – from one focusing on the needs of the manager to one concentrating on the needs of the business.'

THE BURKE–LITWIN MODEL

The Burke–Litwin Model[7] shares many of the components of Egan's Model A. But whereas Egan's model lists the necessary processes to allow organizations to be assessed (or designed), the Burke–Litwin model shows, in diagrammatic form, the causal nature of the interactions, either for the purpose of improving the quality of the transactions or for managing wider transformation. The boxes (i.e. the variables) in the model are shown in Figure 8.3. The way the model links these is shown in Figure 8.4.

From this model it will be seen with which boxes manager training and develop-ment activity is usually concerned, and some options for taking development action in other areas. A broad definition of management development allows us to work with any of them, or more importantly, with a mix of them.

KEY TIPS

❖   When you have identified the high-priority solvable management problems, seek out the high-leverage variables.

❖   Dovetail interventions in two or more boxes.

FIGURE 8.3 DESCRIPTION OF COMPONENTS IN THE BURKE–LITWIN MODEL

External environment. Any outside condition or situation that influences the performance of the organization. These conditions include marketplaces, world financial conditions, political/governmental circumstances, and so on.

Mission and strategy. What employees believe is the central purpose of the organization and how that organization intends to achieve that purpose over an extended timescale.

Leadership. Executives providing overall organizational direction and serving as behavioral role models for all employees. Includes followers' perceptions of executive practices and values.

Culture. 'The way we do things around here.' Culture is the collection of overt and covert rules, values and principles that are enduring and guide organizational behavior, and that have been strongly influenced by an organization's history, customs, etc.

Structure. The arrangement of functions and people into specific areas and level of responsibility, decision-making authority, communication and relationships. Structure assures effective implementation of the organization's mission and strategy.

Management practices. What managers do in the normal course of events to use human and material resources at their disposal to carry out the organization's strategy. 'Practices' means a particular cluster of behaviors.

Systems. Standardized policies and mechanisms that facilitate work. Systems primarily manifest themselves in the organization's reward systems, management information systems (MIS), and in control systems such as performance appraisal, goals and budget development, and human resource allocation.

Climate. The collective current impressions, expectations, and feelings of the members of local work units. These, in turn, affect members' relations with their boss, with one another, and with other units.

Task requirements and individual skills/abilities. The behavior required for task effectiveness, including specific skills and knowledge required of people to accomplish the work assigned and for which they feel directly responsible. This box concerns what is often referred to as job–person match.

Individual needs and values. The specific psychological factors that provide desire and worth for individual actions or thoughts.

Motivation. Aroused behavior tendencies to move toward goals, take needed action, and to persist until satisfaction is attained. This is the net resultant motivation; that is, the resultant net energy generated by the sum of achievement, power, affection, discover, and other important human motives.

Individual and organizational performance. The outcome or result, with the indicator of effort and achievement. Such indicators might include productivity, customer satisfaction, profit, and quality.

Reproduced by courtesy of W. Warner Burke

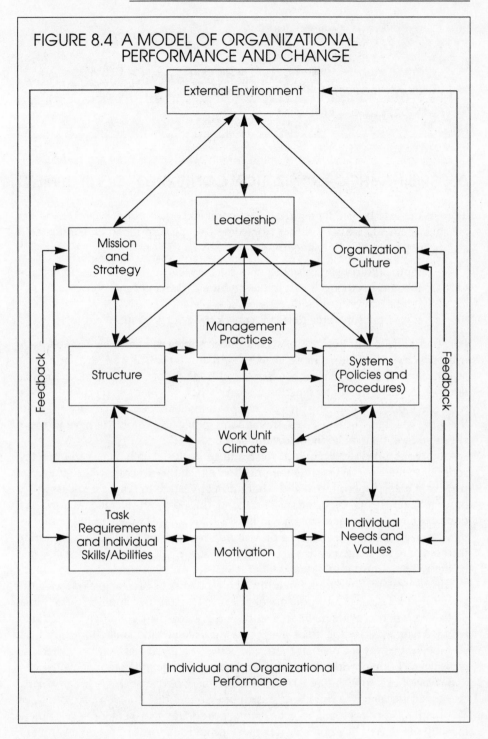

FIGURE 8.4 A MODEL OF ORGANIZATIONAL PERFORMANCE AND CHANGE

Reproduced by courtesy of W. Warner Burke

ACTIVITY 8.3

Consider current instances of isolated development activity where the effort risks are being dissipated through a lack of meaningful connectivity. How could this activity be supported by interventions in other boxes in the organization model, and vice versa?

DESCRIBING THE ORGANIZATION CONTEXT FOR DEVELOPMENT

There is much to be said for a widescale survey of an organization's climate, culture and management practices, either from time to time or prior to embarking on a significant programme of change:

○   It provides considerable data that can be useful in designing interventions.
○   It begins to change perceptions and the dynamics of those involved.
○   It builds awareness and readiness for change.
○   It generates material for feeding back to the organization.

But the formality and expense of such a public survey will often be claimed to be inappropriate. The truth is more likely to be that it is too scary an idea for many a top management who may only expect, and hope, to see training recommendations. If they *are* willing to sanction a survey, they may happily discuss the data, provided it doesn't point any fingers, and provided it appears descriptive of something detached from themselves. But at some point discussion will have to move closer and will then make them feel uncomfortable.

A way round this predicament, which still generates useful data, is to interview some of the key managers. It is then not too difficult to describe where the company is in management terms and where it might aspire to reach. If necessary, in order to meet clients' expectations of training, this portrayal can take the form of a descriptive analysis of the context within which individuals will need to be trained. In other words, before embarking on training, you can begin by describing where the company's management style or culture is at the moment and where it would be desirable to move it to.

This picture can then be refined through a process of checking it out with the power holders or ultimate sponsors of any management development. The initial impressions may provide powerful feedback to the top management and itself may be a learning exercise for them. The resulting dialogue and ability to ground the training in this way means that there is a better chance of a good fit between the goals which both individuals and the company should be trying to reach.

By way of example, Figure 8.5 shows a summary of one such portrayal which I developed for a client. The client was the personnel director of a medium-sized corporation, who was trying to get a fix on appropriate management development through the lens of head office's relationships and support to the line customers. It was self-evident that the company as a whole, and head office departments in particular, were undermanaged, while at the same time being overburdened by bureaucracy and administration. This latter aspect is the subject of the next chapter.

FIGURE 8.5 EXAMPLE OF ORGANIZATION CONTEXT FOR DEVELOPMENT

Present
- Control
- Centralization
- Explicit costs
- Equality of treatment
- Predetermined rules
- Short term
- Corporate
- Centre stage
- Status quo
- How?
- Means
- Tasks
- Maintenance
- Reactivity
- No chance of mistakes
- Known
- Order
- Maintaining norms

Future
- Freedom
- Decentralization
- Implicit costs
- Discretionary judgement
- Logic and common sense
- Long term
- Line
- Background
- Change
- What?, why?, who for?
- Ends
- Results
- Development
- Proactivity
- Speed of response
- Unknown
- Disorder
- Breaking norms

ACTIVITY 8.4

What particular management shortcomings are currently holding back the successful management of your business?

IDENTIFYING AND STATING THE NORMS

Figure 8.5 suggests that managers – certainly at senior levels – should be developed to challenge norms. One company's personnel director even said he wanted 'norm-busters'! Some examples of areas of norms are indicated in Figure 8.6. We are not interested in answering these at the individual level, but judging whether they are group norms – at departmental or company level (some will reflect national culture).

FIGURE 8.6 EXAMPLES OF NORMS WHICH MAY NEED CHALLENGING AND CHANGING

- How fast things typically get done
- What standard is considered good enough
- What kind of performance earns a pay rise or promotion
- How incompetent you have to be to get fired
- How much work is done through committees
- Whether paper qualifications are over- or undervalued
- How strongly you can speak your mind and still keep your job
- Whether new ideas are generally welcome
- Whether managers take work home with them too frequently or too rarely
- Whether managers will work late without expecting compensation
- The level at which managers cease to refer to higher levels as 'the management'
- How willingly managers take on additional responsibilities and are willing to answer for their decisions
- Whether appreciation is shown for a job well done
- How much initiative is generally expected
- What happens to those who display ambition
- The extent to which managers have freedom to act
- Who is allowed to speak to whom without giving offence
- Whether attending punctually matters more than performing well
- Whether doing a task to the rules matters more than achieving results

KEY TIPS

❖ Appoint a resilient and powerful norm-buster and give lots of behind-the-scenes support.

❖ Hunt out disciples in key areas of the business and manage them as an informal team of corporate change agents.

ACTIVITY 8.5

What norms do you consider need to be busted if your management culture is to develop positively?

REFERENCES

1. W. Warner Burke (1972) 'The Role of Training in Organization Development', *Training and Development*, **26** (9).
2. Simon Caulkin (1993) 'The Lust for Leadership', *Management Today*, November.
3. Harvey Hornstein (1986) *Managerial Courage: Revitalizing your Company Without Sacrificing your Job*, New York: John Wiley and Sons Inc.
4. William Tate (1995) *Developing Managerial Competence: A Critical Guide to Methods and Materials*, Aldershot: Gower.
5. Management Charter Initiative (1995) *Senior Management Standards*, London: MCI.
6. Gerard Egan (1993) *Adding Value – A Systematic Guide to Business-Driven Management and Leadership*, San Francisco: Jossey-Bass, pp. 21–30, 48–64.
7. W. Warner Burke and George H. Litwin (1992) 'A Causal Model of Organizational Performance and Change', *Journal of Management*, **18** (3), pp. 523–45.

APPENDIX: THE ROLE OF TRAINING IN ORGANIZATION DEVELOPMENT[1]

Training of individuals to perform their jobs more effectively seldom has positive impact on the organization. The type of training I have in mind is in the area of behavioral or attitudinal change, not manual skill development. The training I am discussing does include, however, managerial skill development, like learning to communicate more effectively interpersonally. In this paper, I argue that individual training programs which are not integrated within the context of an overall organization improvement effort will have little if any positive impact on the organization.

Training, as the term is employed by most organizations, is generally an individually oriented educational strategy which assumes that individual change is the prime mediator of organization change. This leads to the belief that if the person can be changed, for example, made more democratic in his managerial practices, the organization will, as a consequence, operate more effectively.

... individually oriented strategies of change, such as training, are not effective in producing organizational change. This is due to at least three basic problems. The first relates to the age-old issue in training – transfer of learning. The simple fact that most training occurs in a location other than the individual's work space produces the problem of re-creating the training milieu and learning back on the job.

Critical mass is a second problem. How many people must one train to obtain the desired impact on the organization? In a large organization, the answer to this question is difficult to formulate.

A third problem relates to the social psychological principle ... that individual behavior in a group context is considerably shaped and regulated by social norms. Individual training often requires individual deviance from accepted norms, e.g. the individual is trained to be more 'open' in his interpersonal communication when the norm of his organization is to be diplomatic and to 'play things close to the vest' in interpersonal relationships. Since conformity to social 'regulators' is a powerful determinant of human behavior, organization members are more likely to conform to patterns of expected behaviour than to violate such norms by applying what they learn in a training environment.

Given these problems with training, why do many trainers still rely on individual approaches to organizational change? One reason may be that trainers know skill training (training people to meet immediate needs of production) does have immediate and observable impact on the organization, and therefore implicitly believe that training in behavioral or attitudinal change should have the same degree of observable success even though other dynamics – group norms – are more directly involved.

Another reason may be that trainers do not have enough power and influence in the organization to produce an effective process of organization change, so they rely on the one strategy they can command, i.e. training individuals. Of course, as I have implied, ... they do not understand that groups are easier to change than individuals.

... Training should *facilitate* organizational change, not attempt to *provide* it. The providing of organizational change comes from managers and subordinates collaboratively diagnosing problems, and strengths, planning action steps for improvement, and then implementing solutions on the basis of joint plans. The OD specialist, and therefore the trainer, can facilitate this process when he functions diagnostically and catalytically, i.e. as a consultant and helper rather than as a specialist who is isolated from any of the real problems facing the organization.

[1] Extracts from W. Warner Burke's paper in *Training & Development*, American Society for Training and Development, **26** (9), September 1972, pp. 30–4. Reprinted with permission. All rights reserved.

9

THE FALL AND RISE OF THE

ORGANIZATION

OVERVIEW

This chapter provides a context for developers who engage in organizational renewal by helping them understand how organizations naturally decline unless actively rejuvenated. It offers many ideas for renewal, concentrating mainly on a key problem which besets most organizations – engulfing bureaucracy.

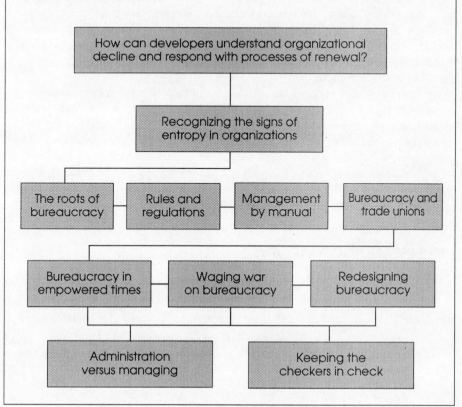

INTRODUCTION

Most development activity in practice aims to improve individual competence. Occasionally the word renewal is heard. But little interest is shown
in understanding just what is breaking down inside the organization that
gives impetus to the need to act. This important subject of how organizations
inexorably degenerate – called entropy – and require regeneration receives relatively
little recognition and discussion compared with occupational competence. Yet
understanding, recognizing and responding to signs of entropy are key skills for
fully rounded developers, who have to be vitally concerned with the never-ending
process of renewal.

What is it that breaks down? Why? How can we identify the symptoms? How can
we diagnose the root causes? And importantly, what strategies can we evolve for
restoring the organization to full health? When the organization falls down, how
can we help it rise again?

The chapter begins by explaining the natural process of organizational entropy –
disorder, disintegration, disorganization, decline, degeneration, disease or decay –
call it what you will. Armed with a fuller understanding of entropy we can better
apply its antidote: renewal.

Decay in organizations takes many forms. It can mean a decline in standards,
authority, relationships, efficiency, quality, cooperation, morality, and so on. Nowadays, the ethical aspect attracts considerable interest, as we frequently witness
decline in the principled conduct of business. In this chapter we touch on various
manifestations of entropy, but our prime focus is that of growing bureaucracy, a
disease which seems to permeate all organizations, unless we actively take steps
periodically to cut it back.

We try to understand the different sources of bureaucracy in order that we can
be realistic about what can be achieved. Then we examine the various levels of
bureaucracy to get down to the roots in the organization's culture so that we can
tackle the problem at source, not simply alleviate the symptoms. We work through
a real example of how a worn out bureaucracy was rejuvenated. We see how the
term *manager* can be a cover for what is better described as *administration*. And
finally, we examine the role of the checkers in organizations and how to keep a
sense of proportion about auditing and control.

UNDERSTANDING ENTROPY

The term 'entropy' is borrowed from science. It derives from the second law of
thermodynamics, which says that everything that is organized will break down or
run down unless it is maintained. According to science writer Boyce Rensberger,

> Examples of entropy can be found throughout the everyday world. Desks will get
> messy. Cars will wear out ... Without librarians, books get scattered and jumbled.
> Lacking nutrients, organisms die and rot. In each case, a highly organized system
> will inevitably proceed to a state of disorder and chaos unless energy (which is
> equivalent to work) is brought into the system to re-establish order.[1]

Robert Waterman, in *The Renewal Factor*, argues that 'A company, even one with a long history of good performance, needs to introduce fresh management energy into its system to stave off the inexorable forces of decay.'[2]

Interest in entropy in organizations is just beginning to develop through the analogy with party political behaviour in a healthy democracy. The argument runs that if a single party remains in power for a very long time, it tends to become corrupt. There are innumerable examples all over the world, as well as close to home.

I use the word 'corrupt' loosely in a number of ways, not just to mean financially corrupted or even corrupted by power, though the latter aspect is probably the biggest problem. The excessive confidence which comes from a long and untrammelled period of holding office leads to arrogance, a sense of infallibility, a narrow concentration of power, and browbeating. This can be fatal for a company and for all those who have a stake in it, as with the Robert Maxwell empire, for example.

It doesn't start like this. Leadership usually begins life with a strong sense of mission, determined to sort out certain problems, and with much positive energy. It may even achieve a culture change for the company, or the nation as it can be argued Margaret Thatcher did in the UK (whatever you may think of it).

Once new leaders have accomplished their initial agenda, they tend to lose the driving force of their vision and they run out of steam. A series of new challenges may work for a while, perhaps with stimuli like take-overs to liven things up and provide adrenaline. But the high cannot be sustained indefinitely. A different order of change is needed.

The problem is that leaders become blinkered and can't and don't want to see this new need for themselves. They come to enjoy the familiar comforts and the trappings of power. Their agenda becomes simply one of staying there. Instead of continuing to add value of their own, the leaders start to diminish that of competitors, both outside and inside. Recognizing the tell-tale signs, those around begin to mumble 'It's time for a change.' Entropy has had its way – as we knew all along it would – with the individual and with the organization.

Whether we are talking about government at the level of the nation or a business, without renewal the organism will wither and die. Entropy is a process that cannot be prevented. But developers can respond to it, not merely replacing the sick elements to restore the status quo, but improving the general fitness of the organization and moving forward.

We can probably recognize a little of this in ourselves. Our personal motivation and creativity proceed along a declining path. We grow stale if we stay unchanged and unchallenged for too long. We get tired and bored. Others begin to see us as part of the problem rather than part of the solution. We probably don't want to admit to it – perhaps because we see no easy way out. But developers should be able to see what is needed and when, and they should be able to initiate timely corrective action for the good of the company and the people concerned.

KEY TIP

❖ Refresh managers' careers before they start to grow mould.

RECOGNIZING ILLNESS OR DECAY

Developers who work as part of organizations can spot decay in a way that hired helpers can't because they have the benefit of a past reference point. They can remember when times were different and possibly better. This doesn't necessarily mean all-round, but in a particular respect, such as managers' general morality in dealings with customers, the quality of interpersonal caring relationships, the freedom with which information flows, the creative buzz, or the amount of bureaucracy.

But insiders may equally have difficulty seeing the wood for the trees. Worse still, they may be part of the degeneration themselves. If this sounds heretical, think of developers who form alliances with the top management. They often need to do this to be effective, but in doing so their own objectivity is compromised.

Outside consultants lack the earlier reference point against which to make a comparison, but they usually have more tools and can facilitate the diagnosis with the help of insiders. A doctor doesn't need to have seen a previously fit body to diagnose illness, but it helps. We ourselves are better placed to notice a sudden loss or increase in weight, for example, and want to find out why. The doctor can help us find the answer. But, like their internal counterparts, external consultants too have to please the client. In my own experience the best solution is an inside–outside consulting team.

Most developers who understand the need for renewal operate at the level of the individual manager. But developers' main value should be reserved for cases of organizational entropy rather than personal entropy.

SOME OF THE SIGNS

An organization which is on the slide feels like a lost community. Managers pull in multiple directions, following their own agendas. Individual interest is put ahead of the team's. Managers blame each other (sometimes labelled the 'blame culture'). But what are some of the more tangible signs of organizational decline that need to be nipped in the bud? Figure 9.1 contains a selection from my own experience.

FIGURE 9.1 THE NEED FOR ORGANIZATIONAL RENEWAL: SOME SIGNS OF ENTROPY

- When managers (even directors) begin to speak of 'the management' as something to which they have no feeling of belonging or sense of responsibility, and which is either a euphemism for the company boss, or something unidentifiable and amorphous.

- When the conduct of business comes to resemble the prosecution of war: using negative advertising to attack competitors' products or poaching their customers, rather than husbanding one's own business.

- When some very good people start to vanish, or are paid large sums to leave.

- When exasperated leaders increasingly seek solutions in top-down exhortations, policy edicts, systems, structures, rules and codes, rather than in relationships and the unique and diverse gifts and goodwill of people.

- When staff turnover is so slow for some years that the age profile of those in power rises to the point where the leadership qualifies for free bus passes.

- When a note comes round saying that anyone who wants to see the boss will in future have to make an appointment with the secretary.

- When the most talked-about news is either the size of the company's profit, the announced need for more job cuts, or the size of the boss's pay rise.

- When constructive argument is replaced by intellectual bullying or rank.

- When everyone frequently has to stop productive work to provide reams of figures.

- When company equipment is labelled 'property of XYZ section' and cannot be borrowed.

- When junior personnel officials become trade union representatives on consultative committees or when senior managers feel the need to be represented by a trade union.

- When elected members on institutions' governing boards are replaced with appointees.

- When the 'unfair' distribution of annual bonuses is blamed on computerized 'normalizing'.

- When it appears necessary for any company success to be credited to the chief executive.

- When the boss sends round a letter 'to all you folks' informing them that from now on 'Fridays are informal dress days', and how he is 'going to enjoy not having to wear a tie'.

- When the MD writes to all staff to say he's discovered that informal walkabouts are useful, and his new policy will be to take them every week.

- When a company resorts to hostile take-overs and publicly engages in a war of words over the current owners' past stewardship.

- When the reward system is regeared to pay out large bonuses based on short-term financial results.

- When general managers begin to say privately that they can't tell their directors what they need to because they have a mortgage to pay.

- When general managers complain to their chief executive that the company lacks a strategy, but don't see that as part of their own role.

- When the company blames government departments and outside agencies for imposing bureaucracy but fails to tackle its own.

Max De Pree, chairman of Herman Miller Inc. (named by *Fortune* magazine as one of the United States' ten 'best managed' companies), puts forward his own fascinating list of signs of entropy in *Leadership is an Art*, which includes the gem 'a loss of grace and civility'.[3]

CASE EXAMPLE: TAKEOVER BEHAVIOUR

An engineering company bought out the electronics subsidiary of an ailing conglomerate. The new owners instructed the acquired company's personnel director to carry out their plans on pain of dismissal without anything more than statutory redundancy pay.

Most of the directors were removed immediately. Discussion then centred on the standard terms which would be available for the levels below. It transpired that the acquired company's normal terms were far more generous than the buying company's, and the new owners were not prepared to honour them. All they would offer was the statutory minimum. They then set about publicly humiliating the senior managers, implying that they must have been incompetent to let their business get into such a parlous state. Managers were attacked on a personal basis, irrespective of their performance. One was told he must be a rotten husband. The new bosses seemed to go out of their way to be aggressive, rude and spiteful, demonstrating their absolute power. Several managers couldn't take it and quickly left of their own accord, as the new owners hoped. Others were made redundant on the inferior terms available, happy to be out. By such dubious methods the company saved itself a considerable sum. So how can we be sure 'a loss of grace and civility' doesn't pay off? Why is it bad business?

Morale and commitment in the old company slumped. People worked strictly within the confines of their jobs. Deadlines were missed as staff didn't put in the extra effort they would have done willingly in the past. More telling, when a head-hunter advertised for a Product Manager, he called the (by now ex-) personnel director to tip him off, saying he had never received so many applications from one company, and to ask what was going on. The chickens were coming home to roost.

You can compile your own list of warning signs. But be careful. Lists like these are very subjective. They are based on one's own unique experience. They reflect prejudices, opinions on management style, and judgements about past bosses, among other things. They can easily end up as little more than pet hates and disguised arrows aimed at persons unnamed. To be useful, such lists need to remain general indications of organizational decline, that the culture is losing its way, and that there is a need for developers' interventions to restore full health.

KEY TIP

❖   Keep a look out for signs of entropy in your own personal behaviour.

ACTIVITY 9.1

Draw up your own list of signs of entropy in your organization. Which ones cause you serious concern and need urgent action?

THE ENEMY IS WITHIN

Companies blame government for imposing bureaucracy (possibly with some justification), but they cause much more of it themselves and do little about it. Blaming outsiders for problems is one sure sign of decay. Externalizing the enemy is a convenient diversionary tactic, but the real enemy is within.

The enemy is vested interest. The enemy is believing that the way to solve yesterday's problems is the way to solve tomorrow's. The enemy is the insecurity that prevents managers from feeling free to challenge the status quo. The enemy is the yes-man who can be relied upon to agree with the boss. The enemy is weariness, powerlessness and fear. The enemy is the system that allows experience and talent to be flushed away with scant regard to either the individual's or the company's long-term interest. The enemy is the natural decay that moves all organizational life through its peak and into decline unless we keep clearing away the debris – of paperwork, of rigid structures, of old solutions, of tired policies, of outdated values, of power-corrupted leaders. The enemy is the internal swamp of bureaucracy which bogs managers down.

If companies would only recognize this and pull themselves together to harness their management capability, the battle to beat the external competition would be a foregone conclusion.

THE ROOTS OF BUREAUCRACY

Bureaucracy can be observed both when particular task processes are carried out and in many people's generalized and ingrained patterns of behaviour. An excess of paperwork provides the most tangible evidence of bureaucratic procedures and behaviour, and most of us instinctively associate bureaucracy with volumes of unnecessary paper. For managers, the daily in-tray serves to remind us that bureaucracy, like entropy, is ever with us. Of course, it is other people who behave like petty bureaucrats and inflict their paperwork on us; we are never bureaucrats ourselves. Our own work procedures and methods are always justified. No one admits to being a bureaucrat – at least not in Britain.

But behind the tangible manifestations of bureaucracy lie underlying causes which have their roots in the national and organization culture's values, as well as in individual personality. These background values to a greater or lesser extent hold the bureaucracy in place. We shall take a look at these various causes in a moment. But first we should reflect on the link between excess bureaucracy and the relentless process of entropy.

In a lecture delivered to the Institute of Administrative Management in 1975 entitled *The War on Paper Bureaucracy*, Sir Derek Rayner, then Joint Managing Director of Marks & Spencer (later Lord Rayner, the company's chairman), observed that,

> It is an inescapable fact that as an organisation grows larger, the whole paraphernalia of bureaucracy ... will grow and flourish. Unless steps are taken to the contrary, the urge to formalise and record everything will predominate to the

detriment of the organisation and to the frustration of the people who work in that organisation. Paper will become more important than people. Forms will multiply and stand firmly in the way of common-sense transaction. Rules and regulations will develop which will prevent human beings acting as individuals ... People will have no time to talk, management will be desk-bound in order to keep the in-tray empty, and no decisions will be taken without reference to rules, regulations, statistics ... [4]

We expect this and we expect to be infuriated by it. Bureaucracy has a bad time in the UK. Yet most of the world and our neighbours in Continental Europe don't see it as such a big problem. There are two reasons for its especially poor reception here.

KNEE-JERK REACTION

The first reason is quite simply that the word 'bureaucracy' has acquired entirely negative connotations in the UK. At the mere mention of the dreaded word, we expect the worst. Yet logically bureaurcracy should be a neutral word; we should expect to encounter both efficient and inefficient examples of it. But in the UK we have come to associate the term with too much red tape, gobbledegook, excess labour costs, unnecessary form-filling, backward practices, unresponsiveness to customers, make-work schemes, slavish decision taking and protracted timescales. To most of us, bureaucracy gives off bad vibes.

We may describe a bad dose of bureaucracy as a 'joke'. This is ironic, since in his design for the ideal organization, bureaucracy's originator, Max Weber, grafted the classical Greek ending onto a modern French beginning as a deliberate joke.

CULTURAL DIFFERENCES

The second reason we have problems with bureaucracy is cultural. The UK is fairly strong on masculine traits, for example, believing heavily in the virtue of competition. Its people feel comparatively comfortable with uncertainty and variety, and those who lack power don't willingly accept wide differences from those who enjoy it. In particular, the UK culture espouses individualism. We take the view that 'bureaucracy is the subjugation of the individual to the system, instead of the system serving the individual'.[4] These cultural conditions favour what Henry Mintzberg calls 'adhocracy'.[5]

Other countries don't quite see it the same way. Generally speaking, other cultures are characterized, in various permutations, by more collectivist attitudes, more nurturing views of society, a greater need for predictability, and wider tolerance of status differences.[6] Given these cultural constructs, anthropologists tell us that bureaucracy offers these people a degree of reassurance. Unless it is clearly badly applied, that is. In the UK we prejudge that it *will* be badly applied and can be only detrimental in its effect. Most other cultures do appear to practise and accept bureaucracy to a somewhat greater degree than does the UK.

Let's take one example of the practice of bureaucracy. France controls its own language and legislates what words its people may speak. Britons would never stand for that, believing that the English language is a living thing and should be allowed to follow a natural and evolutionary meander.

The French admire a well-run centralist bureaucracy. The word derives from the French *bureau* (desk), which gradually came to include the room containing the desk, then the activities conducted in that room as well, and finally the entire organization. As bureaucracy expanded, so did the meaning attached to the word. The British, however, remain suspicious of the word and all things bureaucratic.

It is this difference in attitude which explains why the UK government and its people have so much difficulty with the idea of a powerful European Commission in Brussels run on Continental lines. The irony is that once provided with this security blanket, other countries feel more relaxed than do the British about how they act under its cover. We play by the rules even if we don't like them; we think those who vote for rules and then break them are hypocritical. But they think that if you don't break the rules you must be stupid. The French have an expression for this, meaning 'strict in the regulation, flexible in the application'.

Organizational bureaucracies, of course, differ from state ones, and they differ from one another. But the main differences are in their activities rather than in their inherent approaches towards systems and people. Research, for example, shows that despite IBM's attempts to instil a transcending corporate culture in all its offices world-wide, the local culture remained the dominant ingredient.[6] Thus factors such as the significance of signatures will vary across cultures. Similarly, the importance of academic qualifications and titles in a society will be reflected in dealings in company hierarchical relationships.

KEY TIPS

❖ Be sensitive to trappings and symbols of bureaucracy which may be explained by their roots in a culture different from your own.

❖ There are more gains to be found inside organizations than there are by resisting social legislation without. It may be inconvenient to admit it, but the enemy is within.

SMOOTHING THE DIFFERENCES

Interpreting cultural models in terms of the implications for bureaucracy has only limited utility these days for most developers. Western societies are heterogeneous and are becoming more so. The USA is the prime example, both historically and currently with the rapid growth of the Latino population. It is claimed that 88 languages are now spoken in Los Angeles.

Supra-national political models are slowly replacing and unifying national practice, especially in Europe. Company organizations are going the same way. Firms are acquiring more diverse workforces. Labour is moving freely within the European Union. And the unstoppable process of the internationalization of business means that many companies are losing some of their previous national identity. Overtly British companies, such as the national airline, are seeking international alliances and global partners. Some even acknowledge that the time will soon come when the prefix 'British' will become a trade handicap by implying nationalistic parochialism. The British Institute of Management dropped 'British' to become the mere Institute of Management. When Japanese firms set up business in the west they impose their own cultural norms on their indigenous workforces. In some cases they import their own managements. Homogeneity is on the run.

We may therefore expect this continuing process to dull some of the edges of the cultural model and lead gradually towards more standardized forms of bureaucracy. But the process will be slow because in most cases the management tier in organizations tends to remain more nationally based than either the general workforce or the expectations of customers in the sphere within which the international trade is conducted.

In one respect, these developments will increase at least one aspect of bureaucracy. To cope with its diverse ethnic population, state businesses in California now have to produce written instructions in sixteen languages. European legislation requires corporate purchasers to tender throughout the European Union in all the leading languages. The fastest growing sector in the bureaucratic firmament is that of translation services.

Whether these developments are to be viewed as progress is for you to decide. I am concerned only with examining bureaucracy. In the context of this book, I am going to assume that developers are entirely concerned with examples of *excess* bureaucracy that their clients want cured, tamed or rid of in some way.

RULES AND REGULATIONS

As we have seen, rules and regulations lie at the heart of any bureaucracy. The idea is very simple and indeed rather admirable. The American pioneer of organization theory, Mary Parker Follett (1868–1933), explained the motivation.

> How can we avoid the two extremes: too great bossism in giving orders, and practically no orders given? ... My solution is to depersonalize the giving of orders, to unite all concerned in a study of the situation, to discover the law of the situation and to obey that. ... One *person* should not give orders to another *person*, but both should agree to take their orders from the situation.[7]

As Guy Benveniste shows in *Professionalizing the Organization: Reducing Bureaucracy to Enhance Effectiveness*, rules conveniently enable us to do the following:

O   Explain why something was done.
O   Justify failures.
O   Depoliticize decisions.
O   Ensure egalitarian treatment.
O   Wield power.
O   Avoid the need for trust.[8]

But, in spite of these uses (and sometimes abuses), this view of bureaucracy increasingly appears out of tune with the times in which we live. In truth, it is probably fair to say that it never wholeheartedly lived up to its intended promise, often becoming entirely dislocated.

CASE EXAMPLES: EXCESS BUREAUCRACY

1. A company has a published instruction for all employees on how to obtain a salary certificate from the personnel department for use with banks and building societies. Employees have to pay the company for the privilege of obtaining a certificate. This is designed to deter them from requesting too many. They have to visit personnel to request their certificate, then arrange to go to the finance department to make the payment, then return to personnel with a receipt. There are certain times of the day which personnel set aside for this activity. Work in personnel has been broken down into small specialisms to make mistakes less likely and there is one person whose sole job is to issue salary certificates. Line managers complain that they lose their staff for hours, but personnel have a secure power base and can run its affairs in a way which suits its own purposes.

2. The training department of an overseas nationalized company has a five-page regulation on what trainees should do, and what kind of punishment they will suffer, if they do not attend training courses. The regulation includes the memorable clause 'In case of apologising, the Training Department should be informed not less than three weeks from the date of apologising by filling in an apologising form.' In the event of a conflict between work and training, the regulation states that the training manager can overrule the trainee's line manager. It begins by stating the Act of Parliament under which the company claims to have the necessary authority.

One of the chief problems for bureaucrats is knowing when to stop. They develop an obsessive mentality about the process whereby every form of company life must be catered for, otherwise 'someone might ask a question and we shan't be able to turn up the answer'. So manuals come to state the obvious. One nationalized industry I worked with even published an employment regulation on the subject of ashtrays. At its heart was the policy that 'ashtrays shall be provided for smokers'! (I should add that this policy was not needed to resolve any doubt in these healthier times of no-smoking policies; this was when smoking was the norm twenty years ago.) I managed to have the regulation withdrawn along with many other superfluous ones.

MANAGEMENT BY MANUAL

These policies, rules, regulations, instructions, procedures, orders and notices grow like Topsy. One company had shelves full of the following employment manuals published by its personnel department. (N.B. These were in addition to finance manuals, safety manuals, property maintenance manuals, etc. emanating from all the other head office departments.)

- ○   Staff regulations.
- ○   Information and advisory notices.
- ○   Employment policies and procedures.
- ○   Welfare services.
- ○   Personnel managers' instructions.
- ○   Pay and conditions.
- ○   Standing instructions.

What starts out as manageable and well-intentioned grows into a monster over a period of years. It begins when the first manual starts to burst at the seams. Then new specialisms are created. Their managers want to make names for themselves and feel the need to show evidence for the distinctiveness of their new services, so they choose to publish new manuals rather than be sections in existing volumes. But the new manuals seem so thin – indeed hardly worth publishing – so more has to be written to pack them out. New directors come along and want to communicate their own orders. Rather than try to understand the current system or reform it, they find it easier to invent new Standing Instructions manuals.

I have been there. I recognize this in myself. None of us is immune from the disease. Most of the wounds are self-inflicted.

KEY TIP

❖   Put your energy into beating the competition outside and the bureaucracy inside, not the other way round.

BUREAUCRACY AND TRADE UNION POWER

The dynamics of the bureaucratic process described reflect an administrative mind-set rather than a managerial one – something we shall look at in more depth at the end of this chapter. But real managing is rather a novel experience for many managers. It wasn't mind-set which stopped them from managing: they were not allowed to manage. The daily life of line managers in larger companies used to consist mainly of fire-fighting and damage limitation in a love–hate relationship with trade unions.

The days of beer and sandwiches at Number 10 were mirrored at corporate level. Personnel directors struck deals with their opposite numbers behind closed doors, some even sharing holidays together. Each party needed the other. This state of affairs directly affected corporate bureaucracy. Union power and bureaucracy went hand in hand. It suited the unions' purposes to have a heavily regulated environment because it stripped line managers of power. Indeed, personnel's powerful bureaucracy had developed out of the perceived need to constrain supervisors' arbitrariness.[9]

The unions found it easy to negotiate favourable rules with personnel. And identical day-to-day decisions by line managers meant that union officials weren't always being troubled over petty matters concerning varied treatment to their members. It also suited personnel. Unions gave personnel its *raison d'être* and power base. The bureaucracy was seen as an extension of the industrial relations function.

BUREAUCRACY IN EMPOWERED TIMES

Times have changed. You might say they have come full circle. We now have 'empowerment' and decentralization of power. Line managing has regained some of its lost respect. From this current perspective, the issues with old-style bureaucracy now include the following:

○ Self-serving power. Rather than neutralizing 'bossism' (as Mary Parker Follett conceived it), regulations are the tools by which regulators have their wish for dominance met.

○ The antithesis of putting the customer first, whether the customer is the line manager or the individual employee.

○ Undermining the spontaneous application of common sense and discretion by line managers who need to be able to tailor solutions to a given local situation.

○ No longer affordable machinery for keeping manuals up to date.

○ A move towards minimizing the size and overhead cost in running services from head office, its role becoming more strategic than administrative.

○ Line managers being given delegated powers in functional areas that were hitherto the preserve of specialists, especially personnel. Their appetite has now been whetted, and they are increasingly prone to act unilaterally, not even bothering to check whether a manual deals with a particular subject.

Added to this is the fact that bureaucratic systems eventually collapse under their own weight – the relentless laws of entropy at work. The comparison with the collapse of the Soviet Union's centrally managed economy is apposite. The planners had for years tried to provide for every need. It was all written down in mountains of manuals. For example, the number, shapes and colours of the nation's toothbrushes for the next year were calculated (so that their manufacture could be ordered by the government from the country's only toothbrush maker). Every taxi driver had an annual mileage to be achieved and not exceeded. The bureaucracy even laid down the amount of scrap metal which laundromats had to generate each year from old washing machines. When the planners could no longer cope with the paperwork, along came computers to save the day. But after a while even that was not sufficient. There were now too many planners and not enough doers. Mikhail Gorbachev saw the light and the whole edifice crumbled.

Paradoxically, in the west, the mood of decentralization is taking over in industry rather more rapidly than in the political arena. Decentralizing power from the centre is in many cases accompanied by a fragmentation of power as monolithic giants like IBM and ICI break up as the best means of staying alive and competitive. Where there is privatization, this further means there is less need for armies of bureaucrats to collect data for passing back to government departments.

ACTIVITY 9.2

Identify the outward manifestations of excess bureaucracy in your organization in terms of particular tasks and patterns of behaviour. Which ones cry out for a priority assault?

WAGING WAR ON BUREAUCRACY

Bureaucratic behaviour needs to be considered and assaulted at three levels: task processes, general behaviour patterns, and underlying company values and the structures which reflect them. The first two are easily visible:

1. Task processes

The way in which particular activities are conducted. For example, the process by which vacancies are filled. Customers of such services tend to notice and complain about these: 'Why does it have to take so long to …?'

2. Behaviour patterns

Underlying these processes are general patterns of bureaucratic behaviour, irrespective of the functional activity or service delivered. An example is the way in which management approval has to be sought and how it is communicated.

SYSTEM COMPETENCE, NOT PERSONAL COMPETENCE

Bureaucracy is essentially a system problem, not a personal one. To their customers, bureaucrats may appear incompetent, but one cannot simply view these signs of excessively bureaucratic behaviour in terms of personal competence. If you could wave a magic wand and replace whoever you wished, it would make little difference, as long as the staff were required to perform under the old constraints and pressures to conform.

KEY TIP

❖   Blame and change the systems before the people.

SUSTAINED ENERGY

To mount an attack on bureaucracy first requires energy. Although we live in a world of change, the strongest force in an organization is inertia, as Sir Derek Rayner points out:

> Unless priority is given to setting time aside to probe continuously, and question why the business is being conducted in the way it is, bureaucracy will win. Top management must create the necessary activity and encourage others to do so at

all levels of the company, otherwise the systems which have become anachronistic and irrelevant to the future of the organisation will dominate management time and may even destroy the business. … Unless a business does get down to looking at its organisation and finding out why the symptoms of bureaucracy grow like weeds, it will be engaged in an endless battle.[4]

Second, the war on bureaucracy needs tactical purges.

FREQUENT PURGES

It is not possible to maintain control over bureaucracy all the time. It is inevitable that after carrying out any review, the bureaucracy will eventually start to reappear. New rules and regulations will be dreamt up. Power will creep back to the centre. Recognize this by implementing a substantial reorganization or culling operation every few years. One company I worked with used to call in consultants every ten years to undertake an *overhead value analysis*, whereby the costs of its head office overheads had to be cut by 40 per cent.

Another idea is to conduct a narrowly aimed assault on a specific feature of the bureaucracy. Some examples are as follows:

O   Forms.
O   Distribution lists.
O   Committees.
O   Monthly statistics.
O   Checking procedures.

KEY TIP

❖   Stimulate activity on a narrow front with which people can identify and expect to see a result.

STRATEGIES FOR CURBING BUREAUCRACY

The above are merely tactical responses. We need a strategy. But before we become serious, there is a light-hearted strategy which may appeal to cynics and those close to giving up. This approach is to boost the bureaucracy so that it sinks under its own weight. For example, keep manuals thick so that no one wants to use them. This tongue-in-cheek approach comes from the same stable as the view that the last thing you want is an efficient bureaucracy; if we have to suffer bureaucracy, then let's hope it is inefficient! This sounds to me like a counsel of despair. It constitutes a high risk because it depends on users knowing the subtext, the real name of the game. I prefer serious attempts to prune the bureaucracy.

Behind the outward manifestations of bureaucracy (tasks and behaviours) are various systems and structures which derive from the values of the organization's culture. It is this deeper level which is usually overlooked in the attack against bureaucracy. Instead of making war on bureaucracy, we merely engage in frequent skirmishes. But it is pointless to put effort into redesigning detailed work

procedures to try to make them more streamlined without attacking the fundamental causes which lead to these bureaucratic modes of behaviour and which
underpin and sustain them.

There are three underlying causes on which to concentrate:

1.   The organization's power structure.
2.   Departmental purposes.
3.   The recognition and reward system.

Together, these encourage or discourage certain types of behaviour. Left unchanged, they will maintain the status quo, despite periodic purges.

THE ESSENTIAL STEPS

The essential steps of a strategic assault on bureaucracy comprise the following:

1.   Move beyond the symptoms and diagnose the underlying causes and the
       values in the system which need to be addressed. Draw up a force-field
       analysis[10] to indicate the forces which are facilitating change and those
       which are restraining change; you will then be able to plan how to add to
       the former and weaken the latter.
2.   Reform the formal and informal recognition and reward system. For
       example, reward initiative and risk-taking, even breaking the rules where it
       makes sense to do so. If the bureaucracy is making systems too safe (e.g. a
       practice of over-checking) license a little anarchy.
3.   Restructure to remove excessively centralized power bases in head office
       support departments. Demonstrate the value you place in the line by
       where you allocate resources and what you back.
4.   Change the formal mission of support departments in discussion with line
       departments to emphasize their role in providing business-driven service.
5.   Develop the notion of everyone having (internal) customers. Build internal
       customer feedback into the appraisal and reward systems.
6.   Give head office departmental directors specific targets to meet in (i)
       terms of making specific changes to organizational arrangements and pro-
       cesses, and (ii) faster response times, etc.
7.   Revisit this subject every few years.

INFORMATION TECHNOLOGY

The use of information technology (IT) may be another strategic response. But too
often IT is used tactically and fails to achieve more than an apparent change. It may
even increase the problem. To the arch-bureaucrat the computer can seem a
heaven-sent means to continue handling and processing customary data which
serves little useful purpose.

KEY TIP

❖   Overhaul procedures before computerizing them.

NORM-BUSTERS

Another strategy is to send in a norm-buster, someone whose style is the antithesis of bureaucracy.

CASE EXAMPLE: NORM-BUSTING

A newly appointed chairman (an external political appointee) discovered that directors and managers talked in abbreviated job titles. For example, memos went from PD (Personnel Director) to GIRM (Group Industrial Relations Manager). People even said 'PD' when speaking with the director face-to-face. Office doors gave job titles, but no names. The new chairman immediately broke this convention and ordered that all doors should show names without job titles.

This approach doesn't work for long. Newcomers quickly lose their ability to see from an outside perspective. What is more, the strength of the culture puts up stout resistance to this kind of intrusion into its comfortable conventions. It is highly likely that a norm-buster will quickly become disillusioned and give up.

REDESIGNING BUREAUCRACY

CASE EXAMPLE: MANAGEMENT BY MANUAL

I earlier cited the instance of a company with a plethora of manuals. I was asked to prepare a new system. The features were as follows:

Discretionary guidance
The previous system had been characterized by 'rules and regulations'. By the late 1980s this language was felt to be too hard and controlling. It left no place for common sense and discretion. The new scheme deliberately used the softer language of 'guide' and 'guidance'.

Non-hierarchical, open access
The previous manuals had been for 'staff'. This term had acquired a narrow usage, whereby all matters were the property of the so-called 'two sides of industry' – staff and management. To get round this, we used the term 'employment'. Staff Regulations became Employment Guide.

Worse than this, some of the previous manuals had either been for staff or for their managers. One had three different-coloured sections within each policy area. The first was for all managers on the distribution list. The second was more secret and for the eyes of only a small number of senior managers. The third comprised an even more private section for senior personnel managers. This structure reinforced the sense of secrecy, lack of trust and a them-and-us attitude. It was even divisive among line managers and within the personnel hierarchy.

The answer lay in producing a single manual, open to all. As well as stating the company's policy and procedure in black type on one side of the page, the manual offered guidance and advice to managers on how to exercise their judgement and carry out their part of the process.

Of course, the trade union officials didn't like this because it licensed variability. Many managers didn't like it either; it meant that their staff could see how managers were expected to behave and the parameters governing their actions. Previously, less-confident managers had been able to hide behind their ignorance and their prejudices. One of managers' favourite games was to claim (wrongly) that 'Personnel won't let me'. Now everyone knew what they were entitled to and how managers could and should exercise discretion. Dismantling bureaucracy means removing crutches and nannies.

Why as well as what
Previously, the purpose of the manuals had been to state the rule and the procedure. Switching to open access within a discretionary framework, it was now necessary to begin with a statement of policy and rationale. So the introductory tone became more philosophical. This proved a valuable discipline: as experts began rewording the content, they had to justify it.

Simple language
The earlier versions had been long-winded and somewhat legalistic. The new version attempted to be more accessible in tone and style, more personal, with shorter sentences in the first person using the active voice wherever possible (e.g. 'When you have filled in the application, give it to your manager', rather than 'Completed applications should be passed to management'). The anonymous and divisive word 'management' was avoided as far as possible.

Reduction in size
The aim was to reduce all personnel business to one manual and to scrap around two-thirds of all previous material.

THE PROCESS OF CHANGE

Change will always be resisted by organized labour, but especially so when it means dismantling bureaucracy and empowering line managers. This kind of change will also meet with a mixed reception from the managers themselves, as I have explained. For this reason, the process needs careful handling. It is necessary to get the top management on side first, and to enlist someone very senior, preferably the chief executive or the personnel director, to explain to all managers what is being done and why. Many people then need to be involved in the process of culling the old regulations, and recasting the remainder. The trade unions need to be kept informed too and consulted where appropriate on new wording.

IS THIS MANAGEMENT DEVELOPMENT?

Development activity spans a broad range. At one end is working with individual managers on their personal skills. In the middle is working with groups of managers on shared corporate problems. At the other end are system changes like the bureaucratic ones described here. It doesn't matter to me whether this kind of renewal is called organization development or management development. It finds a place here because it directly impacts on the way managers go about their work and the manner in which the organization's daily business is effectively managed.

What matters is that here was a case of organizational entropy being diagnosed and dealt with. Not a bolt-on as had happened before, not a quick fix, but a fundamental programme of reform. In microcosm this was culture change, re-inforced by other complementary action. What I have explained in some detail is only one small part of the story. At the same time line managers were being given responsibility for conducting their own selection interviews, for example, and the role and size of the corporate personnel department was being reduced drastically as part of a programme to devolve everyday employment administration to each line department. Here I have chosen to concentrate on just one particular example of entropy and how to counter it.

ACTIVITY 9.3

Examine the way your own company is managed via rules and regulations. Where is there scope for trimming this back?

ADMINISTRATION VERSUS MANAGING

Administration is very closely associated with bureaucracy. It risks going the same way in the public's mind. We are growing to the point where we assume admin-istrators don't add value; they have to be tolerated as a regrettable overhead. But it need not be this way: like bureaucracy itself, administration can be vital – in both senses of that word. However, my interest in administration here is when it is a substitute for managing, or put another way, where 'manager' is a misnomer for 'administrator'.

An important context for development activity will often entail shifting the perception of an organization's so-called management team away from admin-istration towards more true managerial behaviour. This is particularly so with clients who are trying to cut overhead costs and weed out unnecessary or excessive bureaucracy.

The problem is common when working with clients in developing countries. These companies have often inherited an administrative tradition, but have failed to move with the times. Having large amounts of administration may, in many cases, suit their national employment structures. Bureaucracy may also be ingrained culturally:

O   It serves to hold back the individual to the condition of the group (in collectivist societies).

○   It provides a bulwark against uncertainty (in uncertainty-avoiding societies).

○   It offers numerous opportunities to demonstrate status and power differentials (in high power-distance societies, and those which insist on identical male outward appearance).

○   In societies strongly characterized by so-called 'feminine' traits (e.g. caring and support) it moderates excessive arbitrary power used against the under-privileged.

But, in spite of the uphill task, foreign companies which want to compete on the international stage have to try to move their administration upstream and concentrate more on managing.

In the west it is only in comparatively recent times that there has been a growing acceptance of the useful distinction between managing and administration. This is not helped by the fact that so many administrators have managerial job titles and are part of their company's management cadre. Since 1915 the UK has had an Institute of Administrative Management. The potential for confusion between administrating and managing is not helped by the quaint name of the foremost managerial qualification, the Master of Business Administration. This should go the same way as the Administrative Staff College, a high-level institute for bosses that began to sound more suited to their secretaries.

But there are some useful distinctions. Put very crudely, we expect managers to be better able to cope with uncertainty. In times of rapid change we therefore expect managers to be able to identify when old methods are no longer appropriate and to be able to design new methods to replace them. Whereas we look to administrators to carry out currently defined tasks efficiently. We expect managers to be proactive and behave strategically, but administrators to be reactive and behave tactically.

But it is not so much the activities of managers and administrators that are different. Many are similar and the edges are somewhat blurred. Much managing involves paperwork, figures and scanning computer screens, indeed some elementary administration. What matters more is the frame of mind. Figure 9.2 sets out, starkly to make its point, some of the stereotypical differences between managing and administration. It may be a shade cruel on administrators, but I have come across some who conform to this stereotype masquerading as managers. And I am sure we have all come across many managers who fail to live up to the stereotype. The realization of different purposes and different skills between managing and administration has probably come too late in the day to save swaths of local government, though it has worked commendably hard to make the switch.

The area of current high-profile is the National Health Service, where there has been substantial growth in the numbers of non-medical staff. The NHS is a political hot potato, and as such it is inevitable that this change, like any other, receives sustained criticism. The problem is that many people don't understand what they are criticizing, beyond the salaries of the so-called 'administrators'. They confuse administration and managing, or pretend they do. I don't know whether the NHS was under-administered, but it was certainly under-managed, and therefore I'm not

FIGURE 9.2 THE MANAGER'S MIND-SET: MANAGERIAL AND ADMINISTRATIVE STEREOTYPES

A *managing* way of thinking

- Regards self as part of 'the management'
- Accepts responsibility
- Takes initiative for proposing action
- Strategic focus on the big picture
- Results-oriented
- Achievement is important
- Deals with the appropriate people
- Expects the job to change
- Skilled at bringing about change
- Has a different role from subordinates
- Manages relationships
- Externally well informed
- Seeks feedback from users and acts on it
- Develops links and networks
- Spends personal time with customers
- Uses discretion and common sense
- Delegates the little issues
- Seeks opportunities to learn in the job
- Relishes a challenge
- Wants to solve problems
- Spots opportunities
- Accepts a share of the blame
- Expects the unknown
- Prepared to speak out

An *administrative* way of thinking

- Speaks of those above as 'the management'
- Shuns responsibility
- Waits to be asked to take action
- Narrow tactical focus within job
- Process-oriented
- Status is important
- Deals with people at own level
- Expects the job to remain static
- Unskilled at managing change
- Does rather similar work to subordinates
- Manages paper
- Local knowledge only
- Closed view of own world
- Works mainly alone
- Uses paper to interface with customers
- Obeys procedures and rules
- Delegates the big issues
- Considers he or she has already learnt it all
- Frightened of a challenge
- Wants to clear the backlog
- Misses opportunities
- Blames others for what is wrong
- Assumes things are predictable
- Keeps a low profile

one of the critics of the idea of putting in managers to run the hospitals. Readers involved in developing the management profession should need little convincing that technicians are not necessarily capable of managing a business, certainly not a large complex one.

It should go without saying that there are countless valuable and efficient administrators whom we could not do without. Many are members of The Institute of Administrative Management and hold that Institute's diploma. They simply do not call themselves or pretend to be managers in the full sense of the word. Ensuring the right language is used in organizations is a good place to start.

ACTIVITY 9.4

Consider your junior and middle management grades. Is a clear distinction drawn between those who are paid to be administrators and those who are required to be true managers? Are there people in manager jobs who behave as administrators?

KEEPING THE CHECKERS IN CHECK

An overseas state-sector company I advised was engaged in what it variously called 'audit' and 'control' at four levels. First was the government's audit department, which was part of the finance ministry, members of whom were permanently located on the company's premises. Second, was the business's firm of external auditors. Then came the company's own internal audit department, whose mission appeared to be to stop anything untoward arising and coming to the notice of the other auditors. Finally, both the finance department and the personnel department had their own internal sections which tried to stop any mistakes and malpractices coming to light outside their departments.

This seemed to me to be both excessive and obsessive. On further investigation, it transpired that auditing had become entirely synonymous with checking. At the higher levels, the true function and breadth of auditing for corporate quality assurance had been sacrificed in favour of detailed checking in narrow areas. At the lower levels it took the form of a 100 per cent pre-audit of other sections' work in the same department. No one in these other sections was assumed either competent or trustworthy enough to undertake their own work correctly. The following consequences ensued:

O   There was a widespread atmosphere of distrust and demotivation.
O   Supervisors were not held accountable for the work of their sections.
O   No training was needed, since mistakes would always be spotted and corrected.
O   The most qualified people became checkers.
O   Work throughput for internal customers was exceedingly slow.
O   The overhead manpower cost was excessive.

The recommended solution was drastic and predictable. These departmental control sections had to be closed down and the staff redeployed to more creative work. Supervisors had to be managed, held accountable and appraised quite differently. The role of the audit department needed to become one of 'carrying out an independent evaluation of the adequacy and effectiveness of the controls, informing top management of areas that need new or revised procedures'.

ACTIVITY 9.5

Examine the various checkers, whatever they call themselves. Are they in proportion to their productive units? Do their working arrangements have any negative effects on supervisors' responsibilities, staff training, speed of work output, where talent gets promoted, etc?

REFERENCES

1. Boyce Rensberger (1986) *How the World Works: A Guide to Science's Greatest Discoveries*, New York: William Morrow, p. 139.
2. Robert Waterman (1987) *The Renewal Factor: How the Best Get and Keep the Competitive Edge*, New York: Bantam Books, p. 19.
3. Max De Pree (1989) *Leadership is an Art*, London: Arrow, p. 111.
4. Sir Derek Rayner (1975) *The War on Paper Bureaucracy*, (Occasional Paper No. 4), Beckenham: The Institute of Administrative Management.
5. Henry Mintzberg (1989) *Mintzberg on Management: Inside our Strange World of Organizations*, New York: Free Press, pp. 196–205.
6. Geert Hofstede (1991) *Cultures and Organizations*, Maidenhead: McGraw-Hill.
7. Henry Metcalf and Lyndall Urwick (1940) *Dynamic Administration: The Collected Papers of Mary Parker Follett*, New York: Harper & Row.
8. Guy Benveniste (1987) *Professionalizing the Organization: Reducing Bureaucracy to Enhance Effectiveness*, San Francisco: Jossey-Bass, pp. 1–25, 255–70.
9. Keith Sisson (ed.) (1989) *Personnel Management in Britain*, Oxford: Blackwell, p. 212.
10. Oscar Mink, James Shultz and Barbara Mink (1986) *Developing and Managing Open Organizations: A Model and Methods for Maximising Organizational Potential*, Austin, Texas: Organization and Human Resource Development Associates, Inc., pp. 107–9.

10
CREATING A POSITIVE ENVIRONMENT

OVERVIEW

This chapter explains what we mean by climate and culture in organizations, advises on the practicalities of trying to make changes, and describes some healthy types to strive for.

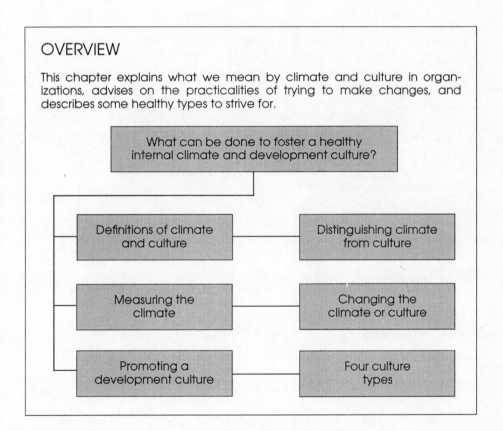

INTRODUCTION

Developers have a twofold interest in an organization's internal environment. First, several of its aspects directly impact upon managers' own development and learning. To help these managers, developers have to understand that environment. Second, developers have a role in helping to develop a more positive environment. The improvements which then result in behaviour change can in turn contribute to improving the environment. The process is circular: an improved environment can lead to the kind of behaviour which can further improve it.

This chapter describes the components of environment; namely, *climate* and *culture*. It distinguishes the two, and shows how each fits with an organizational model of performance. It then investigates some culture types, highlighting those of most interest to developers.

SOME DEFINITIONS

What do we mean by climate? How is it different from culture?

Organization climate is sometimes likened to the weather. Taking the temperature of an organization finds out how it feels. Expressions like 'a great place to work' or 'one big bureaucracy' give clues about the climate. People's perceptions and feelings, as in these quoted expressions, directly affect their performance and productivity and that of the organization, and their joint ability to grow and prosper.

There have been several attempts to produce a definition of climate and to distinguish it from culture. From George Litwin *et al.* comes:

> Climate is a set of measurable properties of a given environment, based on the collective perceptions of the people who live and work in that environment, and demonstrated to influence their motivation and behavior ... what it is like to work in a given environment.[1]

Culture, on the other hand, is often considered to be 'the way we do things around here' (rather than 'how it feels at a particular time'). Gerard Egan describes culture as:

> ... the shared beliefs, values and norms of the company in so far as these drive shared patterns of behaviour ... including strategic behaviour, operational behaviour, decision-making behaviour, information-flow behaviour, managerial behaviour, supervisory behaviour, leadership behaviour.[2]

DISTINGUISHING CLIMATE FROM CULTURE

The work of developers is, of course, *affected by*, and may also have an *influence on*, climate and culture. While they are closely related, developers are required to make a clear distinction between them, for example when using the Burke–Litwin Model (see Chapter 8).

Compared with climate, culture is more deep-seated, more difficult to measure, and more resistant to modification. While drawing on long-established anthropological principles, culture is a much newer subject than climate for discussion at organizational level.

Culture and climate have entered every political commentator's vocabulary. They speak of a 'blame culture' and a 'climate of fear' in such-and-such an industry or institution. These two phrases help a little to differentiate the concepts. We may create a climate in which something *can* happen, but it is left to culture to reveal the consistently important norms of what *does* happen. Thus, a consciously engineered and pervasive climate of fear may lead to a permanent blame culture, or a culture of survival in which people generally keep their heads below the parapet. Climate is something to which you *respond*. Culture is something of which you are *part*.

The key point about climate is that it is easier to have a short-term impact in this area. According to Burke, Litwin *et al.*, climate is 'relatively malleable … could be modified by managerial behavior and by systems'.[3] Development work undertaken with a head of a department can, for example, purposefully tackle his or her need to improve the climate in that department. Aspects of the climate may also be immediately affected by a new boss – for better or worse – without an under-standing of the model. Climate is therefore a psychological state; either a positive one as with a climate of openness, or a negative one as with a climate of fear which may be readily intensified or lessened by an incoming leader.

We can also distinguish climate from culture in terms of *manager* development versus *management* development, as discussed in the opening chapter. Developers can intervene to help improve the climate in order to reinforce and support individual manager development action and improve its chance of success. Culture change interventions, on the other hand, are management/organization development interventions in their own right.

MEASURING THE CLIMATE

What is the climate composed of? Expert opinions vary, and it is here that we again risk confusing the elements of climate and culture. The problem is that in order to be able to make inferences about the climate, we have to look at consequences, manifestations and systems. To find out *why* we have to look at *what*. And some of this behaviour (as Egan shows) is driven by 'shared beliefs, values and norms'. Notwithstanding this difficulty, suggested items in a list of climate questions might include those listed in Figure 10.1. This gives the broad idea, indicating how a positive climate holds clear implications for job satisfaction, productivity and per-formance. There is no definitive list. Indeed, according to Burke, Litwin *et al.*, 'there could be no universal set of dimensions or properties for organizational climate … one could describe climate along different dimensions depending on what kind of organization was being studied'.[3]

Questionnaire-based surveys help developers test the temperature and discuss improvements, as well as monitor changes over time. Some surveys explicitly test climate, others test culture, some test a mix of both under headings like organization survey or attitude survey. Some concentrate on a particularly topical issue such as smoking at work.

FIGURE 10.1 ESTABLISHING CLIMATE: POSSIBLE AREAS TO QUESTION

- **Clarity.** Do people know what is expected of them and how it relates to the company's goals?
- **Commitment.** Are people dedicated to achieving their goals?
- **Standards.** Are standards of excellence emphasized and set by example?
- **Responsibility.** Do individuals feel personally responsible for their work?
- **Dependency.** How much dependency is there? Who is dependent on whom?
- **Freedom.** How much freedom is there? Are people tightly controlled?
- **Recognition/reward.** Do people feel that they are recognized and rewarded for their work?
- **Team spirit.** Is there a feeling of belonging, warmth, mutual support and cooperation?
- **Interpersonal relations.** Are there strong cliques which are difficult to break into?
- **Flexibility.** Are people encouraged to develop new approaches?
- **Supervision.** What is supervisors' influence on employee motivation?
- **Problem management.** How does the organization view and solve problems?
- **Management of mistakes.** What are bosses' attitudes towards personal errors?
- **Personal risk taking.** Are people prepared to take risks? What happens when they do?
- **Organizational risk taking.** How does the organization handle risky situations?
- **Conflict management.** What processes are used to resolve conflict?
- **Decision making.** How are decisions made, by whom, about what?
- **Trust.** Who trusts whom for what?
- **Management of rewards.** What types of behaviours are positively reinforced?
- **Innovation/change.** Who is responsible for instigating change, by what methods?

ACTIVITY 10.1

In what respects would you consider your organization climate unhealthy at the moment? If the climate were to be measured formally by a survey, what factors would you regard as the most pertinent? Are there any topical themes?

CHANGING THE CLIMATE OR THE CULTURE

Social scientists describe the dynamics involved between systems and other organization variables in the above lists as being associated with the transactional level of human behaviour or the everyday interactions and exchanges that create the climate. On the other hand, if a company needs to transform itself radically, then it needs to address its culture rather than merely its climate – a much bigger challenge.

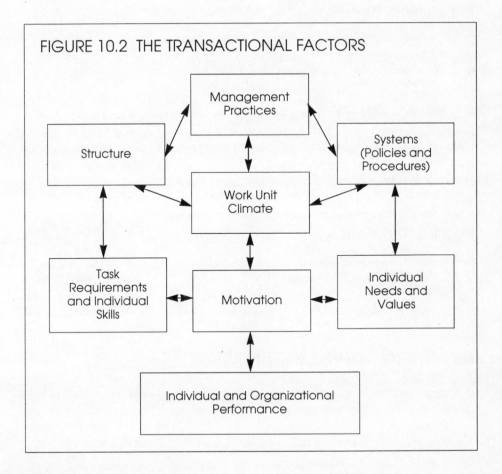

FIGURE 10.2 THE TRANSACTIONAL FACTORS

However challenging and tempting for developers, culture change is not the place to start. Roger Harrison and Juliann Spoth offer common sense advice when they suggest,

> there is much that can be done short of "culture change", and those things should be undertaken first. ... culture change is not a substitute for integrity or for good management; rather, it is what you come to after you are managing the best you can. Some examples of intra-level improvement at the Transactional level are such mundane matters as managing with honesty, justice and consistency; and improving the organization's systems and structures and technology until they are as good as we can get them.[4]

KEY TIP

❖   Manage the climate before attempting culture change.

The Model of Organizational Performance and Change,[5] shown in Figure 8.4 (p. 153), includes the factors of both climate and culture, and shows how they interact with the other variables. The model can be considered in two halves.

TRANSACTIONAL CHANGE

The first half of the model (see Figure 10.2, p. 189) consists of the *transactional* factors which the model's authors consider should be addressed if the need is to make the easier kinds of improvement about which Harrison and Spoth talk.

TRANSFORMATIONAL CHANGE

Beyond this level, according to Burke and Litwin, fundamental change can be brought about only by changes in the external environment, or internally by working on the factors of mission and strategy, leadership, or organization culture, as shown in Figure 10.3.

ACTIVITY 10.2

Contemplate the degree of change which is needed in your organization at the moment. Is it just fine-tuning (transactional) or is it fundamental (transformational)?

PROMOTING A DEVELOPMENT CULTURE

In writing about climate and culture – especially the latter – I am conscious of how easy it would be to fall between two stools. Volumes have been written by experts on the complex processes entailed in bringing about change in an organization's culture and I will not attempt that here. But I shall give an indication of where the

FIGURE 10.3 THE TRANSFORMATIONAL FACTORS

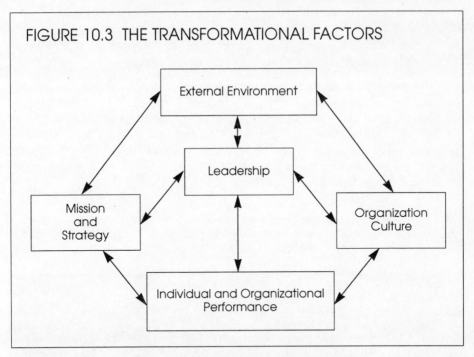

questions of culture and development share a common interest. I will then leave it to readers to decide for themselves on any appropriate action to suit their own organizations and circumstances.

PROCEED WITH CAUTION

People love talking about their organization's culture; it is full of potential for gossip which typifies culture's everyday manifestations. Developers equally love talking about culture change; it sounds much more fun than running training courses. But there are many consultants who argue that an organization's culture is so deeply rooted it cannot be changed. Or they take the position that it is so monumental a task that people should be warned off trying it. There are three good reasons for this advice.

1. The organization's ability to handle culture change is itself dependent upon its present culture, which if it is not presently adequate may not be well suited to *coping* with its own change, let alone actively *managing* it.
2. Those currently in charge of the business are unlikely to be the right people to drive a substantial culture change programme and will themselves need changing. The current leadership has a vested interest in the status quo; this is what got them there and what sustains them in power. This is part of a paradox: to change anything you have to work with the status quo.
3. Any attempt to change something as deeply embedded as culture will generate opposition, which will produce its own problems and may entrench features of the present culture.

KEY TIP

❖   Much that is worthwhile can be done to improve an organization's effectiveness short of attempting full culture change.

One of the troubles with these arguments is that they imply that culture change is either all or nothing. There seems no room for a grey area of marginal culture change – an element of culture *shift*. Nor does this gloomy scenario help us to close in on limited aspects of the organization. A large organization will have subcultures, both functionally and hierarchically. For example, there may be a distinct engineering (sub)culture, and there will be a management (sub)culture – which is what we are most interested in here.

According to Egan,

> The goal is not a full personality transformation. The goal is sustainable patterns of behaviour change that serve the business in key areas. The goal is to effect enough change to make a difference.[2]

ACTIVITY 10.3

Summarize your managerial subculture's shortcomings. With reference to points 1–3 above, how closely identified with the present culture is the current leadership? What support could you count on? Would the present culture be able to manage change to itself? What practically can be attempted short of full culture change?

IS CULTURE CHANGE REAL?

Many service companies have traditionally been negligent in taking overtly good care of their customers and appearing to put them first. They have typically concentrated on hard factors, such as accuracy and punctuality, rather than soft factors such as greetings. If, say, a ferry company wants to move in this soft direction without compromising its values of seamanship and safety, does that constitute a culture change or just a shift?

The banks have put considerable effort into trying to introduce a customer-service culture, yet in spite of all the publicity and seductive advertising, their reputation of putting themselves first remains the dominant public perception. This lends support to the view that values are too entrenched to be changed, and that the banking revolution we hear about is primarily to do with information technology, mergers, number of outlets and staffing levels. But even if this is not the same as changing the organization's heart, it's still fundamental and it does improve the received service.

Having been at the centre of the well-publicized culture change experience in British Airways throughout the 1970s and 1980s, I know what it is like from the inside. There is no doubt in my own mind that the airline's culture *did* change. Remarks such as, 'We could get the aircraft away on time if it wasn't for the passengers!', really are a thing of the past. Making money has permeated the blood-stream. Doing a good job or expecting to pay the price has become the norm.

Some of the norms have changed in BA, and so have some of the values under-pinning them. So it seems to me self-evident that culture can and *does* change – albeit to a greater or lesser degree, and gradually. Not everyone will come on board. Some will have to be jettisoned, with golden parachutes or lifebelts (depending on the culture!). So those who say culture cannot be changed probably mean that the change cannot be *planned* and actively *managed*. But if so, that would mean culture change had a life of its own. If that was the case, the change would have to be a natural response to other forces. What forces?

CAN CULTURE BE MANAGED?

There are many forces outside an organization in its environment – commercial, economic, political, regulatory, technological and social. In BA's case, some of these were being actively managed from outside, such as the government's privati-zation agenda. These in turn become managed inside, and – with something as fundamental as privatization – they become part of the culture change experienced by employees and customers alike. But is there more to it than that?

The many reviews written about culture change in BA clearly reveal a consider-able post-hoc rationalization – or, to be kind, wisdom after the event – which years later retrospectively imposes plans and models on the process. These make the culture change appear to conform to more of a top-down managed grand design than is actually the case.

The truth, in my opinion, is that the dynamics of bringing about change are a mix of attempts to stimulate, half-plan and manage the process according to some partially developed ideas, concepts and models, in accordance with a chosen direc-tion, as well as considerable intuition, experience and drive. The rest is, and can only be, a fluid and largely undefined and unpredictable process which finds its own course through the terrain over the (many) years, according to the following factors:

○   Who is then in positions of power.
○   How at that time these people consider events are turning out.
○   The environment (which will have changed in the meantime in un-predictable ways).
○   Where further opportunities lie and progress might be made.

This view accords with a pragmatic concept of planning, as espoused by Henry Mintzberg in his **emergent strategy**.[6] The idea of a grand plan is wishful thinking, even though there are respectable writers who present their past successes in this light and may claim it as their own approach. Emergent strategy gives a place to learning in the light of events; whereas the idea of detailed strategy formulation for subsequent top-down communication to the strategy implementers precludes learning.

Several vested interests are always at stake in such a high-profile and political activity as culture change, and there is therefore a good deal of mythology created subsequently.[7] As journalistic wits say, 'Never let the facts spoil a good story.' One

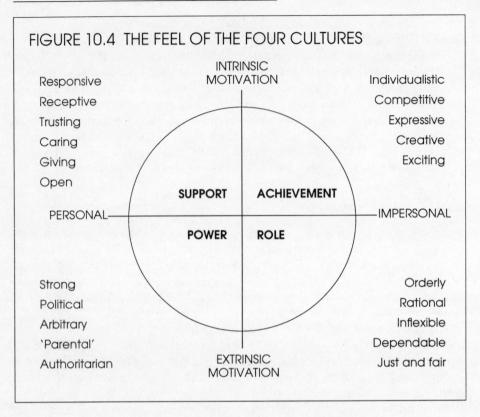

FIGURE 10.4 THE FEEL OF THE FOUR CULTURES

Reproduced by courtesy of Roger Harrison and Celest Powell[10]

needs to read the accounts and take them with a pinch of salt. But with a few million pounds at your disposal, a number of years available, and an external threat that makes you feel you have no choice, substantial culture change can be effected.

CULTURE TYPES

How can we best describe and label the organization culture?

There are many tools and models available for developers to use in connection with mapping their organization's culture. One of the most sympathetic is that designed by Roger Harrison.[8] This is supported by some interesting work about what these culture types imply for organizations whose prime business is to offer customer service.

Harrison's model contains four archetypal culture types:

1.   The power orientation
2.   The role orientation
3.   The achievement orientation
4.   The support orientation

FIGURE 10.5 SOME OF THE WAYS IN WHICH CULTURES EMPOWER AND DISEMPOWER EMPLOYEES

CULTURE ORIENTATION	The culture empowers employees through:	The culture disempowers employees through:
POWER (focus on survival)	• identification with a strong leader	• fear and inability to act without permission
ROLE (focus on security)	• systems that serve the employees and the task, reducing confusion and conflict	• restricting autonomy and creativity and erecting barriers to cooperation
ACHIEVEMENT (focus on self-expression)	• identification with the values and ideals of a vision • the liberation of creativity • freedom to act	• burnout and stress • treating the individual as an instrument of the task • inhibiting dissent about goals and values
SUPPORT (focus on community)	• the power of cooperation and trust • providing understanding, acceptance and assistance	• suppressing conflict • preoccupation with process • conformity to group norms

He provides a diagnostic tool for use with a group of senior managers to find out how their organizational opinions map against the four descriptions.[9] A brief idea of the four cultures is offered in Figure 10.4 (on p. 194).

From a developer's standpoint, the most appealing of the four culture types are achievement and support. It is worth pointing out that each culture has its advantages and disadvantages which have to be traded off against each other. For example, an achievement-oriented culture might utilize its members' talent to the full, yet at the same time suffer from high burn-out. A support-oriented culture might be nurturing to its members, but it may be insufficiently task-oriented.

On the key question of empowerment (always of interest to developers), Figure 10.5 (on p. 195) shows how the four cultures empower and disempower people.

The power- and role-oriented cultures are easily recognized as the traditional forms. Most of us have worked in cultures where the job is what the boss wants done. Similarly, most of us have experienced the bureaucratic manifestations of role cultures, from the outside if not the inside. Fewer of us have experienced organizations where the culture is overwhelmingly achievement- or support-oriented, but at face value these cultures sound far more attractive. But it is all too easy to dismiss wholesale the earlier types of organization culture as being out of tune with the times and to rush for the more recent variants. All cultures have strengths and weaknesses. The trick is to try to achieve, for your organization, a well-balanced culture which exploits the best features of each type. Figure 10.6 is Harrison and Powell's depiction of this balance.

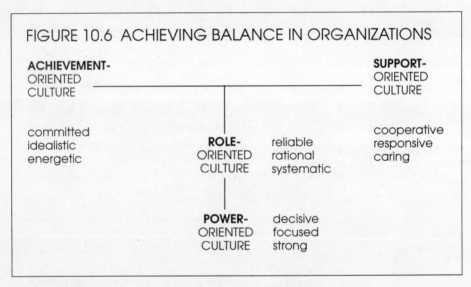

FIGURE 10.6 ACHIEVING BALANCE IN ORGANIZATIONS

ACHIEVEMENT- ORIENTED CULTURE		SUPPORT- ORIENTED CULTURE
committed idealistic energetic	ROLE- ORIENTED CULTURE reliable rational systematic	cooperative responsive caring
	POWER- ORIENTED CULTURE decisive focused strong	

Reproduced by courtesy of Roger Harrison and Celest Powell

CASE EXAMPLE: CHANGING THE MANAGEMENT CULTURE

A medium-sized private ferry operator is the modern offshoot of a large nationalised transport company which divested itself of non-core business several years ago. The new company inherited a management culture which best fits a mix of Harrison's traditional 'power' and 'role' models.

The organization was characterized by long service and very little new blood. With safety paramount, people worked to prescribed roles and procedures, and were not expected to show initiative. The pace of change was slow. Some bosses behaved like paternal barons; no one challenged their authority, but their own departments' staff were protected from incursions by other departments. Most so-called managers were really administrators. Even today the word 'clerk' is sometimes used by old hands to refer to these levels.

A new Managing Director was appointed in 1993 and immediately set about changing the culture in the direction of introducing the best features of the 'achievement' and 'support' models. His approach was highly sensitive to the company's history, and realistic in terms of what could be achieved without significant disruption. His method was to give a strong lead from the front, to 'walk the talk' and visibly demonstrate the kind of behaviour he wanted to see. He broke all the norms, especially focusing on giving direction rather than trying to manage and control managers' everyday actions. Where possible, he gave managers who had repressed potential the developmental resources to prove their ability. Where managers seemed stale, rather than dispose of them he swapped them around. Any softness with individuals was complemented with firmness about how the business needed to change, become competitive, be flexible and keep control over costs.

Two years later the green shoots of success are starting to appear. While there is still much frustration at how long it takes to make this kind of internal change without resorting to blood-letting, there are clear signs that it is paying off financially. Revenue is up by £1m and profits by £1.6m. In terms of behaviour, a few managers who were initially wary now speak openly of being 'converts', feeling free to unleash their opinions and demonstrate their impatience. While this positive energy is welcomed in one sense, unless channelled carefully it antagonizes those who are not yet ready to march in step. Making this kind of evolutionary change is exhausting and calls for the patience of Job. But in a tough economic environment, the improving bottom line buys time to persist with the culture-change programme.

ACTIVITY 10.4

Compare your own company's development culture against the dimensions shown. How does your culture foster, or fail to foster, positive attitudes and processes concerned with development?

REFERENCES

1. George Litwin *et al*. (1978) 'Organizational Climate: A Proven Tool for Improving Performance', *The Cutting Edge*, The Forum Corporation of North America.
2. Gerard Egan (1994) 'Cultivate Your Culture', *Management Today*, April.
3. W. Warner Burke, George H. Litwin *et al*. (1991) 'Organizational Climate', *Theories and Models in Applied Behavioral Science*, San Diego: Pfeiffer & Co.
4. Roger Harrison and Juliann Spoth (1992) 'Matching Change Interventions to Organizational Realities', *Industrial and Commercial Training*, **24** (2).
5. W. Warner Burke and George H. Litwin (1992) 'A Causal Model of Organizational Performance and Change', *Journal of Management*, **18** (3), pp. 523–45.
6. Henry Mintzberg (1989) *Mintzberg on Management: Inside our Strange World of Organizations*, New York: The Free Press, pp. 29–34.
7. William Tate (1991) 'The Human Side of Corporate Competitiveness' (book review), *Human Resources Development Journal*, **1** (4).
8. Roger Harrison (1995) *The Collected Papers of Roger Harrison*, Maidenhead: McGraw-Hill, pp. 149–260.
9. Roger Harrison and Herb Stokes (1992) *Diagnosing Organization Cultures*, San Diego: Pfeiffer & Co.
10. Roger Harrison and Celest Powell (1987) 'Organizational Culture and Quality of Service' *From Organization ... to Organism: A New View of Business and Management*, A conference of the Findhorn Foundation.

11
BUILDING A LEARNING
ORGANIZATION

OVERVIEW

This chapter explains what we mean by 'learning organizations', describes what they feel like, discusses approaches to training and learning which are consistent with the concept, and sets out some practical steps which can be taken to move in the desired direction.

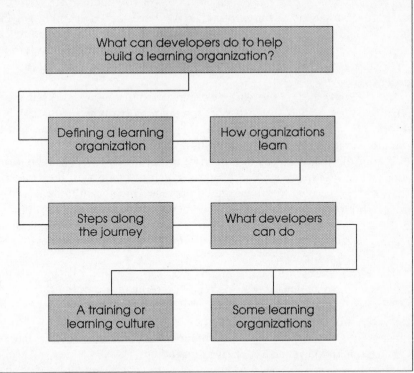

INTRODUCTION

There seems to be an assumption that the features of the **learning organization** are good *per se*. I know one human resources director who expressed the opinion that he did not need to spend time with his fellow directors understanding their business, because it would not influence his advice one jot. He claimed to already know the features of a favourable organizational climate which would be good for *any* company. This was not received favourably.

The HR director's judgement may have been correct to a degree, but it sounded arrogant and was probably not a wise tactic. Line directors and managers have an expectation that developers will need and will want to spend time trying to understand their business. There are, in any case, many other aspects of development activity which *do* need tailoring to the current business circumstances. There seems little choice for developers but to commit time to company business discussions and committees, and then sift the information afterwards for its relevance to development action and options.

But as far as the learning organization aspect is concerned, we shall here assume this HR director's stance; namely, that at the very least, taking the first step in the direction of the learning organization is a good move, that for most companies it will result in a more productive climate, however you define that.

There is a second assumption: that we have lacked learning organizations hitherto, and that the concept is new. Some people have challenged this assumption. It depends on what you mean by a learning organization. Isn't it the same as an organization which learns, and haven't they always needed to do this anyway in order to survive?

If there is an aspect of the learning organization that is controversial, it's whether it has been over-hyped. Is it just another word for a favourable climate? Where does the idea fit with thoughts on climate? Might we alternatively speak of a learning climate or, moving beyond this, a learning culture?

Two of the culture types discussed in the previous chapter (achievement and support) appear to have some features which resonate with the concept of the learning organization. Yet there are companies which claim to be learning organizations but which don't appear to operate under achievement or support cultures. Is this a case of wishful thinking, cunning PR, or muddle-headedness? Or do learning organization claims inevitably amount to legitimate long-term aspirations, rather than current reality?

That's the trouble with bandwagons: you can't be sure who intends going the full distance. Some pay for the ride based on reputation alone without doing their homework. Some receive a jolt and doubt whether they should be on board. Certainly, no one knows where their journey to the land of the learning organization will end. It's a magical mystery tour. By definition, it can have no fixed destination. You never arrive; learning has no end.

Nonetheless, we still need to know something about the journey. What is our own road here to greater understanding? Using the military training principle, we shall begin with the equivalent of naming of parts, i.e. defining terms and explaining concepts. But a learning organization is perhaps less about what you do and more about who you are. So our exploration will need to seek out the values which underpin the concept, in particular the value which most leaderships have a struggle with – openness. This is discussed in detail in the final chapter, 'Developing the Organization to *Be*', where our journey will end with a call for a very different kind of organization from that with which many people are familiar.

WHAT IS A LEARNING ORGANIZATION?

At its simplest, the learning organization is defined by Mike Pedler *et al.* in *Learning Company Project*:

> A learning organisation is one which facilitates the learning of all its members and continuously transforms itself.[1]

In their 1982 bestseller *In Search of Excellence*, Peters and Waterman defined the learning company as:

> the truly adaptive organization [which] evolves in a very Darwinian way. The company is trying lots of things, experimenting, making the right sort of mistakes; that is to say, it is fostering its own mutations.[2]

Writing about his systems view of management in *The Fifth Discipline: The Art and Practice of The Learning Organization*, Peter Senge has added his own definition:

> Organizations where people continually expand their capacity to create the results they desire, where new and expansive patterns of thinking are nurtured, where collective aspiration is set free, and where people are continually learning how to learn together.[3]

Gerard Egan in *Adding Value – A Systematic Guide to Business-Driven Management and Leadership* also puts it very simply:

> What we do around here is learn; we learn continuously and use our learning to improve everything we do.[4]

What these definitions immediately tell us is that an organization which merely makes training opportunities available for all its staff – however imaginative, frequent or well funded – falls a long way short of being a learning organization. Not only is 'training' not the same as 'facilitating the learning of all its members', but it takes no account of the more significant need for the organization itself to be able to adapt.

ADAPTIVE ABILITY

In *Images of Organization*, Gareth Morgan invites us to use metaphorical images to understand organization forms.[5] The learning organization can be likened to a living organism. This conjures up the idea of the organization having the capacity to transform itself. The organization has to contain in its very being – its culture and its climate – a favourable and facilitating environment. This clearly goes far beyond merely having a generous training budget and high-quality provision of resources.

Egan describes the adaptive process:

The more turbulent the environment, the more open these firms must be to learning from the environment and the more quickly they must gear the organization of work, the nature of authority and decision making, communication systems, and employee involvement to constantly evolving conditions. As we approach the twenty-first century, more and more companies are moving toward the 'need to adapt' philosophy because economic, political, social, and industry environments have become more and more turbulent.

Yet organizations, other than in the legal sense, are not entities. They are composed of their individual members. As Alan Mumford reminds us in *Industrial and Commercial Training*,

The actuality of learning is that it is achieved or not achieved by individuals.[6]

And Mumford again:

We all know of individuals who manage to learn with little or no help from 'the organisation'. It is, however, impossible to conceive of a learning organisation, however defined, which exists without individual learners. The learning organisation depends absolutely on the skills, approaches and commitment of individuals of their own learning.[7]

HOW DOES THE ORGANIZATION ITSELF LEARN?

According to Argyris and Schön in *Organizational Learning: A Theory in Action Perspective*,

Organization learning occurs when members of the organization act as learning agents for the organization, responding to changes in the internal and external environments of the organization by detecting and correcting errors in organizational theory-in-use.[8]

This immediately suggests at least three areas of response:

Organization as environment

We need to think of 'the learning organisation as environment', as Mumford expresses it. This favourable environment has to both work for individuals and build up from them too. In my own experience, those whom Mumford describes as 'individuals who learn with little or no contribution from the organisation' often find their organization equally unresponsive to the fruits of their learning. The learning organization must not only value and foster individual learning, but also find ways of using it synergistically.

Changing the framework of rules

It suggests a second and higher level of learning. The first level is simply learning to do things better within the current system rules, presuppositions and constraints. The second level is challenging and changing that framework. It is what Argyris and Schön call double-loop learning. We need to do this for the simple reason which Senge gives that:

as the world becomes more accessible and even the smallest companies can obtain whatever skills and technologies they require at a reasonable cost, so the only way in which competitive advantage is to be achieved is through a company's ability to learn and react more quickly to a fluid market, to be always one step ahead of the rest.[3]

Migrating learning

We need to **migrate** learning around a company. It may be helpful to think of **migration** as relating to the business's core competences in the same way that **transfer** of learning relates to the individual's personal competencies. In their landmark *Harvard Business Review* article 'The Core Competence of the Corporation', C. K. Prahalad and Gary Hamel defined a business's core competencies as 'the collective learning in the organization, especially how to co-ordinate diverse production skills and integrate multiple streams of technologies'. They describe how these core competences reside in individuals and how to manage them as a corporate asset.

LEARNING ORGANIZATIONS VERSUS ORGANIZATIONS WHICH LEARN

Cynics might say that the concept of the learning organization is merely playing with words. In a sense, organizations have been learning as long as there have been organizations, a point well argued by David Boje in *Management Learning*.[10] Organizations have simply lacked the jargon and have not felt under the same modern-day pressure for rapid adaptability. But organizations which failed to learn in the context of their times have always been vulnerable.

There is truth in this. But whether the learning organization constitutes mere evolution along a continuum as Boje claims, or is a paradigm shift as P. Lyons[11] and others declare, the fact remains that there is considerable interest today in what a learning organization looks like, and how, at the very least, it can be further encouraged.

From their research, Hayes, Wheelwright and Clark set out a number of elementary assumptions about human nature in their 'people first' approach, which they claim are preconditions for a learning organization (Figure 11.1).[12]

Lyons presents a list of organization practices (Figure 11.2). Such features of learning organizations both help to describe the concept and contain the forces for making change in this direction.

Calling oneself a learning organization, or aspiring to be one, is clearly not a precondition for the practices listed in Figure 11.2. Equally, an organization might possess many of these, yet still fall short of the ideal. Furthermore, factors in society and world-wide trade are shaping some of these changes, especially the first; they are not all true choices. What is more important is what organizations' power-brokers are doing either to encourage or resist these elements, and why and how they want to capitalize on them.

Baser motives than those which would appeal most to learning organization advocates may be behind the pressure to adopt these modern practices; namely, fashion and copying what the best are claimed to be doing, a search for higher productivity, a wish to bathe in favourable publicity, or sheer competitive pressure. Perhaps I am naïve to believe that the most honourable motives are not necessarily

FIGURE 11.1 LEARNING ORGANIZATION ASSUMPTIONS: A 'PEOPLE FIRST' APPROACH

- All employees are responsible, thinking adults who inherently want to do their best.
- Human resources are too valuable to waste or to leave untapped.
- Creative talents and skills are widely distributed at all levels of an organization and society.
- Workers will surface important problems and concerns if they feel the organization will respond appropriately.
- Work is more interesting when people are challenged in performing it.
- People take pride in training others.
- Better performance occurs when artificial differences in how people are treated are removed.
- Real responsibility motivates high performance.
- People make better decisions, and implement them better, when they work together.

FIGURE 11.2 ORGANIZATIONAL LEARNING PRACTICES

- Embrace diversity in race, gender, age, experience and global perspective.
- Grant importance to continuous improvement; reshaping products or services; refocusing missions.
- Leverage learning with the use of multi-functional and/or cross-functional teams.
- Treat employees as assets or investments.
- Encourage managers and employees to be self-controlled, self-disciplined, self-managed.
- Share important information at all levels.
- View change not as an event but a condition.
- Encourage risk-taking by helping people to be free from a fear of failure.
- Emphasize openness, shared values and information.
- Play down command and control authority/hierarchy.
- Carefully reinforce double-loop or generative learning while retaining single-loop or adaptive learning for routine functions.

market-driven ones or that learning organizations need to be proclaimed loudly. This could lead to a variation of the famous Groucho Marx paradox: don't join a company that boasts about being a learning organization if you really want to belong to one.

KEY TIP

❖   Claimed learning organizations' motives tell you something about whether
        they actually are learning organizations.

STEPS ALONG THE JOURNEY

The climate and culture of a learning organization develop through a number of
phases. It is therefore not so much a case of *being* one, but *seeking* to become more
of one. The journey is more important than the destination. The former manager of
the distance learning unit at the Post Office describes how her organization is 'moving towards an environment in which working and learning become inseparable' as
part of the Post Office's plan to become more a 'learning organization'.

> Success is a journey,
> not a destination.
>   (Anon)

As we said in the chapter's Introduction, by definition the journey has no end.
Herein lies another paradox. An organization which claims to be a learning organization cannot be one since it would deem itself to have arrived there. A true
learning organization can only be one that is still trying to become one!

FIVE PHASES

A comprehensive review of literature and practice by Alan Jones and Chris Hendry[13]
on the subject of learning organizations claimed that companies have to pass
through five phases to qualify for the term 'learning organization':

1.   Foundation/dependency stage
2.   Formation/transitional stage
3.   Continuation/independency stage
4.   Transformation stage
5.   Transfiguration stage

Supporters of the idea (including, presumably, most developers) will want their
organizations to try to move through these stages, or at least some of them. The
start is easy – at least to sign up to! It gradually becomes more demanding. Stage 1
is described as concerned with the following:

○   Learning how to learn.
○   Developing a natural instinct for learning.
○   Creating motivation and confidence.
○   Showing that investment can produce success of various kinds.

If you progress satisfactorily through all the five stages then, in the eyes of Jones
and Hendry, you end up with **transfiguration**. This ultimate stage is said to be
concerned with the following:

○   Transformation plus elevation leading to idealization.
○   People coming first and a concern for society's general welfare and betterment.
○   Asking crucial questions about why the organization exists in the forms that it does.
○   The organization representing a way of life to be cherished because of its values.
○   The organization developing to accommodate and understand global cultures, tolerance, integration and cooperation.

CAN ANYONE HANDLE THIS?

Line managers are almost certainly going to see the language of transfiguration as outlandish. It seems about as far away from bottom-line profits and beating hell out of the competition as you can possibly reach. The learning organization concept contains jargon that frightens many line managers; even the term 'learning organization' itself is too much for some.

This uphill task for developers may eventually moderate by the next century as the hard business talk of the 1980s further recedes, and as the term gains growing acceptance through the natural process of osmosis. Patience and hope are the watchwords. Remember that when *empowerment* broke on the scene in the mid-1980s, it raised eyebrows among advanced trainers who saw it as West-Coast USA, but several years later line managers grasp it willingly (though they do think it has just been invented!). New jargon and ideas always take time to become accepted. But for the moment at least, the more developed forms of the learning organization sound out of reach, certainly for companies in the mainstream of today's business.

A DOSE OF REALISM

Developers would be well advised to stay clear of any talk about the later stages of the development of the learning organization for a long time. If so, they may have little difficulty at the *start* of their journey through their organization's learning milieu. Their line bosses are likely to be positive initially, since it assumes that the learners are still dependent on their organizations and are not showing too much independence. But by the end of the journey, it is expected that the dependency relationship will be reversed. Many traditional bosses may feel that could threaten their control and authority. As parents need and want children, so leaders need and want followers.

'The reality of managerial life determines the nature and effectiveness of any development process,' as Mumford explains, 'and those realities consist of achieving managerial objectives and specific tasks primarily, not achieving the development of others (or even oneself).'[7] But in highlighting the need for developers to both acknowledge and work within those realities, and at the same time seek to change them radically, he provides a test for any management development function:

Unless our management development system provides a counterweight to the dedication to task achievement, there is no prospect of achieving the learning organisation.[7]

KEY TIP

❖   Initially restrict discussion to the early phases of the learning organization.

YESTERDAY'S IDEA FOR TOMORROW

Whether the learning organization will catch on eventually – like empowerment – remains to be seen. It certainly isn't a new idea; it's older than empowerment. For all the publicity which the concept attracts, Reg Revans, the Action Learning pioneer, was writing about this as long ago as 1969. In his paper *The Enterprise as a Learning System*, he stated that among the conditions needed were:

> that its chief executive places high amongst his own responsibilities that for developing the enterprise as a learning system; ... persons at all levels should be encouraged, with their immediate colleagues, to make regular proposals for the study and reorganisation of their own systems of work.[14]

Perhaps the learning organization's time has come.

WHAT CAN DEVELOPERS DO?

There are a number of actions developers can take now to promote the kind of environment in which a learning organization can flourish. On the advice of Jones and Hendry, the organizational factors identified in Figure 11.3 are those which facilitate and inhibit learning. A good place to start is to examine the present learning climate – an important aspect of a learning organization. The Institute of Personnel & Development (formed out of the Institute of Personnel Management (IPM) and the Institute of Training and Development (ITD)) has published a very helpful code of best practice called *An IPM Statement: Continuous Development: People and Work*, available from the IPD's Publications Department. This code may be used as an auditing tool to assess how well an organization fosters continuous development, and it can serve as a planning guide for those attempting to introduce what the IPD calls a continuous development culture.

Such a culture obviously has much in common with references elsewhere in this book to a positive learning climate and to a learning organization. Whilst most thorough and professional, the IPD's code does, however, sound very procedural and appears to have its origins in large, traditional companies, where hierarchies, plans, committees, manuals, representatives and assumed rationality are the stuff of everyday life. For some of the newer, fast-moving, less hierarchical sunrise industries, something looser and more centred on culture and climate than policies might be more in tune. To be fair, the code itself recognizes that 'The CD culture has many and varied characteristics, and each individual organisation that promotes CD will develop its own unique version.' Nonetheless, the IPD considers

FIGURE 11.3 ORGANIZATIONAL FACTORS WHICH FACILITATE OR INHIBIT LEARNING

Factors which facilitate learning

- Opportunities to learn transferable skills
- A wide variety of assignments in a wide variety of situations
- Job challenges, job enrichment and job enlargement
- Time for self-development
- Room for reflection and 'personal space'
- Appraised and fostered teamwork
- Movement between departments and functions
- Open channels to organizational information
- Tangible commitment to training and development
- Well-funded facilities linked to career progression and rewards
- Training linked to the business plan
- Clear understanding of mission and objectives
- Participation and communication

Factors which inhibit learning

- Too much work
- Unrealistic deadlines
- 'Too large' an organization
- Too much specialization
- Where you can't see the end result of your work
- Labelling people with a specific task or status
- Interfunctional rivalries
- Bureaucratic decision making
- Directive management styles
- Mechanistic appraisal schemes

that there are certain key characteristics which are likely to emerge. These are shown in Figure 11.4.

Bear in mind that continuous development, in the IPD's terms at least, is concerned with the individual; the code has nothing to say about teams. This might be taken to imply that the unit of productivity and the source of productivity gains is necessarily the individual, but much of this book has been devoted to explaining that it is the organization and its systems which holds the productivity key. Likewise, the learning organization concept stresses the primacy of teamwork and team learning.

ACTIVITY 11.1

Examine the factors listed in Figure 11.3 and those of the IPD's Code of Best Practice for Continuous Development in Figure 11.4. How well do you think your own organization stands up?

FIGURE 11.4 IPD'S CHARACTERISTICS OF A CONTINUOUS DEVELOPMENT CULTURE

- All understand and share ownership of operational goals.
- Immediate objectives exist and are understood by all.
- New developments are promoted; change is constructive, welcome and enjoyed, not forced and resisted.
- Managers are frequently to be heard discussing learning with their subordinates and colleagues.
- Time is found by all the team to work on individual members' problems.
- Reference documents (manuals, specification sheets, dictionaries and the like) are available to all without difficulty, and are used.
- Colleagues use each other as a resource.
- Members of teams do not just swap information; they tackle problems and create opportunities.
- Team members share responsibility for success or failure; they are not dependent upon one or more leaders.
- Individuals learn while they work, and enjoy both.

Reproduced by courtesy of the Institute of Personnel and Development

MEASURING THE LEARNING CLIMATE

Pedler *et al*. offer a Descriptive Framework (shown in Figure 11.5) which sets out a number of fields of action.[15] Some of the items point clearly at action (e.g. item 11); others are removed from the action and describe how it appears (e.g. item 10). Some are doubtless much easier than others (given agreement by those with the power and resources). Most require considerable planning and lobbying. (Who said that this was supposed to be easy?) What the list does offer, and what this book contributes elsewhere, are pointers for developers to use as they see fit and tailor to their own organizations. This is consequently a mixed list and is not intended to be definitive. The very point about the subject matter is that it should be enabling rather than prescriptive. You can therefore add examples of your own.

FIGURE 11.5 LEARNING ORGANIZATION: DESCRIPTIVE FRAMEWORK

Strategy

1. Learning approach to strategy — Company policy and strategy formation, together with implementation, evaluation and improvement are consciously structured as a learning process enabling continuous improvement through flexibility.

2. Participative policy making — Sharing of involvement in the policy- and strategy-forming processes by all

		members, including the ability to generate and resolve conflict; members include not simply staff but all stakeholders in the company such as customers, owners and neighbours.
	3. Informatting	The use of information technology to inform and empower people, encouraging wider access to information and more 'open' systems.
	4. Formative accounting and control	Systems of accounting, budgeting and reporting are structured to assist learning and add value, encouraging individuals and units to act as small businesses and think about who their customers are.
Looking in	5. Internal exchange	Perception that all internal units and departments are both suppliers to and customers of each other, encouraging wider sharing of expectations and information, negotiating, contracting and providing feedback on goods/services received; fostering an environment of collaboration rather than competition.
	6. Reward flexibility	Using different methods of reward and questioning the use of financial rewards.
Structures	7. Enabling structures	Create opportunities for individual and business development.
Looking out	8. Boundary workers as environmental scanners	Asking for, respecting and using the experience of all members who interact with external customers to feed back information on customer needs.
	9. Inter-company learning	Initiation of mutually advantageous learning activities such as joint training, sharing in investment and job exchanges, including from non-competitors.
Learning opportunities	10. Learning climate	Perception by managers that their primary task is to facilitate experimentation and learning from experience.
	11. Self-development for all	Resources and facilities for self-development are made available to all members, employees at all levels and external stakeholders.

Reproduced by courtesy of McGraw-Hill

Pedler *et al.* offer a questionnaire for measuring the quality of your company's learning climate. This is reproduced as an Appendix at the end of this chapter.[15]

ACTIVITY 11.2

Use the Learning Climate Questionnaire in the Appendix. See if you score highly enough (50–70) to qualify as a legitimate aspirant to become a learning organization

FLATTER HIERARCHIES

Against 'Structures' in Figure 11.5, I would personally add the prevalent idea of flatter hierarchies. One of the principles of a learning organization is that ideas flow freely. Most people have experienced the frustration of having what they consider is a good idea and seeing their boss stamp on it; whereas if it had gone further up it might have enjoyed a sympathetic airing. If a good idea has to go up through a chain, extra levels do nothing to increase its chance of success, but each additional level can put a stop to it. In this respect, the power of the intervening hierarchy up to decision level is wholly negative. Reducing two intervening levels to one increases the odds of the ultimate decision-maker hearing about the idea from two-thirds against to evens.

INFORMATTING

I think this element of the framework should be widened beyond the IT context mentioned in Figure 11.5. In Chapter 9, in dealing with bureaucracy, I mentioned a case example of how to redesign *management by manual*. Those principles were consistent with the concept of the learning organization. I have therefore repeated the salient aspects here.

CASE EXAMPLE: INFORMATTING

One company had a hierarchical and secretive approach to staff rules and entitlements for hundreds of matters such as requesting compassionate leave. There were several manuals, some with coloured sections denoting restricted access above a particular level. This artificially stratified the organization, encouraged a them-and-us attitude, and implied that managers did not have these needs themselves as employees.

I replaced this system with a single open one. The new principle was that staff would now be able to see what discretion their managers had and on what basis they were guided in exercising it.

At the same time, the 'rules' became 'guidelines', with the express right for managers to use their common sense.

Some traditional managers felt exposed by this openness. The trade unions didn't like it because they didn't trust managerial discretion. But we won! The learning organization will not come easily without battles along the way. Established norms will have to be broken; it will take 'norm-busters'.

Companies can produce their own definition and embody this in the form of checklists against which they can benchmark their progress. ICL has done this as a means of measuring its own view of progress towards the holy grail of 100 per cent, and currently claims to stand at around 60 per cent.

ACTIVITY 11.3

Reflect on your company's progress in the direction of a learning organization. What obstacles stand in the way of its adopting the factors in Figure 11.5?

A TRAINING OR LEARNING CULTURE

The above discussion implies a strong need to adopt a new model to replace the **systematic training model**. That model is already in demise without the need for the learning organization to push it, though more nudging wouldn't go amiss! In Chapter 2 we discussed the merits of the **integrated learning model** as its replacement; this is congruent with the learning organization. If you believe whole-heartedly in the learning organization concept, then there can be no fair contest between the models.

But the learning organization is a journey. Even the pioneers are still at their early steps. So shouldn't we expect various shades of transition from training to learning? Should we not be grateful for mere improvements to the systematic training model?

In *A Handbook for Training Strategy*, Martyn Sloman makes a thoughtful and valuable contribution to the discussion with his analysis of various training models.[16] He concludes with views on a more flexible and business-oriented version of the systematic training model. Sloman argues that any new training model must take into account three factors:

1. Training activity needs to be firmly embedded in the organization, thus securing links to strategic objectives and permitting training to operate in a corporate context.
2. The training function has a role in articulating training needs as well as reacting to them.
3. Different organizations are at different stages in terms of training sophistication, and different approaches may therefore be necessary.

For any new model to succeed, Sloman rightly believes that,

> the training function in an organization should not be equated solely with the role and activities of those people who carry the designation 'trainers' ... if the latter are succeeding, training will have become a pervasive activity delivered by many people at all levels – a concept which finds its extreme expression in the learning organization.

But Sloman effectively rejects the full concept of the learning organization on the practical basis that he considers that it is beyond the reach of virtually all developers' line clients. But, even if we accept the reality of this, as I showed in Chapter 2, the alternative of even an improved systematic training model would, *inter alia*, still fail to meet the need for a systems-wide and integrated approach to learning and performance improvement.

ACTIVITY 11.4

Consider what training model your organization is currently working to and how it might move further in the direction of the integrated learning model. What might impede progress?

SYSTEMS-WIDE LEARNING

In *The Fifth Discipline: The Art and Practice of the Learning Organization*, Peter Senge argues that learning organizations successfully manage the convergence of five disciplines:[3]

1.   Personal mastery: the capacity to clarify what is most important to the individual.
2.   Team learning: based on a dialogue in which assumptions are suspended so that genuine thinking together occurs.
3.   Mental models: the capacity to reflect on internal pictures of the world to see how they shape actions
4.   Shared vision: the ability to build a sense of commitment in a group based on what people would really like to create.
5.   Systems thinking: the capacity for putting things together and seeking holistic solutions.

It is this fifth discipline, systems thinking, which holds the key as far as Senge is concerned. It gives his book its title.

> It is the discipline that integrates the disciplines, fusing them into a coherent body of theory and practice. It keeps them from being separate gimmicks or the latest organization change fads. Without a systemic orientation, there is no motivation to look at how the disciplines interrelate. By enhancing each of the other disciplines, it continually reminds us that the whole can exceed the sum of the parts.

Jones and Hendry argue that 'looking holistically at what happens in organizations is likely to provide richer and more authentic analysis and information'.[13] They identify their own five key elements:

1.   Team learning.
2.   Changing power structures.
3.   Leading change.
4.   Giving vision.
5.   Concern for social and ethical issues.

Egan[4] and Burke[17] likewise argue – from slightly different standpoints – for integrated, system-wide perspectives and interventions. However you classify the elements, the message remains the same: take an holistic approach.

In spite of this powerful advocacy, it is clear that many trainers nevertheless remain prone to compartmentalizing the concept, conduct, organization and evaluation of training. Most organizations' models are still heavily training-led and largely unintegrated with other system variables.

ACTIVITY 11.5

Reflect on how management training and development activity is conducted in relation to other organization system variables. Are interventions wholly training-led or are they well integrated?

We should be disappointed when training interventions are accepted as independent interventions, but we should not be taken aback. Given the incessant talk nationally of 'training' as *the* cure, coupled with the vested interests in training departments, the search for new *training* models, rather than *learning* models, comes as no surprise. Training has a strong political attraction, both inside and outside the company.

But we should at least accept that this emphasis on 'training delivery', even at 'its extreme expression',[16] including line manager involvement falls well short of any attempt at the learning organization concept. The learning organization clearly demands a *learning culture*, not a *training culture*. BP recognized this in appointing a Head of Organizational Learning. In the same vein, the Prudential has a Manager Change and Learning Development. Changing titles like this has a powerful psychological effect: it switches attention away from the giving process. For managers in particular it brings home the truth that seeking specific and predictable needs for which training has the answers is a vain search for fast-vanishing stability.

The problem is that many companies already have inadequate training functions, and a full-blown switch to a learning orientation is beyond them. For many, therefore, perhaps there *is* a case for an intermediate stage, one which merely sets out to improve training. (Chapter 12, 'Forming a Development Strategy', includes sections on 'Conducting Training Strategy Reviews' and 'How Best to Structure Training Activity'.)

DO WE HAVE ANY LEARNING ORGANIZATIONS?

Whether the fully developed learning organization is attainable, let alone desirable, remains to be seen. Could such a radically different ambience and power structure still deliver results? What would we then accept as results? We still need more experimentation and research so we can learn more about learning organizations: the necessary conditions for their evolution, their processes and their consequences.

Jones and Hendry claim that no learning organizations exist at present.[13] If they did, we should probably fail to recognize them as they would not look like businesses as we know them today. This has not deterred several companies from already claiming to be learning organizations. Many more have been credited by others with that accolade. Figure 11.6 contains a list of some of the better known examples.

It is sometimes assumed that because a particular company has successfully undergone profound change and transformed itself in the eyes of its customers, and if it can claim to have actively managed that process, then by definition it is a learning organization. That is an over-simplification. Transformation can be achieved in a variety of ways and manifest its new-found being in a variety of forms which may be unsympathetic to some of the key values of the learning organization. Furthermore, who is to be the judge?

A good test would be how it feels to employees inside such organizations, particularly those companies claiming the label for themselves. Perhaps it is the people who work there, rather than customers, owners, boards and admirers, who should be allowed to confer the honour. It may then not be granted quite so readily. While alleged learning organizations may proclaim their new-found values, to those working inside them they may still seem like hire-and-fire companies, appearing to capitalize on fear and insecurity, and merely using the catch-phrase for propaganda purposes.

Cynicism apart, the list shows a welcome interest and awareness and probably considerable effort in the right direction. There is certainly a different feel to some of these organizations. As Jones and Hendry say: a company 'which does not attempt to develop itself into a full learning organisation will remain "an unfinished

FIGURE 11.6 CLAIMED EXAMPLES OF LEARNING ORGANIZATIONS

Their own claim

TMI	Sun Alliance	Sheerness Steel
Grandmet	TSB	Newlands Preparatory School
Russell & Brand	Nabisco	Manchester Airport
Canon	Digital	Royal Borough of Windsor & Maidenhead

Others' attribution

JCB	British Airways	Guardian Royal Exchange
Tioxide	Gatwick Airport	American Express
ICI	Lucas	Shell
ICL	IBM	Cadbury-Schweppes
Rylands Whitecross	GKN	Greater Glasgow Tourist Board
Komatsu	Massey Ferguson	Rover Cars

business" '.[13] While they may not be there (almost certainly are not by the previously mentioned yardsticks) these companies are at least trying.

PERMANENT TRANSITION

One of the features of learning organizations is that, like any learning organism, they are permanently in transition – they are learning! They are therefore likely to display many characteristics of uncertainty and confusion, as they struggle to balance contradictions like top-down controls and bottom-up responsibility, and maximizing profit for the shareholders while showing a social responsibility towards the community.

The trouble is that the organization, while having values in one sense, is not an entity, but a collection of individuals with their own values and favoured direction for the company. Developers are probably trying to pull the company in the direction of a learning organization's values and features, while the chief executive may at best understand only the label's publicity value. It is not easy to test where a company is on the spectrum of the learning organization.

The question of an organization's motives for seeking either the actuality or the publicity of labels such as 'learning organization' or 'investor in people', is discussed in the final chapter when we consider some ethical issues.

REFERENCES

1. Mike Pedler, Tom Boydell and John Burgoyne (1988) *Learning Company Project: A Report on Work undertaken October 1987 to April 1988*, Sheffield: Training Agency, p. 1.
2. Tom Peters and Robert Waterman (1982) *In Search of Excellence: Lessons from America's Best-Run Companies*, London: Harper and Row.
3. Peter Senge (1990) *The Fifth Discipline: The Art and Practice of The Learning Organization*, London: Business Books, p. 12.
4. Gerard Egan (1993) *Adding Value – A Systematic Guide to Business-Driven Management and Leadership*, San Francisco: Jossey-Bass, p. 168.
5. Gareth Morgan (1986) *Images of Organization*, London: Sage.
6. Alan Mumford (1990) 'The Individual and Learning Opportunities', *Industrial and Commercial Training*, **22** (1).
7. Alan Mumford (1991) 'Individual and Organisational Learning', *Industrial and Commercial Training*, **23** (6).
8. Chris Argyris and D. Schön (1978) *Organizational Learning: A Theory in Action Perspective*, Wokingham: Addison-Wesley.
9. C. K. Prahalad and Gary Hamel (1990) 'The Core Competence of the Corporation', *Harvard Business Review*, May–June, p. 82.
10. David Boje (1994) 'Organizational Storytelling: The Struggles of Pre-modern, Modern and Post-modern Organizational Learning Discourses', *Management Learning*, London: Sage, **25** (3).

11. P. Lyons (1993) 'People Skills and the Learning Organization', *OL: The Organizational Newsletter*, 4 (March), pp. 7–9.
12. R. H. Hayes., S. C. Wheelwright and K. B. Clark (1988) *Dynamic Manufacturing: Creating the Learning Organization*, New York: The Free Press.
13. Alan Jones and Chris Hendry (1992) *The Learning Organization: A Review of Literature and Practice*, London: Human Resource Development Partnership.
14. R. W. Revans (1969) 'The Enterprise as a Learning System', Fondation Industrie-Université, Brussels, May.
15. Mike Pedler, John Burgoyne and Tom Boydell (1991) *The Learning Company – A Strategy for Sustainable Development*, Maidenhead: McGraw-Hill.
16. Martyn Sloman (1994) *A Handbook for Training Strategy*, Aldershot: Gower, pp 21-42, 165.
17. W. Warner Burke and George H. Litwin (1992) 'A Causal Model of Organizational Performance and Change', *Journal of Management*, **18** (3), pp. 523–45.

APPENDIX: LEARNING CLIMATE QUESTIONNAIRE[1]

One of the defining characteristics of the Learning Company is of being a place that encourages everyone in it or who has contact with it to learn. It has the 'learning habit' so that actions taken for reasons of production, marketing, problem-solving or customer service also yield a harvest of reflections, insights and new ideas for action.

Here is a simple questionnaire that you can use to measure the learning climate of your company, department or team.

For each of the following ten dimensions, ring the number that you think best represents the quality of the Learning Climate in your company, 1 being very poor, 7 being excellent:

1. Physical environment

The amount and quality of space and privacy afforded to people; the temperature, noise, ventilation and comfort levels.

People are cramped with   1 2 3 4 5 6 7   People have plenty of
little privacy and poor   space, privacy and
conditions.   good surroundings.

2. Learning resources

Numbers, quality and availability of training and development staff, also books, films, training packages, equipment, etc.

Very few or no trained   1 2 3 4 5 6 7   Many development
people, poor resources   people and lots of
and equipment.   resources; very good
                                                  facilities.

3. Encouragement to learn

The extent to which people feel encouraged to have ideas, take risks, experiment and learn new ways of doing old tasks.

Little encouragement to   1 2 3 4 5 6 7   People are encouraged
learn; there are low   to learn at all times and
expectations of people in   to extend themselves
terms of new skills and   and their knowledge.
abilities.

4. Communications

How open and free is the flow of information? Do people express ideas and opinions easily and openly?

Feelings kept to self;   1 2 3 4 5 6 7   People are usually
secretive; information is   ready to give their
hoarded.   views and pass on
                                                  information.

5. Rewards

How well rewarded are people for effort? Is recognition given for good work or are people punished and blamed?

People are ignored and then blamed when things go wrong.	1 2 3 4 5 6 7	People are recognised for good work and rewarded for effort and learning.

6. Conformity

The extent to which people are expected to conform to rules, norms, regulations, policies, rather than think for themselves.

There is conformity to rules and standards at all times – no personal responsibility taken or given.	1 2 3 4 5 6 7	People manage themselves and do their work as they see fit; great emphasis on taking personal responsibility.

7. Value placed on ideas

How much are ideas, opinions and suggestions sought out, encouraged and valued?

People are 'not paid to think'; their ideas are not valued.	1 2 3 4 5 6 7	Efforts are made to get people to put ideas forward; there is a view that the future rests on people's ideas.

8. Practical help available

The extent to which people help each other, lend a hand, offer skills, knowledge or support.

People don't help each other; there is unwillingness to pool or share resources.	1 2 3 4 5 6 7	People very willing and helpful; pleasure is taken in the success of others.

9. Warmth and support

How friendly are people in the company? Do people support, trust and like one another?

Little warmth and support; this is a cold, isolating place.	1 2 3 4 5 6 7	Warm and friendly place; people enjoy coming to work; good relationships = good work.

10. Standards

The emphasis placed upon quality in all things; people set challenging standards for themselves and each other.

| Low standards and quality; no one really gives a damn. | 1 2 3 4 5 6 7 | High standards; everone cares and people pick each other up on quality. |

SCORING

If your score comes to 30 or less, you're working in a *poor* learning climate. Learning companies aspire to scores in the 50–70 range as the best guarantee of future survival, maintenance and development.

If you carry out a survey of the company, you may find differences in the various parts of the organisation. How do you explain this? The person in charge of a department usually has the biggest influence on the learning climate. Does that person have the development of an excellent learning climate as a key objective?

[1] This questionnaire is reproduced by kind permission of McGraw-Hill.

PART FIVE
STRATEGIES FOR THE FUTURE

❖

12
FORMING A DEVELOPMENT STRATEGY

OVERVIEW

This chapter presents a strategic framework to help readers compile action plans for the future of development in their organization.

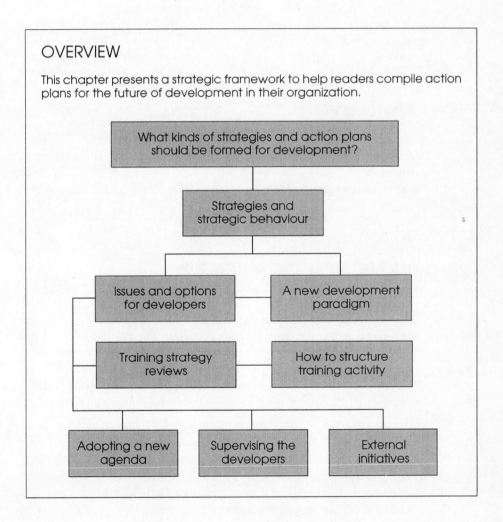

INTRODUCTION

I f a company's development function is to fulfil its own potential and achieve a significant impact on the company's future well-being, it needs well thought-out action plans which draw on a development strategy. Or, more precisely, it needs a number of development strategies. We therefore first need to reflect on the various forms which strategies can take, the processes used for deriving them, and who should be involved. Only then can we begin work on their content.

As well as needing development strategies, a company has – or should have – a number of other strategic requirements of its development function and its professional members. Among these are the following abilities:

O   To demonstrate strategic thinking and strategic behaviour.
O   To understand, listen and interact openly with the environment – inside and outside.
O   To take account of the business, organizational, political and social context.
O   To develop a vision for the function and take control over purpose and plans, rather than being swamped by reacting to day-to-day operational and delivery issues.
O   To stand to one side, reflect afresh, and challenge the ways things are.
O   To take an independent, values-driven stance, when required.
O   To envision and operate across a broad perspective of potential development activity.
O   To apply techniques for looking piercingly at *what is*, as well as *what might be*.

STRATEGIES AND STRATEGIC BEHAVIOUR

We are traditionally led to expect that clarity of purpose will be delivered in the form of well-considered, sustainable, and clearly promulgated strategies that bosses will pass down to us so that we know what we have to do. But this hierarchical model is deferential and disempowering, quite out of tune with the times in which we live. Henry Mintzberg of McGill University of Montreal has also shown it to be naïve and fraudulent.[1] He blew the rational strategy–plan–act concept out of the water with his radical ideas some years ago. In particular, Mintzberg showed us that:

O   Strategies have a habit of *emerging* from and as part of a fluid, interactive process with what is already happening and changing. As they evolve, these incipient strategies rely on feedback from a learning organization. How strategies form is more important than how they are formulated.
O   Conventional wisdom equates strategy with 'plan'. But there are several other ways of looking at the concept of strategy, which Mintzberg calls the *5 Ps*: plans, positions, perspectives, patterns and ploys.[2]

TYPES OF STRATEGY

Mintzberg has helped open the mind to what strategy may look like. To help exemplify the concept for readers, I have set down in Figure 12.1 some examples of a few implicit and explicit strategies from a context I am familiar with: British Airways.

FIGURE 12.1   EXAMPLES OF IMPLICIT AND EXPLICIT BRITISH AIRWAYS STRATEGIES – A PERSONAL VIEW

Position
- To be the best.
- To cover the world, even if thinly.
- To be in favour of lower fares in Europe.

Plans
- To seek partners and alliances.
- To decentralize resources away from Heathrow.
- To exploit revenue opportunities outside airline context (e.g. selling information technology).

Perspectives
- Let the customer be the judge.
- Accept the inevitability of deregulation.
- View the airline business like any other commercial/marketing activity.

Patterns
- Over-engineered and over-complex.
- No expense spared on product.
- Freedom for subsidiaries at expense of Group image.

Ploys
- Put pressure on foreign competitor nationalized airlines to privatize.
- Talk a lot about the need to cut costs.
- Support the green movement.

It has to be admitted that when faced with this broad and imaginative model for looking at strategy, the more hierarchically minded managers can be found rushing for the security of their boss–subordinate dependency structure. Either they don't want the responsibility of being seen to be concerned with strategy other than implementing someone else's, or in their own role as boss they don't want subordinates thinking they can mess with the boss's strategies.

But assuming that developers do not behave so defensively, as a starting point you may find it helpful to classify your own current development strategies using this 5P taxonomy. You may discover you already have more strategies than you realize. You are then better placed to start challenging them and to see where the gaps are.

OVERT AND COVERT STRATEGIES

There are far more unannounced strategies than public ones. Many remain covert, for a variety of reasons:

○   Some strategies cannot be publicized for tactical reasons, so that competitors will not hear about them and will be left guessing.

○   Some employment strategies need to be kept from the employees, general
public and press, because they may be considered unpalatable or suspect
(e.g. those for insurance salesmen).

○   Some remain unfinished business and are therefore never announced for
fear of criticism or early obsolescence.

○   Some are so sensitive that they can't be written down or even given the
label 'strategy'; they are undiscussed, and their existence in any form is
undiscussible and has to be inferred privately.

○   Some exist in the form of a long-established and significant pattern of business behaviour, and may be construed as constituting strategy by default.

○   Some strategies are what Mintzberg calls 'ploys'. They are not quite what
they seem.

○   Some might receive a quizzical look, even a cynical reaction, from those
hearing them. An example might be 'Let the customer be the judge'. Some
strategies are better left to permeate the organization's bloodstream and
seep subliminally into its environment by osmosis.

ACTIVITY 12.1

You may find it helpful to draw up a list of your current development
strategies, overt and covert, using the 5P model. See which need
reconsidering, and look for any obvious gaps. How good is the fit with the
company's business strategies?

DEVELOPMENT'S PROBLEMS WITH THE OLD STRATEGY CONCEPT

From a development perspective there are many problems with the old way of
thinking about strategy:

○   Bosses are neither sufficiently clever nor informed.
○   The conventional top-down view of strategy dissemination is disempowering to managers at large who can play a much fuller role in developing
strategies.
○   The world of business, its environment, and the complexity of most organizations militates against a handful of people having sufficient information
and understanding to carry out all the strategy-setting work on their own.
They need all the help they can get.
○   There are many functional areas which need strategies: competitor
strategy, cash-flow strategy, advertising strategy, employment strategy,
even management and organization development strategy. There is no
shortage of strategizing work to go round, and it needs the expertise and
involvement of many managers and specialists.

○   The environment is changing so quickly that strategies need continued vigilance, updating, and flexibility in form and interpretation, so all managers need to be involved.

○   Traditional thinking fails to make a distinction between strategies on the one hand, and a strategic way of thinking and strategic behaviour on the other. If we defer to the former, we might all miss out on the latter.

A strategic way of thinking

One of the biggest failings in senior managers is the inability to think strategically – never mind *having* strategies. We appoint senior managers based on all sorts of criteria, but often overlook this key one. Many lack the ability to work out what is really worth their time and what not to bother with. We train managers in *how* to delegate but not in *what* to delegate.

I earlier cited the case of the executive board that wanted to know how many people I had trained in the last month. They were more interested in monitoring my efficiency than my effectiveness. How short-sighted. What they should have wanted to know was whether my training department was making a difference. Behaving strategically means knowing what questions to ask and what data to call for.

Functional analysis

Strategic thinking is one of the problem areas with the process of functional analysis – the means of understanding what managers do. The technique of functional analysis is used to establish competences, which are then applied to selection, training, assessment and compensation. Unfortunately, strategic thinking is not readily observable. When you repeatedly cascade the question, 'And what do you need to do in order to achieve that?', you tend not to receive the answer, 'I think strategically.'

Strategy abdication

I mentioned under 'Signs of Entropy' in Chapter 9 the danger signal of managers complaining to the chief executive that they lack a strategy. Even worse is when the boss half accepts the criticism, believing that his or her only mistake might be in a failure in presentation; the managers have simply failed to understand. It is rather like the unpopular politicians who refuse to re-examine their policies, and instead blame their publicity departments. The chief executive should tell the managers to get in there and lend a hand.

Strategy protectionism

Many directors misguidedly try to over-differentiate their role from their managers' by claiming a unique responsibility for the company's strategy – a role they guard jealously. Directors would be on safer ground if they differentiated between the process of evolving strategy, holding legal responsibility for it, and communicating it. And they should distinguish between macro business strategy and multiple consequential and functional strategies.

STRATEGIC RESPONSIBILITY FOR THE ORGANIZATION

A key difference between the role of senior managers compared with lower levels (as highlighted in MCI's management standards) is senior managers' strategic organizational responsibility: they are required to 'review and improve the organization's structures and systems', and 'plan how to develop the effectiveness of the management team'. This is the organizational equivalent of double-loop learning: not simply managing what is there, but also changing it.

But this statement of responsibility should not fool developers into thinking that if they develop individual senior managers, all will be well with the organization. As I pointed out earlier, the holy grail of corporate competence isn't to be discovered as simply as this. Many strategic organization changes cannot be promoted, let alone managed, by individual senior managers: they require developers to be proactive at this supra-manager level of intervention.

DEVELOPING BUSINESS STRATEGIES

Given that strategy-making is often held close to the chest, it is a surprise that developers quite frequently get involved in running business strategy programmes for senior managers. Potential directors are trained in how to undertake the activity, often by playing at the real thing. In other words, the aim of such a programme is to 'develop an alternative business strategy for your company'. Earlier in the book I mentioned a company, a large bakery, which tried this. The directors sanctioned it, but didn't take part themselves. The senior managers hoped their play/real strategies would be well received by the Board of Directors. Inevitably, the Board rejected them. How could they do otherwise without committing job suicide? The senior managers felt badly let down. Playing with business strategy is playing with fire. For any readers involved with this kind of strategy development programme, there are several lessons here.

KEY TIPS

❖   Attempt to develop the directors and their business strategy first.

❖   Don't confuse play with real. And don't think you can get round this by repeating 'the strategies are only a learning vehicle'.

❖   Develop managers for current responsibilities before possible future ones.

Also bear in mind that while all managers can probably behave more strategically than they do, not all are cut out to be strategists. People's interests, strengths and energies differ. Nor should you want it otherwise. You are unlikely to find the highest levels of long-term strategic reflection combined with the short-term ability to drive action forward. We want a rich and practical ability mix within teams.

RELATING DEVELOPMENT ACTION TO BUSINESS STRATEGY

Developers frequently attend meetings where the company's detailed business is discussed. If you attend a developers' conference, you will find that speakers spend considerable time talking impressively about their company's business. It has become *de rigueur*. Why?

In reality, much of the detailed business transacted at such meetings is not directly relevant to development. But the developers cannot easily predict this, and they may be genuinely interested and need to appear so. There are two types of business, and it may be helpful to pass them through the appropriate filter. Developers' work on improving the company climate is largely unaffected by what they are likely to hear at such meetings. Concepts such as the learning organization have merit in their own right. But a policy such as developing local management overseas to take over from expatriate management would clearly be affected by business plans. At such policy-type meetings, the interdependence runs both ways: some business plans may be affected by development's ability to deliver.

BEING OPEN ABOUT YOUR STRATEGIES

Openness is a highly sensitive matter. Earlier in the book we discussed the need for organizations to develop empowered followers who have the means and courage to challenge their leaders and keep them on the straight and narrow, citing Robert Maxwell as a case in point. Powerful leaders can develop into the modern-day equivalent of robber barons, arrogant and insensitive, often blinkered and motivated by short-term self-interest. They rarely relish frank advice or having their views challenged. Part of the developer's strategy therefore needs to take political account of the conflict between developing followers who are good for the organization's long-term health, and more compliant ones.

This reminds us of the earlier discussion concerning 'Who is the client?' Where there are painful dilemmas like this, should we still be thinking of the chief executive as the client? Or can we think of the client as being the company, its shareholders, or all those who have a stake in it? Even if you would like to believe that the client is one of these alternative groups, doesn't the chief executive remain the legitimate embodiment and representative of that group anyway? There are no right answers here. Writ small and in a different context, this is the perennial problem faced by whistle-blowers.

The question I am raising is whether any part of the developer's strategy will need to remain covert for political reasons and for self-protection. I am not advocating sedition, only pointing out what may be a painful dilemma. (I discuss some of the choices open to developers, and their ethical ramifications, in the final chapter.)

A PLAN FOR DEVELOPMENT STRATEGIES

Figure 12.2 offers a ten-point plan to help you move forward in this area:

FIGURE 12.2 FORMING STRATEGIES FOR DEVELOPMENT: A TEN-POINT PLAN

1. Don't wait to be given a development strategy. Work on it yourself.

2. Think imaginatively about your company's business and other key strategies (both overt and covert) and relate your own strategy-planning work accordingly.

3. Interpret the concept of development 'strategy' broadly to comprise plans, positions, perspectives, patterns and ploys.

4. Accept strategies that *emerge*, rather than just those created deliberately in isolation for launching on an unsuspecting world.

5. Even if you lack formal published strategies, learn to behave more strategically:
   - Stand back and reflect.
   - Work more upstream (don't just fish bodies out of the water; stop those who are throwing them in).
   - Ask the question where are you headed and why.
   - 'Read' the environment and be informed by it.
   - Recognize and respond to challenges.
   - Confront traditional thinking.

6. Continually monitor and update your strategies as part of the learning process.

7. Help your boss understand your strategies and feel ownership of them.

8. Involve others around you: bosses, clients, peers, subordinates.

9. Develop a strategy for developing your strategy:
   - Who is going to be involved?
   - How long will you give yourself?
   - Who will you regard as your client?
   - Where is the pressure coming from?
   - Will you need to budget for it?
   - How public will it be?

10. Be open with what you are doing as far as practicable.

KEY TIP

❖　　　Don't simply think in terms of a strategy; behave more strategically too.

TOWARDS A NEW DEVELOPMENT PARADIGM

Notwithstanding jokes about US Presidential cynicism and blind spots concerning 'the vision thing', recent years have seen a boom in business for the art of developing a vision. The assumption was that we had no difficulty in seeing where we were; what we lacked was the means of imagining and articulating a better future – more efficient, comradely, prosperous, buoyant, valuable, or whatever.

This analysis of where we lack a key skill may be true at the grand level of envisaging the heart of the business's long-term future, where predicting market winners is an important art (for example, foreseeing the demise of mainframe computers in favour of PCs on every desk). Likewise, making practical and integrated use of our vision as a unifying, motivating and driving force also seems elusive. At the personal level too, envisioning a different future for ourselves can be difficult. But at the detailed organization level, I believe the reverse is often the case. It seems to me that we often have relatively little difficulty in articulating how we would like things to be, but current-state diagnoses are either taken for granted or are lamentably superficial.

In terms of the classic A → B change process, we find B easier to define adequately than A. Developers may have a clear vision of the healthy organization irrespective of the business. On a small scale, we may simply define B in terms of A: B may be no more than the absence of A. Future health may be the absence of current pain. So until we have defined A, we may have difficulty articulating B; but having defined A, B may be self-evident. However, although B may be adequately defined for our purpose, it cannot be pinned down in any permanent sense; B is only a transient aimed-for condition.

I hope the book's earlier chapters on analytical and diagnostic methods will have helped readers to better understand the current state. And I hope this concluding chapter will provide them with the strategic means to achieve their own future – whatever and wherever they decide 'there' might be. In Figure 12.3 I have set out my own vision for a new paradigm for the development function as a whole.

FIGURE 12.3 TOWARDS A NEW DEVELOPMENT PARADIGM

Old paradigm	New paradigm
• Mainly manager development	• Mainly management/ organization development
• Individual focus	• More team and group focus
• People focus	• People, systems and climate focus
• Separated from work situations	• Integrated with work situations
• Solves abstract problems	• Solves real problems
• Independent interventions	• Multi-pronged, supporting interventions
• Job driven	• People driven
• Hierarchically determined	• Learner determined
• Career motivated	• Growth motivated
• Short-term benefit oriented	• Long-term benefit oriented
• Trainer-led needs diagnosis	• Performance-led needs diagnosis
• Mostly training	• Education/training balanced and distinctive
• Formal and infrequent learning experiences	• Varied, all-round, continuous learning experiences

DEVELOPMENT ISSUES AND OPTIONS

There are many detailed options to be considered, for example practical issues like how your company will resource the planned activities. Most of these issues have already been raised in one way or another in the earlier chapters. Figure 12.4 summarizes a number of the bigger questions.

FIGURE 12.4 DEVELOPING THE ORGANIZATION'S MANAGEMENT: ISSUES AND OPTIONS

Business direction and needs

1. How can development best support your company's business plans and chosen direction?
2. How can development best respond to general trends in the business world?
3. What particular current company problems can development directly try to solve with its activities?

Target learners

4. What current level of capability is there generally in your company's managers?
5. What competence do you need to develop?
6. How and how much do you want managers to take responsibility for their own development?
7. On what groups, levels and disciplines do you need and want to expend most effort?
8. What are your highest and lowest priorities?

Corporate culture, values and style

9. Does the organization have a distinct culture or culture shift it wishes to promote?
10. Is development expected to and able to lead this?
11. Is there a core requirement for all managers in order to generate a distinctive corporate style?
12. How good is the fit between the development culture and the organization's culture?
13. How important in the company are managerial qualifications, such as MBAs and NVQs?

Practical response by development

14. Where can line management expertise be home grown, and where will it have to be hired?
15. What skills do we have in the development function and what do we need?
16. What should be resourced inside and what outside?
17. Where can development expertise be home grown, and where will it have to be hired?
18. What should the terms of reference be for the development function?
19. How should development organizationally relate to other personnel specialisms?

---

20. How can we balance traditional learning methods with modern open learning approaches?
21. How can we reinforce learning interventions with other comple- mentary organization action?

Political environment

22. What are the painful political issues that will have to be confronted?
23. Who are your most powerful allies who can support new strategies for development?
24. Where do you need improved access? How might you achieve it?
25. How much freedom do you have to change development's role and develop new strategies?
26. What are the biggest organizational obstacles to your achieving development's aims?

Image

27. What image do you and/or the development function currently have that may need to be worked on?
28. How high a profile should you give development, inside and outside?

Evaluation

29. How will the organization monitor and audit the development function to ensure it's getting sound advice and value for money?
30. How can you help your line boss manage your work and advice in an informed and objective manner?

ACTIVITY 12.2

Review the questions raised in Figure 12.4 and see which are relevant for you at this time.

CONDUCTING TRAINING STRATEGY REVIEWS

One company I dealt with appointed a new training director with a view to undertaking a substantial review of its approach to training. The company wanted to develop a training strategy. In Figure 12.5 I show the range of agenda issues which I developed for us both to consider.

HOW BEST TO STRUCTURE TRAINING ACTIVITY

Earlier in the book we discussed a possible mission for the range of activities we labelled Management and Organization Development. The full mission statement (in the Appendix to Chapter 1, p. 23) laid down broad terms of reference for such

FIGURE 12.5 REVIEWING TRAINING STRATEGY: CRITICAL AGENDA QUESTIONS

On present position and practice

1. What are your unit's strengths and weaknesses? What are its opportunities and threats?
2. What training are you currently carrying out? Where are you 'coming from' generally?
3. How are training needs/performance needs currently analysed and established?
4. What are you achieving?
5. What feedback do you receive from your customers (e.g. learners and their bosses)?
6. What are your managers' current perceptions and expectations of what you provide?
7. What are your current forward commitments?
8. Are you given any targets?
9. How generous a budget are you allowed? What proportion of company revenue is spent on training?
10. What resources and facilities do you have or could be expected to have?
11. How do you balance training to solve known problems versus opening doors to new possibilities?
12. What are your standards for trainers?
13. How does the line get involved in training (e.g. support, mentoring, coaching)?

On the organization's management performance

14. What is currently holding back the organization?
15. What are the main obstacles to managers doing a better job?
16. How skilled are you at analysing these wider management performance issues?
17. What access do you have to these wider management performance issues?
18. How good is teamwork in and across departments?
19. How well qualified in formal terms are your managers for the tasks they need to perform?
20. How capable are your managers viewed generally?
21. Have you any aggregate performance data (e.g. from appraisals or competency analyses)?

On the organization's culture and climate

22. How important are managers' qualifications in this organization?
23. How stratified is the hierarchy (élitism, status, protocol, fast-trackers, etc.)?
24. What is the working climate like?
25. What issues cannot be discussed?
26. How important are means versus ends in this organization?
27. How free and diverse is management style and behaviour?
28. Has the company taken a view on the competence-based approach for management?

29. What sort of people 'get on'?
30. What do people get kicked for?
31. What factors are formally built into appraisal?
32. What is the bottom line?
33. How easily are people satisfied around here?
34. How far down the road is the company as a learning organization?
35. What recognition is given to team performance versus individual performance?
36. Is training seen as something the company provides or something managers do for themselves?
37. Are any management groups deemed beyond need of your training service?
38. How does the organization culture need to change?

On personnel and employment matters

39. How does your labour market affect your hiring or losing of talented managers?
40. What company employment policies and practices have an impact on training?
41. Are there any new policy needs for training (e.g. training vouchers, OU sponsorship)?
42. What performance management and appraisal processes interact with training?

On politics and processes

43. What access do you have to your Board's strategic business plan?
44. What is in that plan that could have a bearing on training?
45. Do you want to be involved in national initiatives (NVQs, IiP, national training awards, lead bodies, MCI)?
46. What are your publicity channels? How well do they work for you?
47. How high profile do you want training to be seen to be, inside and outside?
48. How is training evaluated at macro and micro level?
49. What is your brief? What are your boss's expectations? How long have you got?
50. Who is to be involved in this review process? How private is it?
51. How are you expected to present your new training strategy (e.g. Board paper)?
52. What are the important political issues to be recognized?

a function to establish its boundaries and purpose. This in turn generates a number of (re)organization issues, as will any substantial review of training. A few of these issues are discussed here.

SHOULD MANAGEMENT TRAINING BE LINKED WITH OPERATIONAL/TECHNICAL TRAINING?

There are two schools of thought. Some believe that any kind of training is a distinct professional activity, and that its prime technologies are training and instructional technologies rather than work-oriented ones, including understanding the psychological processes by which people learn. From this viewpoint, training can be carried out only by dedicated career trainers who have training coursing through their veins and who mix with other trainers in a centralized training department that combines all operational and technical training along with that for managers and supervisors.

Whilst the 'one big training department' approach has merit in fostering training expertise, I do not belong to that school. I favour the alternative organization strategy – decentralizing wherever feasible and economically viable on the general premise of getting close to the customer. But I exclude management training from this decentralizing tendency for reasons which will become clear. First, here are the general arguments in favour of decentralizing non-management training:

Accountability

Decentralization enables line directors to feel more accountable for their departments' total performance. It makes it easy for them to say what training they want, when they should release staff for training to be undertaken, and what proportion of their expenditure budget to commit to training versus production.

If, on the other hand, line directors remain dependent on, say, the personnel director to provide them with the right number of suitably trained staff, that presents them with a ready-made excuse for the chief executive when failing to deliver to their business targets. In a centralized arrangement it is commonplace for line directors to compete for the company training manager's resources (classroom places etc.) and to then complain that they receive less than they need.

Self-serving

Training exists only because it has customers and is conducted solely to meet their needs. Separate training departments which are organizationally removed from their line customers can easily lose sight of that fact. They have a tendency to become self-serving and assume too much self-importance. They feel free to decide what needs to be trained, to what standard, and when to call people off the job for training.

Lack of access

Training departments which are not part of the line lack ready access to current day-to-day problems. Their solutions take on the form of fixed, off-the-job courses. Opportunities are lost to provide quick, inexpensive, on-the-job training, one-to-one coaching and other forms of local and spontaneous briefing, instruction and communication.

Relevance

Training activity has to be directly relevant and integrated with each department's requirement to deliver against its mission. Staff returning from centrally run training are often told to forget what they have learnt because 'it's not the way things are done round here'.

Career trainers

Central training departments become staffed with career trainers. They can lose a sympathetic relationship with their customer departments and can become out of touch with technical and other changes in those departments. There is benefit in rotating technical trainers through suitable manager and supervisory positions to keep them abreast of what is happening at the sharp end of the business. But the organization structure and its job classification and grading system militates against this. Furthermore, trainers may be perceived as not good enough to be line managers, the opposite of what should be the case.

Resources

This argument cuts both ways. Central training establishments can become too important in their own right and be overly grand and expensive to run and administer. From time to time they can need cutting down to size. On the other hand, they do permit scope for economies through the sharing of common facilities, equipment, training journals, etc.

By contrast, decentralization is not automatically identified with small, and small is not necessarily beautiful. A number of separate empires, rather than one, can easily grow if allowed to. In any case, some line departments may simply be too small to justify their own separate resourcing.

A DISTINCT FOCUS ON MANAGEMENT

Given that this book is about management, from our point of view the decentralizing of operational/technical training allows us to concentrate more fully on management's unique needs. Without this special attention, the needs of management can easily take second place, since the needs for operational/technical training will usually seem more urgent and more quantifiable.

This suggested split will normally prove acceptable to directors. They generally see themselves as development's client for operational/technical training, but are happy to consider the MD as the client for management training.

Above a certain level managers are therefore best regarded as a corporate resource. That view allows those who advise the chief executive to manage their learning, appraisal, recognition and reward, managerial style, and career development moves in a way which fosters the achievement of corporate goals, not sectional ones. Such activity has to be managed strongly at the centre if the company wants to operate as an entity, whether for reasons of necessary functional interdependence between departments, or for pure choice and a desired single image.

A strongly centralized approach to management training, education and development also permits close links with other personnel department functions such as compensation and benefits, recruitment, manpower planning, etc. If there are some generalist personnel staffs permanently attached to line departments, then these connections can also be coordinated and exploited.

All these links are needed if training is not to be regarded as a stand-alone activity. As this book has argued, training interventions work effectively for the organization only if they are part of a wider intervention consisting of a number of mutually reinforcing activities. Professional staff in the personnel department can therefore help with the analysis, conduct and support of the range of related activities.

But this form of centralized arrangement is not the sole option and may not work well. A chief executive might be persuaded by arguments to centralize development activity, but might not trust the personnel director with it. That depends on the nature of the personnel department, its past role, and its image in the company. In any case, there are some inherent conflicts of perspective, if not of interest, between personnel and development.

DEVELOPMENT'S AND PERSONNEL'S DIFFERENT PERSPECTIVES

We have seen how development's mission is:

> *To provide a strategic focal point for the ongoing development of a modern and forward-looking organization and talented management team, promoting individual and collective management capability and company capacity, able to initiate and manage renewal and change.*

A traditional personnel mission might be summarized as:

> *To provide appropriate professional personnel and employment services and policies to help departments achieve their business objectives.*

From this it follows that:

O   Much personnel work is responsive and reactive to short-term day-to-day demands. By contrast, development is more about anticipating tomorrow's needs and being proactive about developing future capability.

O   Whilst much personnel work is tactical and administrative, development is more strategic, creative and concerned with change.

O   The bulk of personnel work should take place efficiently and with a fairly low profile. Development is rather more high-profile and political, requiring close and frequent access to the top levels of management.

O   Personnel serves the company as a whole and has contact with all employees. Development generally tends to be more narrowly focused on managers and the way the business is managed and organized.

However, given the right conditions and strong leadership in personnel, as I outlined earlier, there are many synergies to be gained by placing the functions together in a combined Personnel or Human Resources Department.

ORGANIZATION CHANGE CYCLES

The structure of organizations tends to go in cycles, especially centralization versus decentralization. This is partly a question of fashion, and decentralization is fashionable at the time of writing. I dare say the mood of centralization will return. But there are more substantial reasons for changing than to keep abreast of fashion. The truth is that there is no ideal arrangement that will endure over time. There are both pros and cons, and these will be seen from the standpoint of present arrangements, leading inevitably toward pressure to reorganize.

The benefits of making a change to decentralize training (or vice versa) will eventually diminish. Disbenefits will start to appear. For example, decentralizing operational/ technical training may eventually lead to lower standards of training and less interest in or compliance with government initiatives. The trainers may 'go native' and display a lack of collaboration with other trainers; this is especially so with scarce or expensive resources, which become regarded as departmental rather than corporate.

If and when such dysfunctional behaviour happens, it may call for a period of centralization to exchange one set of pros and cons for another. And then, once again, after standards have been raised and behaviour modified, the time may return when it is again ripe to decentralize training in order to get close to the customer. One should hope that the cycle takes place over several years to allow for some stability in the meantime.

ACTIVITY 12.3

Using the considerations mentioned, you may find it helpful to re-examine how your own management training function is structured in relation to other company training activity, and how development can best relate to other personnel work.

ADOPTING A NEW AGENDA

The more you think about development strategy, the more you will become convinced that there is no lack of scope. The challenge may seem too daunting, particularly the task of persuading other stakeholders. But does it have to be a huge leap, or can progress be made by taking small steps? If the change is more than simply quantitative, but is also highly sensitive, then it is wise to move forward with caution if not outright stealth. So where to begin? Figure 12.6 contains some practical tips on how developers can start to adopt a new agenda.

FIGURE 12.6 HOW TO GET STARTED ON A NEW AGENDA: TEN PRACTICAL TIPS FOR DEVELOPERS

1. Develop a clear vision about where you ultimately want to get to and an understanding of where you are now.

2. Sort out your own priorities, what to achieve first and what can wait.

3. Be honest with yourself about how much you can achieve if allowed to, and over what timescale.

4. Identify what principles you are prepared to die for in the trenches, and what you are willing to sacrifice if you have to.

5. Identify the obstacles in your path and how you might find ways round them.

6. Conduct a stakeholder analysis, so that you know who you can count on to support your planned changes and who will be against you. Be clear about who will inevitably be for or against you *per se* for personal and past reasons, and who will be for or against your ideas irrespective of the relationship. Work on the latter group.

7. Develop the developers so that they are perceived as credible when matched against any new roles suggested.

8. Always display a full appreciation of the problems facing the business and its forward plans.

9. Use every opportunity to integrate real business issues into development programmes.

10. Involve top managers in your programmes and other activities.

SUPERVISING THE DEVELOPERS

Throughout this book I have tried to be supportive of developers. Readers may also have detected a note of caution when it comes to assuming that their line clients can be relied upon to be equally supportive of developers and their products and services. There are some unquestioned assumptions here about who is the good guy and who is the bad guy. But developers themselves are a mixed breed, with fads and foibles, pride and prejudice. They suffer from incomplete information and poor judgement like the rest of us (e.g. 'I wouldn't touch open learning with a barge-pole – expensive bookends!', as one training manager told me). Some commit their companies heavily to management competences and NVQs, while others block their use entirely.

In-house developers frequently resort to covert strategies with their senior line clients. They feel they have to, believing that it is not in the best interests of their company to disclose their own real values and their long-term aims for the organization's culture. In this and other respects, developers' biggest headaches often lie in their relationship with their chief executive and other senior line directors. Many give up, circumvent this top level, or are content to busy themselves lower down the organization and settle for considerably less for their organization than they might.

Some developers don't need to construct their agenda behind the chief executive's back. They are openly allowed a broad licence to determine at a fundamental level *what* is appropriate for their client organization (as well as *how, how much*, etc.). This too is a problem and is unhealthy for the organization. Many developers would like to keep this freedom and power. But where is the accountability? Whilst developers need a degree of freedom, they also need to accept responsible supervision from their chief executive. Who is to approve the developers' agenda, if not their boss? Who is to endorse the developers' vision? Who is to judge their motives? What we never seem to do with all our management development activity is to set out to equip line bosses with the means of quizzing developers in a structured and searching manner. Arguably, too much is taken on trust or ignorance. That may be convenient for the developers, but is it open and is it ethical?

One of the yawning gaps in the management development market is the lack of practical advice for chief executives on how to derive the best from developers. As this is a field in which few chief executives have had direct management experience themselves, they are often vulnerable. Many lack an objective means of judging whether high-profile and politicized national initiatives are all they are promoted to be and whether they are well-suited to their own organization. This is just one important example. Some retain an independent consultant whose expert opinion is wholly trusted. But it is arguably second best when compared with the well-informed chief executive who has a more hands-on supervisory role. Even where development is well managed by its functional head, it still requires supervision by its line boss. At the very least, chief executives need to be clear about its purpose, long-term aspirations, scope and values. Figure 12.7 contains a checklist of sample questions for top bosses to use with their chief developer.

FIGURE 12.7 CHECKLIST FOR CHIEF EXECUTIVES TO SUPERVISE THEIR DEVELOPERS

1. What are your current development strategies?
2. What strategic changes are you planning to make to the company's development portfolio?
3. What are the biggest organizational problems we face?
4. How do your strategies relate to where the company is currently and where it is going?
5. What development are we doing which is markedly different from our competitors? Is the difference a strength or a weakness?
6. What national initiatives, market trends, etc. are we having nothing to do with, and why?
7. What values and beliefs about development, people and organizations are driving the service you provide me with?
8. What assumptions are you making about how easily off-the-job learning can be applied to the practical benefit of the business?
9. What are you doing to migrate development activity towards action which is most likely to realize a pay-off, to the company and the individuals?
10. What are the biggest obstacles you face in trying to help me and the company?
11. Where do you need improved access?
12. How can you help me supervise you?
13. Where are my blind spots in terms of understanding and supervising your development function?
14. How could you help me put together a plan for my own development and that of my directors?

ACTIVITY 12.4

How would you describe the nature and quality of the relationship between the key developers and those in top management to whom they are formally accountable? How could arrangements be improved from both standpoints?

EXTERNAL INITIATIVES

This book cannot remain oblivious to what is happening in the world of management development beyond individual organizations. This is especially true of the competence movement as applied to managers and promoted in the UK by the Management Charter Initiative (MCI) through its published management standards. Since MCI has thus far been primarily concerned with the individual manager, that agency's role is critically examined in my book *Developing Managerial Competence*.[3] But since my thesis here is that management development can and should be interpreted more broadly than mere manager development, there must inevitably be some comment on MCI's role and contribution here too.

Likewise, the merger of the Institute of Personnel Management (IPM) and the Institute of Training and Development (ITD) to form the new Institute of Personnel and Development presents the IPD with a golden opportunity to marry the best of both fields of professional activity in a new development agenda. The plans to combine the two Lead Bodies' occupational standards (for personnel and training) underscores this need.

The Association for Management Education and Development (AMED) can also make a valuable contribution. It already runs 'Developing the Developers' programmes. There are lessons in this book for government departments too and for the *Investors in People* initiative.

MANAGEMENT CHARTER INITIATIVE

MCI's mission is: 'To improve the performance of UK organizations by improving the quality of UK managers.' Its objective is: 'To increase the quantity, quality, relevance and accessibility of management education and development.' This conceptual platform which underpins its everyday work derives from the important national issues which were much discussed in various reports during the mid-1980s. That scenario has now changed, and it is my firm belief that this particular role for MCI and its underlying logic needs to be reassessed.

MCI's role follows the conventional wisdom of the 1980s that the nation's most pressing weaknesses can be ranged on the supply side of the management equation. This leads to the comparative neglect of issues on the demand side – i.e. organizations' need for, and actual use of, managerial talent. Within certain companies one can see isolated training departments still training managers and supervisors while line directors are shedding those same groups of staff. Whether because of its mission, or because it shares the mind-set that besets so many developers, MCI's role is rather analogous to those training departments, lacking direct connections and inputs to the rest of the management body and the other half of the capability equation which links genuine potential with realized performance. Because of this narrow focus on individual capability (examined more fully in Chapter 8), I believe two other important aspects of management development are being relatively neglected:

○   the organization dimension of management, and
○   nurturing managerial talent other than by formal learning.

The organization dimension of management

The kinds of management problem exemplified in the prison service and financial services sector (discussed earlier) occur because the organization dimension is not developed and managed at the same time as the individual managers themselves. MCI, along with most others, compartmentalizes (or may be forced by its mission to compartmentalize) the box in the organization model called 'individual competence'. Yet ultimate company performance depends on a holistic approach, with other boxes in the model – e.g. managerial climate, ethical matters and values, the recognition and reward system, management structure, cross-functional relationships, etc. – receiving attention at the same time.

Nurturing managerial talent other than by formal learning

This aspect is about how companies audit their managerial talent base and match this against their anticipated needs, and how they then manage their managerial resourcing – *incoming, in situ careers,* and *exiting.* Particularly in times of managerial cost-cutting and delayering, companies tend to undervalue and squander their managerial talent, mismanaging this experienced resource, and often dumping it indiscriminately and prematurely. This scandalous waste receives no co-ordinated national advice.

The development of organization *management* and the development of organizations' *managers* need to share a common perspective, with the latter benefiting from the organizational context. As long as MCI is only able to focus on individual manager development while portraying this as the full answer to management development, these two aspects of development will at best remain only partially integrated. Those who mistakenly believe that manager development is all there is to management development will be reinforced in their view.

If you accept the underlying philosophy behind the competence approach (which I examine in *Developing Managerial Competence*), then MCI has made significant strides to push the concept into British business. But there is a need to move on and address today's needs. To expand MCI's role (in respect of a greater involvement with organization management issues) would be a tough strategy and would risk bringing it into conflict with other agencies, institutions and national programmes, raising possible questions of subsuming or merging roles. There are two other alternatives. One is for MCI to admit to a role as a niche development player, to speak openly of '*manager* development' rather than *management* development, and advise clients to make sure they achieve integration elsewhere, but this leaves unresolved competitor issues with organizations whose product MCI can choose to approve or reject. Another option is to concentrate on the valuable role of national occupational standards setter, leaving *development* to commercial companies.

INVESTORS IN PEOPLE

Investors in People (IiP) is a most valuable programme which complements MCI's focus on individual managers in that it offers the prospect of looking directly at the organization's contributions to key aspects of successful human resource management. It is a healthy sign that the two organizations cooperate in respect of managers.

While the goals are admirable, it is of concern that some of the same core beliefs and flawed thinking mentioned throughout this book are also evident in IiP. Again, there are hierarchical and paternalistic overtones and an over-reliance on individual training and development. Again, there are hints of an overcompartmentalization of the development of capability and overestimation of its independent leverage, rather than managing competence interdependently with other system variables. These frayed threads can be detected running through the programme's four stated principles:

1. An *Investor in People* makes a public commitment from the top to develop all employees to achieve its business objectives.
2. An *Investor in People* regularly reviews the training and development needs of all employees.
3. An *Investor in People* takes action to train and develop individuals on recruitment and throughout their employment.
4. An *Investor in People* evaluates the investment in training and development to assess achievement and improve future effectiveness.[4]

This way of defining a responsible employer's behaviour towards its employees could lead to the provision of 'coping with stress' courses, for example, while subjecting employees – especially managers – to ever greater pressures. A shift of focus is needed, from emphasizing *provision* of training and development towards a healthier *utilization* climate. And instead of stressing the responsibilities of those at the top of organizations, there is scope for sharing responsibility, including helping employees take responsibility for their own learning, growth and well-being.

Investing in people is more about investing in common sense and goodwill than about spending the budget.

INSTITUTE OF PERSONNEL AND DEVELOPMENT

Much of the above philosophical comment on the need to redefine development practice applies equally to the Institute of Personnel and Development. But unlike MCI they are not hamstrung by their origins in quite the same way. With the ITD-

IPM merger they have an opportunity to tackle these conceptual integration issues; on the other hand they are faced with practical membership integration issues at the same time. No one should underestimate the substantial vested interest in the stand-alone training market.

ACTION PLAN

Figure 12.8 puts forward a suggested action plan to cover the various parties' areas of interest. Note that some of the items derive from issues discussed more fully in *Developing Managerial Competence*.

FIGURE 12.8 EXTERNAL INITIATIVES: SUGGESTED MULTIPLE ACTION PLAN

1. Help organizations understand why attending to individual competence development alone will fall short of assuring competent corporate performance.

2. Extend the development debate from individual managers' capabilities and contributions towards the holistic development of organizations' management teams, systems, climate and processes.

3. Encourage development which is the managerial equivalent of Investors in People. Redefine 'quality initiatives' to embrace the quality of internal management conduct, practice and relationships.

4. Develop tools for the direct assessment of management competence at corporate level.

5. Help organizations with the means to diagnose their full range of management development needs.

6. Issue codes of practice for broad management development that clearly go beyond *manager* development.

7. Develop and promote the use of analytical and developmental tools to close the gap between can-do competence, and choose-to-do and allowed-to-do competence.

8. Accept competences as (merely) a generic skills base upon which to build personal managerial artistry.

9. Approve and support development products which set out to engage learners in their own local and timely context.

10. Publish comprehensive management development case-studies (not just for manager development).

11. Break away from dated deferential models which assume top-down hierarchical authority and control.

12. Develop tools to help chief executives evaluate the advice, recommendations and service they receive from their developers.

13. Sharpen the distinction between training which has the purpose of conforming, and education which has the purpose of liberating and fostering challenge. Maintain a healthy balance.

14. Reverse the trend towards a unitary model of management and its development, training and education. Adopt and espouse the cause of pluralism in provision.

15. Remove any pressure for higher education to be based on assessed output competences. Leave competence-based training to management trainers.

16. Shift the balance away from MBAs towards a wider range of higher degrees.

17. Resist politicians' bureaucratic attempts to introduce levies for 'approved training', which emphasize quantity rather than quality, training rather than education, individual development rather than organizational development, and recouping the levy rather than solving companies' real performance problems.

18. Distinguish more clearly between national training initiatives which have a social purpose intended to help the unemployed, and those which aim to improve business efficiency/effectiveness. The two can be diametrically opposed. (NB: Being highly trained does not stop managers losing their jobs.)

REFERENCES

1. Henry Mintzberg (1989) *Mintzberg on Management*, New York: The Free Press, pp. 25–42.
2. Henry Mintzberg (1987) 'The Strategy Concept I: Five Ps for Strategy', *California Management Review*, Fall.
3. William Tate (1995) *Developing Managerial Competence: A Critical Guide to Methods and Materials*, Aldershot: Gower.
4. Employment Department (1991) *Investing in People*, Sheffield.

13

DEVELOPING THE ORGANIZATION TO *BE*

OVERVIEW

This chapter rounds off the book by overlaying its ideas with a value framework to help readers to combine development action with meaning, to benefit all their stakeholders.

> What kind of organization should developers be seeking to create?

> Developing a more open system

> An organization which *is*

> Modelling openness

> Towards more ethical development

> An ethical aim for business

INTRODUCTION

One well-known British company has established an open learning centre for its managers. It is very well planned, generously funded, and lavishly equipped with both hardware and software – strong signs that the company aspires to being a so-called learning organization. Or are they? To answer that question we would need to search below the surface artefacts and seek out the underlying values which currently drive the organization's behaviour.

The company in question is fiercely competitive – inside and outside. It considers that its open learning centre is an arm of its latest business strategy. And why not? After all, writers on these matters have been encouraging companies to view the development of human resources as one of the key means to achieving a competitive advantage. Therefore the open learning centre is a top secret.

I was allowed to visit the centre, but not allowed to see the written guidance the centre gives to its learners on how to assess their preferred learning style in order to match it with the facilities. I was told that the arrangement of the library resources on the shelves gave clues to the company strategy. I was not allowed to mention the company as a good example of an open learning centre for fear that it would attract interest from competitors.

Maybe this unease is understandable. Maybe not. Contrast these values with those implicit in a true learning organization:

O   Openness
O   Sharing
O   Trust
O   Collaboration
O   Confidence
O   Experimentation
O   Feedback
O   Risk-taking
O   'Win-win'
O   Benchmarking

You immediately come up against the centre's dominant value – paranoid secrecy! I saw only two people using the centre. Perhaps the rest hadn't heard about it!

This book is not exclusively about learning organizations, but its values are sympathetic. So a good starting point for moving in this direction is opening up the system.

KEY TIPS

❖   Aim to be congruent with your professed values.

❖   Open your doors. You'll be amazed at what you get back in return.

DEVELOPING A MORE OPEN SYSTEM

What would a more open system feel like? Paraphrasing Warren Bennis and Philip Slater as much as twenty years earlier, Mink, Shultz and Mink summarize an open system as:

> an embodiment of the democratic process. This process is the root requirement for survival of a post-industrial society. An open system with full interaction among all its parts and with its environment has resources for renewal ... . The goal of development, then, is organizational and societal renewal. Renewal will occur through developing organizations which deal effectively with uncertainty, diversity and complexity. An open organization has been characterized as a healthy system with mechanisms for organizing around purposes and information flow, rather than preordained centres of power.[1]

How ironic that this quotation reads so like Mary Parker Follett's age-old justification for bureaucratic management (see Chapter 9) according to rules and regulations ('discover the law of the situation' to 'avoid too great bossism', etc.)! On this occasion I hope we can safely say that this is not a case of history repeating itself cloaked in fresh jargon.

OPEN AND CLOSED PATTERNS

What characterizes an open organization compared with a closed one? Mink, Shultz and Mink have identified contrasting patterns, as set out in Figure 13.1.

ACTIVITY 13.1

Assess the feel and nature of your organization in terms of its qualifying as an open system. What kind of issue is it impossible for developers to discuss in your organization? Where does it need to become more open?

AN ORGANIZATION WHICH *IS*

Running through much of the discussion in this book about how developers can help their clients achieve results for their businesses has been a thread of value-development – not just helping the organization to do, but helping it to *be* as well as *do*. But the idea of intervening with the express objective of developing, say, a more open system is unlikely to be well understood or well received by those on high. Openness means sharing information and power.

It is often confusing to top management at best, and unacceptable to them at worst, for developers to suggest that management problems may not necessarily be best tackled by training their managers to *do* things, and instead to suggest other less tangible interventions concerned with *values*.

Nervousness aside, one problem is that top managements instinctively feel more comfortable with conventional manager training. They understand it. They can

FIGURE 13.1 PATTERNS OF OPEN AND CLOSED ORGANIZATIONS

An **open organization** is more likely to:

- Treat top positions in the hierarchy as broader in scope and more integrative in function but not implying overall personal authority.

- Seek external feedback and respond flexibly in light of the organization's mission.

- Base itself on higher motives (self-actualization, a desire to know and contribute).

- Encourage an overlap in planning and implementing.

- View top-level decisions as hypotheses subject to review and revision at lower echelons.

- Structure itself by temporary task forces, functional linkages, broad role definitions, mobile and regional property, brief amendable constitution.

- Set an atmosphere which is goal-oriented, challenging yet informal.

- Manage through supportive use of authority, i.e. encourage experimentation, learn from errors, emphasize personal development, use resources, tolerate ambiguity.

- Communicate up, down and across – unlimited chain of command. Promote an interactive mode.

A **closed organization** is more likely to:

- Treat occupants of top business as if they possessed overall personal authority (omniscience, omnipotence).

- Avoid external feedback so as to avoid inconvenient changes in the status quo.

- Base itself on lower motives (personal safety, comfort).

- Make a sharp distinction beween planning and implementing.

- View top-level decisions as final unless review is initiated by the top-level staff.

- Structure itself by permanent departments and echelons, fixed property, permanent detailed constitution and bylaws.

- Set an atmosphere which is routine-oriented, deadening, formalistic.

- Manage through intimidating use of authority, i.e. create caution and fear of errors, emphasize personal selection, conserve resources, and avoid ambiguity.

- Communicate one-way, downward through the chain of command – all other communication viewed as insubordinate.

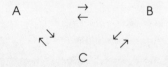

Reproduced by courtesy of Organization and Human Resource Development Associates

discuss it. They can recognize it. They can cost it. They may even have a loose expectation of what will happen at the end of it (often, sadly, not very much!). Yet for all that professed understanding, the quality of their articulation may be limited to wanting 'better qualified managers' or 'better trained managers'. But better qualified or trained to *do* what? Allowed to do what? More importantly, free to *be* what? So how can developers show the organization how to *be*?

MODELLING OPENNESS

It is often not easy for developers to conduct a frank discussion with their chief executives. Some issues may border on the undiscussible. It may not even be possible to discuss what cannot be discussed because the shortcomings of a company's management culture may result in a conspiracy of silence where even the temperature of the water cannot be tested. Some subjects are completely taboo. Even to say 'Do you think it might be possible to discuss xyz sometime?' might be courting danger.

The result is that many training and development departments turn inwardly on themselves. Because of a lack of top-level access, or through understandable trepidation, or even from sheer arrogance, they may come to assume a private mandate for improving the quality of management – that is, according to their own definition and values. It doesn't feel like this. It isn't questioned. It's not unique. In fact, it seems quite normal – the way we do things round here.

But to play this game is to accept the current rules and the dysfunctional company climate. The real name of the game should be changing the rules and improving openness. The product of the training and development department, that is its newly aware managers, should also be part of changing those rules and opening up the organization. This is why they are unpopular, and why any worthwhile development experience opens eyes to risks as well as opportunities, so often demotivating and a little scary after an initial high.

But how to get beyond this? That's the problem. What are the tactical options? Views are polarized.

'Practise what you preach'

Some developers *claim* a preference for being entirely open with their client directors, showing the benefit of modelling open behaviour. They say why they are there and what they want to achieve. Presumably, if they believe wholeheartedly in the goal of the learning organization, they explain what this could look like to their chief executive, no matter how sceptical.

Whether this amounts to shooting oneself in the foot depends on the interpersonal relationship, the character of the parties, and the organization culture. It may also make the developer feel good but achieve nothing for the company.

'The end justifies the means'

The other school of thought is of the-end-justifies-the-means variety. In other words, keep your own counsel. These developers talk of their tactics with S-words like subterfuge, subversion and stealth. Presumably they would follow Peter Honey's practical advice:

> If top management are out of sympathy with the notion of the learning organisation, that is unfortunate but not the end of the matter. Simply use the steps to create a mini-learning organisation in the parts you *can* influence.[2]

Are such developers' methods unethical or simply realistic? Can their approach be justified in the name of the long-term good of the organization, as *they* see it?

'Go where the client is'

There may be a middle course, best summed up by the consultants' expression 'go where the client is'. In other words, listen to what bosses say and try to provide them with what they seem to be wanting. Don't tell them they need something different – at least, not until you've won their wholehearted trust. If you disagree with what they are saying, simply keep silent and fail to reinforce it. Whenever they say something sensible, nod. You'll get there in the end.

This slightly devious approach may amount to nothing more or less than good consulting practice and common sense. But I have met some innocents abroad who will consider any position which is less than fully disclosed to be Machiavellian. The early management theorist perhaps had the answer in the classic *The Prince* written in 1513!

> A prince ... need not necessarily have all the good qualities I mentioned above, but he should certainly appear to have them. I would even go so far as to say that if he has those qualities and always behaves accordingly he will find them ruinous; if he only appears to have them they will render him service. He should appear to be compassionate, faithful to his word, guileless and devout. And indeed he should be so. But his disposition should be such that if he needs to be the opposite, he knows how.[3]

ACTIVITY 13.2

Where do you stand on the ethical and practical issue of how open you can afford to be/need to be/ought to be with your top clients?

TOWARDS MORE ETHICAL DEVELOPMENT

The Mink and Shultz quotation cited earlier reminds us that there are hard and soft business people, typified by their response to words such as 'democratic' and 'societal renewal'. As a very broad generalization, developers are likely to feel inspired by such sentiments and by the prospect of embedding these values in their organizations. Whereas, it is a fair bet that many line managers and directors would cringe. What responsibility, then, have developers in respect of helping organizations with general ethical and moral issues?

Ethics now has a firm place on the agenda. But whose? Like so much management development activity, it is accepted so long as it's off the job, away from the place of work where the real action takes place. Ethics has become the bypass of the work community – we may see the need for it, but 'not in my back yard'. It is discussed as a subject in abstract and philosophical terms, rather than by reference to real in-company case examples. The discussion needs bringing down to earth.

POINTERS TO PROBLEMS

Figure 13.2 suggests a few areas which developers might investigate for pointers to ethical problems.

FIGURE 13.2 TEN POINTERS TO POTENTIAL AREAS OF ETHICAL PROBLEMS

1. How does the company 'let go' its long-serving managers? Is expenditure excessively used as conscience money? Who gets to see whom? Who takes responsibility?

2. To what extent does the company seek to satisfy the interests of the full range of stakeholders, such as neighbours and the local and wider community?

3. Does the company's mission statement contain references to its values and its philosophy? Do these ring true? Would the company be able to conduct an objective audit against them?

4. What is the organization's bottom-line? Does the company stress the need for profit as a means to achieve goals, or as an end in itself – a measure of success along a journey, or its culmination, life blood or life itself?

5. What seems to be the organization's true purpose? Who are the winners and losers? Who appears to do best out of it?

6. Are your company's leaders 'inflicting pain or bearing pain', as De Pree puts it?[4]

7. Do your leaders give people 'space in the sense of freedom ... enabling our gifts to be exercised ... to grow, to be ourselves, to exercise our diversity'? (qv. education vs. training)

8. And in being committed to quality (as most companies claim these days), what evidence is there of 'the quality of our relationships and the quality of our communications and the quality of our promises to each other'?

9. Do those with power exercise it wisely and with due restraint as far as their own self-interest is concerned? If they find a need for excuses to be offered, can they conveniently look to Personnel as a willing accomplice to defend any dubious morality?

10. Do you frequently feel confused, uncomfortable, compromised, inhibited or gagged concerning positions taken by your company?

DEVELOPERS' OWN CONSCIENCES

Before you can claim to help your organization with its morality, you need to be clear about your own. Where do you stand, for example, on the true motives and the consequences behind various development interventions, such as de-layering, which result in slimmed-down organizations? Do you believe that reducing staff is the unfortunate consequence or the desired aim? While a company's position may genuinely be necessary, even laudable, and its handling of the casualties humane rather than merely guilt-ridden, could these change programmes really be a cover for cost-cutting to appeal to none other than the share price god?

ACTIVITY 13.3

Consider your company's various strategies, postures, statements, commitments, plans and methods. Which of these cause you concern from a professional or ethical standpoint?

AN ETHICAL AIM FOR BUSINESS

I was struck by Bob Cumber's pertinent historical perspective in *What Price Development?*:

> A century ago corporate success would have been measured in quite different ways. The great British industrialists seemed to attach quite a lot of importance to improving the world from which they created their wealth – creating new jobs, new homes and new beginnings for people. Just consider Port Sunlight and Bournville, two outstanding Victorian initiatives by businessmen (developers?) who saw their role as much in terms of enhancing society as enhancing the bottom line.[5]

Such philanthropy now seems far removed from most top bosses' creeds, indeed probably directly opposed to it. The chairman of one of the large high-street banks announces record profits of over £1billion for the year's first six months of trading. In the next breath he announces his intention of making 2500 more job cuts on top of the 18,500 to date. When asked why, he says he has to 'seek more efficiency', that 'we are determined to build on the progress achieved in the first half of 1994', and 'they [the press critics] have forgotten banks are supposed to make a profit'. Perhaps *they* have remembered something which he has forgotten. These job cuts mean more computers to do the work of people and fewer local outlets. Is this progress? What price personal service? When financiers can only place staff on the liabilities half of the balance sheet, it shows us what a long road we have to climb.

This is not intended to be a personal attack on the banking sector or one of its chairmen. In his position, with the benefit of inside knowledge of the company and its present business, organization and forecasts, and with his obligations and the pressures of competition, we might arrive at a similar agenda. The fact that the employees are paying the price of their bosses' bad judgement in incurring ruinous bad debts overseas a few years ago matters not a jot now. The developers might well be right to support the boss's cause and help him with the organizational means of achieving the further staff reductions. In any case, they have little choice in the matter. One day it will be their turn to put out the light, since Personnel are usually targeted too. What is wrong?

The problem is that we have become trapped into this way of thinking about the aim of business and the values which legitimately support it. We have taken a closed-system perspective. The interpretation of who are the stakeholders has become, first, the shareholders and, secondly, the customers. This excludes not only the interest of employees, but wider society's too. The fact that 2,500 more people are jobless and have to be supported by those remaining in employment is of no concern to the business.

Soap powder companies take out costly full-page advertisements in the national press directly to attack the opposition. Airlines hack into each other's computers to steal their competitors' passengers. Nowadays business is conducted like a war. But as John Kay in *Foundations of Corporate Success* claims, 'Success in business derives from adding value of your own, not diminishing that of your competitors, and it is based on distinctive capability not on destructive capacity.'[6] Sadly, Kay only espouses the ideal rather than the actualité.

No doubt this view would be supported by Robert Heller, founding editor of *Management Today*. Writing about Top Management Quality (TMQ) and quoting Thomas Kochan and Robert McKersie, he comments that,

> Competitive strategies that stress value added (e.g. enhanced quality) and/or product innovation require high levels of commitment and trust in employment relations [whereas] competitive strategies that stress low costs and low wages produce high levels of labour–management conflict, reinforce low trust, and inhibit innovation and improvement of quality.[7]

ACTIVITY 13.4

What role are you required to play in connection with any controversial, painful or dubious line management strategies, decisions, actions, plans, communications, etc? How do you try to resolve ethical dilemmas and reconcile conflicting professional and organizational responsibilities?

AN INCLUSIVE CAPITALISM CREED

De Pree's 'inclusive capitalism' creed (Figure 13.3) speaks to developers everywhere.[7] Can the torch of developers help to put some enlightenment back into Adam Smith's 'self-interest'? Is not developers' role, as Charles Handy expressed it on Radio Four's *Thought for the Day*, 'to balance high tech with high touch'?

FIGURE 13.3 AN INCLUSIVE CAPITALISM CREED

- Being faithful is more important than being successful. If we are successful in the world's eyes but unfaithful in terms of what we believe, then we fail in our efforts at insidership.

- Corporations can and should have a redemptive purpose. We need to weigh the pragmatic in the clarifying light of the moral. We must understand that reaching our potential is more important than reaching our goals.

- We need to become vulnerable to each other. We owe each other the chance to reach our potential.

- Belonging requires us to be willing and ready to risk. Risk is like change; it's not a choice.

- Belonging requires intimacy. Being an insider is not a spectator sport. It means adding value. It means being fully and personally accountable. It means forgoing superficiality.

- Last, we need to be learners together. The steady process of becoming goes on in most of us throughout our lifetime. We need to be searching for maturity, openness and sensitivity.

Reproduced by courtesy of Business Books

As we reach the moment for parting company, let us cast our minds back to the book's opening remarks and its underlying purpose. In particular, it called for 'a wider discussion and more relevant agenda'. It looked to a better future for developers, one which frees them 'to embark on something more fulfilling', for themselves and for their organizations. A hard but worthwhile struggle on the road to nirvana? Or continue with the sideshow and a walk-on part when prompted?

> Do you have the can-do competence?
> Will you be allowed to do?
> Will you choose to do?

This may be an aptly thought-provoking and resounding chord on which to end this personal venture into the field of management learning and change. More importantly than mere skill, knowledge, insights and resources, I hope this book has given you heart and courage, and has contributed towards your own personal vision for development.

REFERENCES

1. Oscar Mink, James Shultz and Barbara Mink (1986) *Developing and Managing Open Organizations: A Model and Methods for Maximising Organizational Potential*, Austin, Texas: Organization and Human Resource Development Associates, Inc., pp. 13–20.

2. Peter Honey (1991) 'The Learning Organisation Simplified', *Training and Development*, **9** (7), July, p. 33.
3. Niccolò Machiavelli (1967) *The Prince*, London: Penguin reprint, p. 100.
4. Max De Pree (1994) *Leadership is an Art*, London: Business Books, pp. 11, 69–70.
5. Bob Cumber (1994) 'What Price Development?', *Organisations & People*, London: Kogan Page, **1** (3).
6. John Kay (1994) *Foundations of Corporate Success*, Oxford: Oxford University Press.
7. Robert Heller (1994) 'Developing the Lighter Touch', *Management Today* (October).

INDEX

managing business and organizational
processes 147–8, 150
organization diagnosis 75–6
systematic training see Systematic
training model
Modelling behaviour 88
Montaigne, Michel de xvi
Morgan, Gareth 199
Motivation see Empowerment
Mumford, Alan 29–30, 83–4, 200, 204

Nabisco 213
NASA 138
National Forum for Management Education
and Development 146
National Freight Corporation 91
National/government initiatives 139, 233,
237, 244
National Health Service 178
National initiatives needed 243
National training awards 38, 233
National training targets 7
National Vocational Qualifications (NVQs)
xi, 230, 233, 238
Nationwide 104
NatWest Life 105
Needs analysis 43–76, 229, 232
analytical techniques 44
change diagnostic model 75
clients' predefined wants rather than
needs 44
defining the client see Client
individual performance problems 51–2
individual vs. organizational problems
and needs 44, 58, 72, 229
key performance questions 44
problems with training-solution led
analysis 63, 70–73, 76
training needs analysis (TNA) 44, 70–73,
232
via appraisals 50
Negotiating skills 57–8
Networking 25, 36
Newlands Preparatory School 213
Nixon, Bruce 83
Non-executive directors 143
Non-rational management see Shadow side
Norms 12, 39, 52, 88, 101
challenging; norm-busters 32, 80, 129,
153–4, 175
identifying and stating 153–4
Norwich Union 104

Objectives; Objective setting 23, 86, 96–8,
101–5, 110, 120

shared objectives 101–2
Obstacles and blockages 5, 28, 44, 52, 63,
65, 69, 75–6, 88, 96, 140
Olson, Ken 141
Open behaviour 227, 238, 246–50
Open learning 14, 17, 48, 50, 62, 84, 130,
231, 238, 246
Open versus closed systems perspective 11,
17, 253
Organization culture see Culture
Organization development (OD) xii, 7–10,
19–21, 46
Organization structure see Structure
Organization variables/boxes 11–12, 36, 138,
148–52, 187, 212, 241–2
Organized labour see Trade unions
Otis Lifts 22
Outcomes versus outputs 13–19
Outsourcing 20, 124, 139, 230

Paradigm shift 38–9, 201, 228–9
Parker Follett, Mary 168, 171, 247
Partnerships 18
Pedler, Mike 35, 37, 80, 83, 94, 207–8
Performance
improvement, permitting, enhancing xii,
49–50, 69
individual performance problems and
issues 46–7, 51–2, 83, 97–8
organizational and/or individual 62, 72,
148–51
standards 24, 75, 81, 102, 118, 186
Performance management
appraisal and reviews – systems and
processes 24, 75, 81, 95–121, 143, 233
appraising appraisal 116–7
cycle of decline and need for re-gearing
109
effect on motivation 99
focus on end results or means of
achieving 99, 103–6, 143, 232
feedback see Feedback
influencing teamly behaviour 86–8
management practices and behaviours
86, 98–100, 103–6, 110, 118–20, 149,
151
personal development reviews and plans
50–51, 113, 120–1
rating scales and labels 97, 109
sample questions 114–15
team-based appraisal 109–12
Performance needs analysis see Needs
analysis
Performance-related pay (PRP) 96–100, 103,
106–12